A LIFE OF
Gwendolyn Brooks

A LIFE OF
Gwendolyn Brooks

GEORGE E. KENT

THE UNIVERSITY PRESS OF KENTUCKY

Copyright © 1990 by the estate of George E. Kent

Published by The University Press of Kentucky

Scholarly publisher for the Commonwealth,
serving Bellarmine College, Berea College, Centre
College of Kentucky, Eastern Kentucky University,
The Filson Club, Georgetown College, Kentucky
Historical Society, Kentucky State University,
Morehead State University, Murray State University,
Northern Kentucky University, Transylvania University,
University of Kentucky, University of Louisville,
and Western Kentucky University.

Editorial and Sales Offices: Lexington, Kentucky 40506-0336

Library of Congress Cataloging-in-Publication Data

Kent, George E.
    A life of Gwendolyn Brooks / George E. Kent.
        p.   cm.
    Bibliography: p.
    Includes index.
    ISBN 0-8131-1659-7
    1. Brooks, Gwendolyn, 1917-   —Biography. 2. Poets,
American—20th century—Biography. 3. Afro-Americans—Intellectual
life. I. Title.
PS3503.R7244Z73   1989
811'.54—dc20   89-31738
[B]

This book is printed on acid-free paper meeting
the requirements of the American National Standard
for Permanence of Paper for Printed Library Materials.
∞

Contents

Foreword

George Kent completed his biography of Gwendolyn Brooks only a short time before his death in 1982. As professor of English at the University of Chicago for the last thirteen years of his life, Kent came to know Chicago's Black literary world intimately. He first met Brooks at the celebration honoring her at the Affro-Arts Theatre in Chicago on December 20, 1969. Having admired her poetry for years, he introduced himself to Brooks and asked permission to write her life story. She agreed immediately. Thus began an association that was to last until Kent's death.

Kent was born in 1920 in Columbus, Georgia, the son of a master blacksmith and a school principal. His teaching career began at the age of sixteen in the school his mother had established in the backwoods of Georgia. He later earned a B.A. at Savannah State College and, after serving in the military, took his M.A. and Ph.D. at Boston University.

Kent knew the intellectual life of Black America because he lived the 1960s and 1970s as did few having his training and sensibility. At his funeral, Brooks noted that he "respected and enjoyed all kinds of people. He was an *intense* scholar. Authors he took very seriously, and he expected them to take *themselves* seriously, to work as hard as *he* worked." A sensitive observer of literature and humanity, he gained a reputation for his work on Richard Wright and William Faulkner. Kent had hoped to write stories and memoirs. It is not surprising, then, that his criticism has depth and an enabling vision into the creative process.

Kent's most sustained research and criticism concerned Gwendolyn Brooks. He worked on the biography, revising and editing it, until the end of his life, despite the debilitating effects of lung cancer and chemotherapy. Earlier, he had spent many hours interviewing the poet, members of her family, and close friends. He went with Brooks to all the homes she had occupied and even traveled with her to California to interview her aunt,

Viola Leath. In addition, the poet loaned him her early workbooks and other unpublished manuscripts. Although he and I discussed mutual discoveries in the Harper and Row correspondence, he also carefully perused everything for himself at Princeton University Library and in New York City. While Brooks cooperated fully with Kent, it should be noted that this is not an "authorized" biography and that Brooks did not see the manuscript prior to publication.

Had Kent lived, he would unquestionably have brought his biography up to date for publication. American literature lost an invaluable scholar in his untimely death. We are grateful, nevertheless, for his gift to us, this life of a treasure of the nation, Gwendolyn Brooks.

D. H. MELHEM

1

Beginnings

Keziah Brooks first encountered her daughter Gwendolyn's talent when she found her scribbling two-line verses at the age of seven. The verses filled a page and surprised Keziah by their clarity and originality. Legend has it that Keziah stated, "You are going to be the lady Paul Laurence Dunbar."[1] Within two years Gwendolyn was writing surprisingly good four-line verses. Sensing her poetic talent, the family gave her the time she needed to perfect her work. Gwendolyn later declared that she believed in the certainty with which her mother spoke, and never stopped writing. She received inspiration also from her father, David, during and after the preschool years, through his habit of singing in the household and reciting poetry and other literature from Paul Laurence Dunbar and the Harvard Classics. She later felt that her father's readings had made her want to write poems comparable to those she heard from him.

If we seem to be overtaken here by the American Dream, it is one that took different forms in the Brooks family before their arrival in Chicago, and long before Gwendolyn felt that Harper, in its dealings with *A Street in Bronzeville*, was turning her life into a fairy tale. Family history has it that Gwendolyn's paternal grandfather, Lucas, a field slave, threw his master into a hollow stump and escaped to join the Union Army. His daughter Viola, born when Lucas was seventy-two, remembers him as a handsome man, nearly six feet tall, dark-skinned, and of erect, soldierly bearing. Lucas married Elizabeth, a mulatto house slave. The union produced Gwendolyn's father, David, and eleven other children. Lucas and Elizabeth had no time to become literate, though Lucas learned to handle figures well. The harshness of the family struggle in rural Oklahoma and Oklahoma City was scattered with a few rich pleasures but apparently left David, the head of the family after his father died, more anguished and restless than the other children. His brothers turned to trades, and both brothers and sisters married early and centered their lives on home, lodges, and churches, the social and ordering forces of the day. David was not to marry until he was thirty-three. He attended Fisk University, hoping to prepare for a medical education, but was unable to stay more than a year. Early in the century he came to Chicago and made one among the 2 percent of the population that blacks comprised up to 1910. Though there was a small thriving black middle class, David would find the largest number of blacks confined to the service area of the economy. Whites, many of them immigrants, dominated industry, a fact that, after some strife and adjustment, would place them in the mainstream of the economy and give them advantages over blacks.

What David thought of the industrial sector is not known. He went into the service area as a porter with the McKinley Music Publishing Company on East Fifty-fifth Street, a job he would hold for thirty years. In 1914 he accompanied his friend Berry Thompson to the home of Thompson's friend Gertrude Wims at 4747 South State Street, where he met Keziah Wims, a pretty, slender-faced woman, brown-skinned, slightly shorter than David's five feet seven. David and Keziah were married in July 1916 at the home of Keziah's parents, at 1118 North Jackson Street, Topeka, Kansas. Keziah, one of ten children, had lived in a family pattern similar to David's. Her mother, Luvenia, was skilled in domestic arts and devoted to the usual institutions of church and family. Both families suffered losses through hardship and accidents. But the maternal grandparents otherwise seem not to have faced the degree of hardship confronted by the paternal family. Both families stressed order, discipline, and usefulness, and provided personnel for the trades.

Like David, Keziah had made an epic struggle to attain an education, an effort shared completely only by her sister Beulah, who became a sewing teacher. Keziah supported herself at Emporia Normal in Kansas by a loan from her sister and by the not always humane domestic service. Like David, she had aspirations—the dream of becoming a great concert pianist. One of her jokes was that she somehow felt if she could simply persist in taking the music courses, she could accomplish her mission. "This misconception stayed with me throughout childhood and a part of adulthood. I did not give up the idea of becoming a pianist until after marriage." Past fifty, she composed her first song, "Luvenia," in memory of her mother, and later a sacred song entitled "I Want to Be Consecrated to Thee."

The new Brooks family took a series of residences in Chicago. They roomed at 4142 South Evans until Keziah became pregnant with Gwendolyn, when she briefly returned to her mother's in Topeka. Shortly after Gwendolyn's birth in Topeka at 1:00 P.M. on Thursday, June 7, 1917, Keziah and David took an apartment at 5626 South Lake Park Avenue, Chicago.

Led about the apartment by members of the family, Gwendolyn was not allowed to crawl. Sixteen months later Gwendolyn's brother, Raymond, was born and the family was complete.

Although comfortable, the Brookses sought to purchase a home, a quest intensified by the attack upon Keziah by a demented woman. They found a lifelong home in what soon proved to be a changing neighborhood at 4332 South Champlain. It was a short street cut off from the main traffic and marked by family homes, well-kept lawns, beautiful trees, clean streets. The yards, front and back, were pleasant for the children, but what held great attraction for Keziah were the large porches from which she could enjoy the fresh air and see her acquaintances. "Since I had never made a habit of visiting neighbors in their homes, our large porch afforded me this delightful pastime." Being attached to home, she was comfortable in a neighborhood where weekly or monthly visits did not occur. The Brooks family was the second black family on the block, following the Sharplesses. The Mitchell family was the third. By then the neighborhood was secured institutionally for blacks, since they had purchased the Carter Temple Church a few months before the Brookses moved in. Keziah joined the church and attended regularly until her children were married.

Obviously, the neighborhood corresponded to Keziah's own sense of order and quiet rituals. Her neighbor at 4324 had two small children and, like herself, "was greatly concerned about how and with whom they played." The families agreed that their children would play together, and Gwendolyn and Raymond gathered with the other two in the Brookses' back yard, where they played quietly and made mud pies.

A typical day for the children began with breakfast at eight or nine— toast or biscuits with butter and jelly, orange juice, applesauce, or bacon and eggs with cereal and juice. Or, as Gwendolyn still remembers, oatmeal with cream floating on it, graced with butter, sugar, and other additions. Then off to play for Gwendolyn and Raymond when they were preschoolers—or later off to school. Lunch was at noon or thereabouts—often soup, bread and butter sometimes topped with sugar, and applesauce. During the week, dinner might be hamburger patties, pork chops, or lamb chops, and a salad that almost always contained sliced tomatoes. Sundays probably brought roast chicken, roast lamb shoulder, or leg of lamb.

The children were dressed twice a day. Before they were of school age, they put on rough but clean clothes in the morning so they could play freely, and their hair received the first of the day's combings. After lunch they washed and dressed in nicer clean clothes and Gwendolyn's hair was again combed—their afternoon play was expected to be more restrained. Except for making mud pies, Gwendolyn and Raymond's favorite games during early childhood tended not to be of the dirtying kind. Their favorites outdoors were tag and hide and seek. The indoor family games included checkers, dominoes, jigsaw puzzles, and occasionally whist.

The late Lorraine Williams Bolton, head of the art department at Hampton Institute and a childhood friend of Gwendolyn's, pointed out that the pattern of Gwendolyn's rearing was similar to her own and that of many Chicagoans. It tended to encourage inwardness and withdrawal into imaginative resources—a necessity in the face of the strict limits placed upon disorderly play and inquisitiveness. Children read or drew—or soon, as in Gwendolyn's case, exploited other artistic talents. Lorraine Bolton herself became a painter and is said to have written two novels before she was twelve.

As Lorraine explained, there were many Chicagoes in that period. Gwendolyn remembered that Lorraine, a schoolteacher's daughter, was numbered by Gwendolyn and others among the rich. Admired for her stylish dress, she gained even more stature among the children when her awkwardness in athletics exposed her expensive underwear. Gwendolyn's own Chicago was among those Horace Cayton and St. Clair Drake called the "respectables," people not of self-conscious class, color, educational, or aristocratic distinctions but somewhere in the middle, the good-doing people determined to live within a firm moral ordering. Autobiographies have confirmed the existence of the various Chicagoes: the extreme American Dream striving of Katherine Dunham's father in Glen Ellyn and environs; the ostensibly assimilated family of Willard Motley growing up among whites in the West Sixtieth Street area; the hard-pressed, disintegrating migrant families of Alden Bland's *Behold a Cry* and Richard Wright's *American Hunter.*

Wright records the shock of the southern rural migrant's first encounter with Chicago. "My first glimpse of the flat black stretches of Chicago depressed and dismayed me, mocked all my fantasies. Chicago seemed an unreal city whose foundations were sinking slowly into the dank prairie. Flashes of steam showed intermittently on the wide horizon, gleaming translucently in the winter sun. The din of the city entered my consciousness, entered to remain for years to come. The year was 1927." Thinking that his Aunt Cleo lived in an apartment, Wright was disturbed to find that she lived in a single room. "I was baffled. Everything seemed makeshift, temporary. I caught an abiding sense of insecurity in the personalities of the people around me. I found Aunt Cleo aged beyond her years. Her husband, a product of a southern plantation, had, like my father, 'gone off.' Why had he left? My aunt could not answer. She was beaten by the life of the city, just as my mother had been beaten. Wherever my eyes turned they saw stricken, frightened black faces trying vainly to cope with a civilization they did not understand."[2]

David Brooks had struggled through the terrors of Oklahoma and his father's sufferings. He had dealt with institutions and graduated from high school. Keziah too had dealt with urban institutions that to some degree coped with life expectations. Both had been through a refining fire before coming to Chicago, and David had had many years in the big city in which to acquire both poise and a sense of when to bow to necessity. They were ready for tried and true traditions and for submitting their children to them. Although the young Gwendolyn experienced a band of order and a set of values, she also felt anxiety from her contact with less sheltered children, a contact that placed its mark upon her personality and her art.

Gwendolyn had run golden in the quiet, orderly, and restraining environment provided by her parents in her preschool years. But upon entering Forrestville Elementary School at the age of six, she found a different set of values, one for which her quiet and orderly ways offered no support. She did not have what she would later call "sass" or "brass." She had not learned to fight or to be athletic. She was not a player of jacks or a rider of bicycles. Her most exciting moments had come not at any high point of activity but when, on her back porch, she sat facing the dream world in the sky. There she could feel the beauty of the scene and the beauty of her own life and of life in general. Her nearest contact with this brasher world was the strange matters revealed in the overheard voices of the family's tenants. They sometimes cursed or dropped and threw things. Standing at the foot of the stairway, she and Raymond would listen and giggle. She would, of course, discover later that quarreling could invade the warm cocoon of her own family life.

But at the Forrestville School, matters went beyond quarreling. Even her nice dresses, gifts from her Aunt Beulah, created problems. The children ignored her or, seeing her wallflower-like withdrawal, called her "ol' stuck-up heifer" and declared that they wanted "nothin' t' do with no rich people's sp'iled chirren." Among the "rich" were the children of black doctors, lawyers, city hall employees, post office workers, and teachers. They formed a pecking order.

But her major deficiency, others believed, was the absence of light skin and "good grade" hair. Possessing neither the rough and ready skills nor the light color and "good" hair nor the affluent family, Gwendolyn faced a difficult struggle. Even the Forrestville Elementary School building, as she was later to describe it in her novel *Maud Martha* (1953), looked solid and somewhat forbidding: a June day suggested the coming of brightness in little ways but carried a November briskness and chill. The other children, however, blended with the wind and expressed vitality and a world of their own. Contrasting with their worldly topics, Gwendolyn's speech was "of the sweet potato pie that would be served at home."

The conflict in language and in other matters is dramatically registered. But the intraracial color prejudice was the greatest shock for Gwendolyn. To think that skin color was going to be the test for her future worth conflicted with all other principles for being well thought of that she had been taught. For the most part, she could return to neighborhood and home to find the Edenic world she had known. But here too she would find indirect assaults when she overheard adult conversation.

Aunt Ella: "Why did he want Jessie? Jessie is light and has long hair."

Or Aunt Beulah (discussing looks): "I'm sorry for myself."

More direct were the Emmanuels, portrayed in *Maud Martha*, who rejected her and referred to her as "old black gal." In the academic work of the school, there were "the truly nice delights of crayon and chalk and watercolor, of story time, and textbooks with cheery pictures of neat gay-coloured life-among-the-white-folks." Then home again to song ("Brighten the corner where you are!"), food, and help with schoolwork. Keziah invested everything with cheerfulness. Gwendolyn's father also abounded in homemaking skills, artistic abilities, and cheerfulness. Both David and Keziah made all holidays and ceremonial occasions special rituals, times of happiness.

So there were two universes in which to live. At home Gwendolyn gave herself to writing poetry, an act of inner communing that gave pure delight or produced results that could be arranged in a form that would give delight. At the age of eleven, she began to keep notebooks of the poetry she had written. Surviving collections extend from her thirteenth year to her twenty-fifth, with the exception of 1932.

The notebook poetry for the period of 1930–33 seems to carry over the early preadolescent preoccupations and to be a reliable guide to the universe that she found supportive. But it contains at least one example of the lasting penetration of color prejudice. In the notebook entitled *The Red Book or the Merry Book* (1930), Gwendolyn carefully worked out color symbolism:

> red—ashamed, shame, disgrace, fiery, fierce
> brown—songster, gleeful, ambitious
> green—envious, jealous
> gray—shadowy, gloomy

yellow gold—avaricious, desireful, love of riches
purple—beauty, beautiful, fine, artful
blue—heavenly, religious, pious
white—clean, righteous, pure
pink—blushful, pretty mountain maiden
black—flower of crime

Gwendolyn feels today that she was a victim of brainwashing. Obviously the impact of environment and of books would impede the growth of a spontaneous social personality. It formed the shyness that stayed with her most of her life.

Other than the color notation, there is nothing to mar the prevalence of beauty and order in the universe of poems composed from her thirteenth year to her sixteenth. The largest number of poems deal with the beauties of nature and the natural cycle. Despite physical nature's occasional unpleasantness, the constant changes of seasons bring forth the beauties of each and provide joy and lessons for the world. Numerous moralizing poems are on the side of goodness and right behavior, and the domestic circle provides mainly security and love.

These youthful poems seldom break with the poetic diction of the nineteenth century. One feels the presence of William Wordsworth, William Cullen Bryant, Henry Wadsworth Longfellow, John Keats, and the reflection of the thirteen-year-old girl as a keen observer, an avid reader, and a person for whom the universe is as yet adequately explained by authority. On the whole, nature is properly arranged and vital, man's existence has the right fruits, to be harvested by strong will and hard work and choosing of the good. God's in his heaven, in other words, and all's just about right, fundamentally, with the world. The growth of the young poet is revealed in the mastery of traditional forms, the accumulation of vocabulary, and the growing ability to express complex relations.

Not appearing in the available notebooks is Gwendolyn's first published poem, "Eventide," published in *American Childhood*, October 1930.

Eventide

By Gwendolyn Brooks (13 Years)

When the sun sinks behind the mountains,
And the sky is besprinkled with color,
And the neighboring brook is peacefully still,
With a gentle, silent ripple now and then;
When the flowers send forth sweet odors,
And the grass is uncommonly green,

When the air is tranquilly sweet,
And children flock to their mothers' side[s],

Then worry flees and comforts presides
For all know it is welcoming evening.

(The corrections are those Gwendolyn made in the printed copy because of printer's errors.) The peace of nature and domesticity overcome the troubles of the world as the day fades. Obviously the poem derives much from reading. Gwendolyn still remembers the impact of William Cullen Bryant's "Thanatopsis" in her adolescence, and reading Longfellow in a "shiny green book" that she still has.

The 1930 notebooks deal with both personal experience and reading. "Lamentation for a Pet" presents the dying, death, and burial of a goldfish, with a bit of bathos. ("Are you dead, little fish?" "Oh no! But I'm dying.") "Lovely Spring," "April," "Lines to a Flower in Spring," "Summer," "Sweet May the Queen," and "Nature's Children" (flowers) celebrate in various ways Gwendolyn's joy in the physical beauties of nature. The best of such poems are dramatic and make effective use of verbs. "Sweet May the Queen" lightly achieves a moralizing turn:

April gathered her traveling bags,
When May came dancing down the road
With crowns of flowers in her gold hair,
And laughing at April's heavy load.
"Ah", sighed April, "I remember well
When March was sad as I am now,
And I came dancing my merry way!"
"Don't cry, sister April, for you'll come again
With your dewy eyes and great bags of rain;
But now is my turn to dance and play!"
And with a joyous laugh, away went May!

"The Scottish Maid" is notable for its revelation of an early interest in the ballad form, which will be more freely exploited after the apprenticeship years:

"Whither ye to, my faire young maid?
Whither ye to, atrodding so slow?"
"Ime on mye trail to Mother Lon's.
That is whither I go."

"And wha will ye do there, my faire young maid?
Wha will ye do there all daye?"

"I'll roll the dough and make it brown,
And what else who can saye?"

"Then let me wak with ye, my faire young maid.
Let me wak with ye this morne!"
"Nay, nay." She cry, and wide her eye.
Nay, never 'til Gabriel blows his horne!"

Also of particular interest are the moralizing poems, in which one often feels a tensing of the will of the young poet, a habit sustained through the years of struggle before she received her first major breakthrough to publication in *Poetry, A Magazine of Verse*. In the 1930 group there are only the formally pious "A Sabbath Prayer," which simply gives thanks for the bounties of God; "Forgive and Forget," which has the "rise above it" theme of forgiving and forgetting those who hurt and neglect one until recognition comes, by and by; "The Glory of Victory," celebrating "our forefathers" who died during the Revolution and "knew what country love meant"; "A Song of Life" ("Life is but a song of rocky melody. Some play a wrong note."); and "Lines Written In A Sad Moment," which reads in part:

These dearly I want:
The pleasures of life,
Untouched by hate, unbroken by strife;
Free of bores and foul loves and cares,
Free of dead fears and timely gray hairs!
Full of adventure and cheer and good will,
Full of true friendships, without modern chill;
Ambitions and aims that really come true

Obviously not notable as a poem, but something of the struggle in the less pleasant universe comes through the conventional mode of expression.

"The House of Liberty" is perhaps only indirectly related to artistic strivings. It advises struggling over a long road, climbing its heights, and defending rights. The end of the road "is worth a king's gold." "Futures" advises that victory and a future, if promised by talent, are superior to riches and foes. "Voice and Mind" has implications for Gwendolyn's feeling of inarticulateness in responding to others.

The best of thoughts are not revealed
~~seldom said~~
However good they be.
They live within the mind, alone.
And so it is with me.

I cannot in a rush of words
Declare, as some can do,
How much I like a certain thing—
And yet my speech is true.

A grand idea excites my ~~the~~ mind.
But though I try my best,
I cannot for the life of me
That thought in words invest.

And when I'm full of gratitude,
The one thing I can say,
Is "thank you ma'am," and "thank you sir,"
And run off to my play.

It may not be with other folk.
I find to my dismay,
That startling truths formed mentally
My tongue will not betray.

The youthful Gwendolyn must have been satisfied with the precision with which she expressed the issue of inarticulateness. The poem is also one of her top achievements for this period, using a four-beat line alternating with three whose sound pattern reflects the nuances of the thought.

But the most direct evidence of the struggle of the will is in the poem "Ambition."

It hurts ~~so much~~ a lot to see the top—
And know you're at the base;
To know some power holds you back
And yet see glory's face!

But all true climbers know that they
Must rise by base degree.
And so they keep on climbing 'til
They find that they are—free!

The overall feeling of these early manuscripts persuades the reader of being in the presence of one who has chosen her vocation, that whatever the outward circumstances, she is through art increasingly seizing possession of her inner world. Both the passing of time and the necessity for plan are receiving consideration, matters that persist throughout these notebook collections. *My Fancy Book* gives the idea more fully than other notebooks of this period. "This book was started," the poet wrote on the opening page, "on Thursday, June 25, 1931, at the age of fourteen. (Somehow, I can't

realize I am that.)" A skipped space below, then: "Stories, poems, composi-
tions, and character sketches and dialogues will be written here, all composed by Gwendolyn Brooks, aged fourteen and 18 days." In *The Account
Book,* she carefully notes "Beauty Words": "fires, desires, beauty, flame,
blows, flowers, wind, winds, river, wanderlust, wanderlusts, shores, wilderness, quivers, quiver, glows, stars." The quantity of poems mounts and is
frequently noted: "20 new verses herein" (*The Account Book*); "11 new poems
herein to date" (*My Fancy Book*); "44 new verses herein" (*Blue Book of
Verse*); "58 'poems' here" (*The Red Book or the Merry Book*).

The ethical bent of many verses expresses a moral universe of which her
mother would have approved. There are good children, mischievous children, conceited, stubborn, and courageous children. Naughtiness injures
the self, envy is to be avoided, only work done willingly and with pleasure is
inwardly rewarding. In "Reproduction" (*The Account Book*), the poet holds
that the deeds we "do on earth are reproduced after death," and provides a
brief gloss on the meaning of the poem. "We Who Never Learn" advises:
"There's no excusing the first mistake / Which occurs a second time / The
error created more than once / Society deems a crime." A number of poems
console regarding death and indicate that death is a night that passes into
day or that the loved one is to be mourned but remembered as happy in
heaven. Brief poems about God stress His bounty and His provision of
beauty in nature. Thus, the poet dwelt in a unified world in which all was for
the best and all changes were explained, obviously a product of adult
prescriptions and strivings.

But the notebook poems also contain some seeming protest against this
adult world. Actually, some sentiments derived not from Gwendolyn's
home life but from whimsical impressions based on her readings of the
Harvard Classics. "A Dull Moment's Thought" (*The Account Book*) states:
"I am a warrior, imprisoned in a strong / dungeon, with hard walls all about
me. / There is only one soft spot, and that is fast / hardening into a silly
stone." A parenthetical note adds, "It has." An undated comment in *My
Fancy Book* grumbles: "When I am grown, I will let my children stay outside
and talk to other children on a scorching-hot night. *Oh, well.* One learns by
experience." In a lighter tone, a poem expresses the child's joy in the beauty
of the night, and her surrender to the wisdom of parents who feel that
children should be in the house after dark. But in her autobiography,
Gwendolyn says she was allowed to enjoy the night and the conversation
behind the front gate.

Gwendolyn's story "Alice's Brown Dress" (*Account Book*) portrays a
shopping trip during which the mother refuses to buy Alice a bright-colored

dress and insists upon purchasing a drab one instead. "But, Mother," exclaims the little girl in surprise, "*I* like it. Bright colors are *for* little girls! O Mother! Surely you aren't going to get that dull old brown thing." The next day the mother and Alice, wearing the new dress, go to visit Alice's aunt: "It was indeed too dull for a merry little girl of seven. The neck was very high, and the dress was quite straight in line. The color was dark brown." Unknown to her mother (Mrs. Sidney), Alice had "cried herself to sleep over that dress."

Alice's aunt protests the drabness of the dress. "I want my daughter," Mrs. Edith Sidney says, "to be a quiet, reserved child. . . . It is my belief that clothes have an influence—." But the aunt protests that the girl looks dull and unnatural, and that she herself will make Alice a dress if she ever sees "that ridiculous thing on her again." The next day Mrs. Sidney takes her daughter to a shop and buys her "a happy looking red gingham dress."

Gwendolyn herself seems to have later adopted the practice of wearing rather conservative clothes, since a few of her friends speak of their efforts to persuade her to wear more sprightly apparel. But she says her mother had actually encouraged her to wear light colors and cheerful styles.

In "Human Little Beings" Gwendolyn writes against punishment devoid of understanding and sympathy, but she has stated since that the situation had no personal application and that her mother was not, in any case, indulgent with kisses.

> I think that children would be nicer,
> If they had no punishment.
> Silence—shaming—which is wiser?
> Sometimes the child is innocent!
>
> And children dont like ~~pretty~~ mother's kisses,
> Much as they like sympathy.
> They want you to share their troubles—
> "Parents, won't you cry with me?"

In "Me," Gwendolyn states her satisfaction at being herself. The self of most of the poem is sprightly, loving, joyful, at times meditative. Perhaps some conflict among tendencies of the self is expressed in "Tis But a Child" (*Blue Book of Verse*):

> Tis but a child you see here seated
> In this apartment overheated,
> A child with prim and elderly looks,
> Talking of laws and lectures and books.

> Another child—we see her dancing
> Over a hill, so lightly prancing—
> Playing with leaves and grass and flowers—
> Transforming the sand into towers.
>
> If I were to have my choice of one
> I'd favor the child who loved the sun,
> And the brooklet's silvery water—
> The other's a woman, not daughter.

There's something of the model of the "quiet, reserved child" in the first portrait, something of the child happy amidst nature in the second. Most poems involving family are happy ones, or appreciative. There are poems to the mother, to Uncle Luther, to the grandfathers and grandmothers, and to the aunts, and a story representing a father. A highly ethical tone pervades "Mother's Birthday," in which Gwendolyn wishes for her (despite the rain "upon your natal day") "beautiful and gay thoughts and a mind kept in purity," allowing her to age gracefully. A poem dated May 2, 1931, deals with the death of a mother's mother (*The Account Book*, "Tears and Yearning") and offers consolation, but it is not clear that Gwendolyn was speaking of her own mother. "To An Uncle" celebrates the kindness, cheerfulness, warmth, and fun-loving qualities of "Uncle Luther, Papa's Brother." "Grandfather" (*Book of Thoughts*) supposedly celebrates both grandfathers for their piety, discipline ("One glance or glare—no words at all / Would make a haughty spirit Fall. . . . / This man had power in his eye"), and purity, but most emphasis falls upon discipline: "For though the whip was not applied / The guilty one was stripped of pride." Both Grandfather Wims and Grandfather Brooks had reputations for sternness, but the emphasis upon the eye derives from Keziah Wims Brooks's memory of her father. The grandmothers are celebrated for hard work and sacrificial qualities (*Book of Thoughts*).

Gwendolyn began *My Fancy Book* ("This is my first dedication") with a poem to her Aunt Eppie Small, the eldest of her maternal aunts, who raised three small adopted children on a fourteen-acre farm. The poem has something of the solemn tread of one of the lesser Shakespearean sonnets: "When all the love for you drains from my soul / I shall be lifeless in a silent grave." Through Aunt Eppie's friendship, "a tender hope, / the hope in glory grows, and builds the wires / Of work and struggle. These make fame's stout rope."

Much warmer is "A House" (*Blue Book of Verse*), which celebrates the hospitality and gaiety at the home of an aunt.

My auntie's house is very nice.
It is so light and free.
The kitchen often smells of spice.
(She's making things for me!)
There is a tiny, tiny hall
Closed by a bead portiere,
And often, after evenings fall,
Gay music comes from here. ~~pours~~
No matter how much mad rain falls
Or peals of thunder roll;
When once inside these friendly doors
There's comfort in the soul.
The yard is such a lovely yard!
Now, someday when I'm grown
I'll have a house just like this house
All for my very own.

"My auntie" in the poem was Gertrude Robinson of 9248 South Wabash in Chicago, whom Gwendolyn associated with fun, good food, and companionship.

But to place the emphasis upon ethical and family poems would distort the body of the work created during Gwendolyn's fourteenth year. The largest category of poems ranged over the course of nature: the seasons, sun, wind, rain, flowers, birds, night, moon, stars, darkness, morning, evening, and the like. A sizable group fall into the categories of fantasy (fairies, dreamland, and such), play, personalities, and reflections of her reading. Despite her concentration upon nature and upon "prancing," frolicking, gleeful children, Gwendolyn's own favorite pastime was playing with paper dolls. An elaborate picture of this kind of amusement is created in two poems, "Paper Doll Play" and "Paper Dolls." The second poem celebrates such play as an escape from boredom while ill. The first describes in loving detail the process of paper doll playing, and an escape motif appears, beginning with the second verse:

Now place one here and place one there,
(You'd better make a house)
Some paper children may be bad—
Some quiet as a mouse.

The paper dolls which are for sale
Cost but a dime or more.
But best of all are smaller ones
Which are not in the store.

> You find them in the fashion-books,
> And in the papers, too . . .

Gwendolyn's reading is reflected in several poems. The fantasy pieces, both poems and stories, owe something to *Grimm's Fairy Tales* and those of Hans Christian Andersen. She also wrote several patriotic pieces and a moral evaluation of the characters in Shakespeare's *Julius Caesar*, as well as several humorous pieces.

Gwendolyn took an obvious pleasure in creating from her pleasant neighborhood and family universe. By the end of 1931, the fourteen-year-old had written so many poems that a sense of form was hers, and she engaged in self-criticism. Most of her forms are traditional—variations on the ballad meter—but a few poems are in free verse. One of them, "Smoke" (*Blue Book of Verse*), reveals a potential power in the use of the image, as well as the faculty of close observation:

> Smoke is a veil,
> Of greyish, blackish thickness.
> Like a cloak
> It's wide dimensions spread,
> Until the depths grow thick.
> Grayer and grayer
> It grows,
> Fading constantly,
> And soon
> It vanishes.

"Artificial" [*Blue Book of Verse*] also breaks with the metronome effect of rhymed verse, although the final line seems to exist primarily for the sake of rhyme.

> Giant machines—
> Worshipped substitutes.
> Machines and artifice—
> Stamping out the life
> Of the natural.
> Artifice—
> Letting nature's fine resources rot.
> Machines—
> Throwing to the winds the might and right
> Of the muscles of men.
> But always I shall cling
> In heart and mind

If not in actuality
To Nature,
Mother of modernity.

Peeping forth from such poems are temporary escapes from the poetic diction of a considerable number of the rhymed poems. But even in the conventional form, Gwendolyn can occasionally impress by the tight economical line and the degree of flexibility in manipulating traditional tools. "Tis But a Child" has the ring of Robert Frost and of other coupleteers in several lines ("Tis but a child you see here seated / In this apartment overheated"). In this poem and a few others, she was able to go beyond delight in sonority and make the rhymes express part of the informing attitude. She also tried a variety of rhyme schemes.

Gwendolyn made her universe flexible. She lived in it in two guises—one being the real-life girl of quiet games, wild inner delight over the aspects of physical nature, and occasional rebelliousness; the other guise being the prancing, dancing figures of her imagination, of fantasy, and of poetic geographical features: dales, hills, mountains, brooks.

She was actually experiencing a more changeful world than that of her youthful verses—one with both pleasant and unpleasant qualities. With her mother and her brother, Raymond, she went to the movies at Chicago theaters—the Harmony on Forty-third right off Grand Boulevard, the Regal on Forty-seventh and South Park, and the Metropolitan on Forty-sixth and South Park. She delighted in love stories featuring Clara Bow, Jeanette McDonald, Bette Davis, Clark Gable, Spencer Tracy, and Katharine Hepburn. Raymond enjoyed cowboy and adventure stories, featuring William S. Hart, for example. With the characters of Clara Bow and the other romantic heroines, Gwendolyn could "participate" in the stormy but delicate passions of man and woman; later in adolescence, she would write poems that spoke of very passionate love affairs and of the pain of unrequited love.

In a more serious frame of mind, she recited poetry, after excellent drilling by her mother, in the Carter Temple Church. Sometimes she joined Raymond, father, and mother in a game of whist, or she and her brother played with the trains of which both were so fond.

Her Aunt Beulah, visiting from Topeka in the summers, brought into the atmosphere a certain style. In addition to dresses, Gwendolyn received a "natty pair" of beach pajamas, and some of her more stylish attire for parties was made by Aunt Beulah.

But the family occasion most special to her was a trip to her Aunt Gertrude's. Her brother told her, "You just like to go out there because they think you're pretty." Raymond was right. Gwendolyn felt that Raymond was something of a favorite at home. At Aunt Gertrude's, however, Gwendolyn was the princess, and she opened up there. Filled with anticipation at a visit to Aunt Gertrude's, Gwendolyn would ride the streetcar with her mother and brother from State Street to Wabash—a long trip through what was then undeveloped land. Near the "Lilydale" house at 9248 South Wabash, she would see the house built by Aunt Gertrude and Uncle Paul Robinson, who had once played a piano in nightclubs but was now solidly entrenched in "a good job" at City Hall. As Gwendolyn walked closer to her aunt's, a repressed dread of grasshoppers would suddenly break into her consciousness. Nearly closing her eyes, she would run with hysterical straightness over the grassy yard, sticking her fingers into her ears to blot out the sound of the buzzing insects.

Inside the house were ice cream and devil's food cake, deep-dark with white frosting, and she knew things were going to be exciting. Uncle Paul told jokes and played beautiful music. Aunt Gertrude taught her to do the Charleston and other dances. Gwendolyn would stroll through the house pushing back curtains made of colored beads. In the air was flamboyance, and she lost many of the inhibitions that crowded the "reserved, quiet child" of her mother's expectations. The visit touched a part of her being that would develop more expression in her adult life.

Back on her own turf, she played freely and often gossiped with her friend Ida DeBroe about the boys of the neighborhood. But frequently came the moments when she preferred to be alone in her room, or daydreaming in the backyard, playing with paper dolls, or reading, writing, or drawing. With paper dolls, she could organize "governments, theaters, tournaments, . . . wardrobes, . . . feasts."[3] She could give them personalities, and they did not require laundering of any kind. In reading, there was a lot to keep her going with her vocation. With the *Writer's Digest* before her, she felt herself part of a noble group that experienced her kind of pain, fought for the right word, struggled with nouns, received rejection slips, imagined the cold faces of editors, waited with pounding hearts for postmen.

She identified with the Canadian girl portrayed in the Emily books by L.M. Montgomery: she and Emily both kept notebooks, wrote, dreamed, aspired. She would soon be discovering black writers in Countee Cullen's anthology *Caroling Dusk* (1927).

When Gwendolyn was somewhat sated with reading, she would seek the back porch, sky-dreaming in the morning, at noon, or late in the day, at sunset or deep twilight, as she recounts in her autobiography, *Report from Part One* (1972). In the sky she saw red streaks, gold worlds, gods and little girls, angels and heroes and future lovers, all moving in "misty glory or sharp grandeur."[4] She could pretend things about her future, basing her dreams on fairy tales and allowing them to run before her in a vague expanse, a heady extension of being.

As she moved over the threshold of adolescence, she would also fantasize about boys, who behaved differently in these dreams than in her day-to-day life. At night in bed, she would dream of their embraces and of marriage, of being the mother of one child and loved to distraction by this boy/man. More often, she would be the center of attention and the object of the heart-longings of more than one boy. Like the knights of the fairy tales she read, they would fight for her favor and possession.

The "real" world often led to a feeling of aloneness, and whether daydreaming or writing, she was often self-absorbed. She would frequently fail to notice exciting games of tag or hide and seek going on nearby until her mother, anxious for her to rest her eyes and get exercise, would call them to her attention. Once her mother leaned into her room while she was writing and said, "There's a big fire down the street." "Yes," Gwendolyn replied, and continued to write.

But the changes in the world forced their way into her consciousness. For one thing, the street was changing, as whites moved out and more blacks moved in, an event that gave her new friends in the neighborhood. Her mother was concerned about the size of the families and whether the newcomers were responsible property-owners. Some of them were, some were not. The families were larger and spilled over more into the street than did the children of the earlier and smaller families, both white and black.

More serious for young Gwendolyn were the arguments between her father and her mother. The Depression was on, and her parents' quarrels, she vaguely knew, were about money. Keziah felt that David's earnings at the McKinley Music Company—$25 weekly or $30 with overtime—were inadequate. (He often got extra jobs, painting and decorating, with or without his friend Berry Thompson.) When David's wages went down to $18 weekly, then to $10, during the Depression, Keziah felt that he should find some other full-time job. Relatives of theirs were doing better and living better. But David had worked with McKinley for over thirty years and the Word during the Depression was to hold on to what you had—if you had anything at all. Besides, he was well-liked by the people at the company, relied on and trusted. The "goodness" of the company and the personal relations there were not a new topic of breakfast table conversation.

The marital disagreements climaxed one day when Keziah packed herself and Gwendolyn and Raymond off to Topeka, Kansas. The harmony Gwendolyn had known was broken, and she was disturbed by being separated from her father. On another level, she feared that she would not return to Chicago in time to enter school. David solved the problem by coming to Kansas for "his children." One of the aunts urged Keziah to let him take "his children." He did, bringing them back to Chicago, where he took good care of them by himself for a year. Although her father exuded kindness, Gwendolyn missed her mother and felt abandoned by her. In fact, when Keziah returned after a year, Gwendolyn gave her a childish rebuke. Nonetheless, she was happy again, feeling secure in the presence of both loved parents.

At the age of fourteen, Gwendolyn was surging with new feelings. She had accepted earlier parental discipline easily or at least resignedly, dissipating any resentments in the quiet or magic of her room or in the exhilaration of play. Now, however, the patient, firm, tenacious nurturing of her mother sometimes made her feel a minor tempest surging within. Her mother spanked both children occasionally—with either her hand or light "switches," branches from the backyard Tree of Heaven (ailanthus). One day, to the surprise of both mother and daughter, Gwendolyn received such a spanking with stony stillness. When her father returned from work and heard Keziah's report, he gave Gwendolyn the only spanking she ever received from him. Even then Gwendolyn stood stonily and refused to cry. It was Keziah, seeing her daughter's spirit unmoved by the correcting hand, who broke down in tears. Gwendolyn had made a very firm statement regarding her new sense of being. It would be her way of rebellion when parental guidance failed to acknowledge fully her independence.

But that conflict was momentary. What did not pass was the outer world, that other universe beyond neighborhood and family, where Gwendolyn felt she had been greeted with hostility when she entered school at the age of six. She had always enjoyed academic work. But with schoolmates her relations were anxiety-producing—at best only tentative, uncertain. In earlier days, she had suffered from the lack of social and athletic skills, retreating into writing and solitude. But now she had a fuller sense of her neighborhood, where the girls who had talked of "nasty boys" or gossiped with her about "the sharp ones" were moving into new, closer relationships with boys. She herself dreamed about boys. Irresistibly, nature had begun to exert the magnetizing power through which it peoples the world.

In early adolescence, Gwendolyn experienced her most bitter rejections at the parties for which the girls put on their finery and sparkled and the boys came scrubbed, in their best attire. In vain did she enter in the "snazzy" dresses made by her Aunt Beulah, her hair straightened, parted, and waved just right, her tongue primed for witty utterance. In vain had she been taught the Charleston by Aunt Gertrude. The light-skinned girls in their own pretty frocks were the boys' choices, as the girls had foreknown. When the dancing began, it was not the Charleston that prevailed but a sort of one-step that allowed a continuous close embrace. Rarely asked to dance, Gwendolyn sat in her chair feeling stiff and far too proper.

When the kissing games began, Post Office or Kiss the Pilla, the girls sashayed about, laughing lightly and making "smart" repartee in response to some boy's remark. When the girls began to receive "letters from the post of-fice," there would be peals of laughter. The lucky girl would go into the al-cove to meet, for a kiss, the boy who had "sent" the letter. Such girls, who re-turned looking at times demure and wise, at times somewhat ruffled, rapidly acquired boyfriends. Gwendolyn herself attracted few letters. Most often she was "timid to the point of terror, silent, primly dressed. AND DARK. The boys did not mind telling me that *this* was the failing of failings."[5]

Among the ironies, her mind perhaps increased the solidity of the wall that she felt around her. Although she experienced minor feelings of adolescent rebellion, she was probably never more her mother's daughter than when, alone in her room, she classified the behavior of some of the girls as abandoned. In later adolescence this judgment would recur. While she had a liking for flamboyance and freedom from inhibition, the attrac-tion was more or less defined by the arts and graces of Aunt Gertrude and her husband.

Gwendolyn could not consciously feel that there was anything wrong with her appearance. She thought well of her dark skin. She was too much aware of feelings of beauty and excited responses to the universe to accept fully the judgments of this other universe, although she would also yearn for its acceptance. There must be some way the world could be made to appreciate her being. Like Marian, the unfulfilled housewife of *In the Mecca*, she could not feel that she was truly seen. She would dream of burying her manuscripts to have them discovered years later, her I am-ness fully regis-tered. But jangling at her side, too, was the uneasy understanding that others felt her inferior—a knowledge that would follow her all through school.

Later she would look at her autograph albums from school days and see no evidence of rejection. One early album lists the members of the Jolly Three Club: Lillie Sykes, Ruth Dent, and Gwendolyn Brooks. Her class-mates' messages were either moralistic or jolly. Thelma E. Bowles: "Be true to the best you know." Marie Davis: "Love is shaped like a toy and if you want it broken just give it to a boy." (A later note to the comment, written by

Gwendolyn: "About this my nice father, reading it, said with a worried knitting of brows: 'I don't know why she says that.' ")

Lillie Sykes (now Lillie Rhodes): "Make your life like Arithmetic: Friends multiplied, love divided, joy added, and sorrow subtracted." Gwendolyn's later comment: "Just the kind of thing sensible Lillie would have said."

The autograph album has its share of forget-me-not notes, too. Amos Martin: "When you are married and scrubbing the floors / Think of me and scrub some More." Gwendolyn's later comment: "Yeah." Her brother, Raymond: "Remember B / But most of all / Remember me." Thelma Owens ("The It Girl") advised her not to worry, since "the worst is yet to come. Move on."

In another autograph book, from Willard School, Gwendolyn, her mother, and some friends sound a sententious note, others speak of other matters: Gwendolyn: "It is my duty to be faithful to my school. Not only is the real point of loyalty in the statement but the principle of TRUE LOVE involved. *Your* school is what you make it. You, a child, are the representative of your home." Keziah Brooks: "What is worth doing at all is worth doing well." Ocy Hanna "1930": "Remember me at Willard School gate." Mildred Taylor: "If in heaven we do not meet, I hope we both enjoy the heat." Mary Baker speaks of Gwendolyn as her best pal. Leola Jones: "You have crossed the ocean and now the bay lies before you." Ida Louise DeBroe: "In your golden chain of memory, remember me as a link."

Gwendolyn wished that she had the inner certainty, inner poise of her mother. Her mother was kind but did not exude kindness as her father did. Duty, rectitude—for her mother, these were foremost. "Duty and decency," alliterates Gwendolyn, who needed kindness instead to help warm her universe. Later, Gwendolyn remembered, she tried in a childish way to break through to her mother by calling her Keziah, as at one brief phase of her childhood she had called her father David. Her mother easily repelled this crude breach of parental status: "Call him 'David' all you like. Call *me* 'Mother' or 'Mama.' "[6] Her mother was hard to get around. Once Keziah was displeased by the low grade Gwendolyn had received for a really good paper that was blemished by ink smudges. Marching coolly upon Authority at the Forrestville School, Keziah insisted that the teacher read the paper again, since she was sure that the teacher had looked only at the messy smudges and not at the tight, clear sentences. After the teacher reread the paper, she awarded it a "Good" instead of the former mere "Pass," but withheld an "Excellent" because of the messiness. When Gwendolyn was charged with plagiarism because of her skill in composition, Keziah again mounted invasions.

No wonder Gwendolyn lost encounters with her mother, except for that time when she presented a stony, untearful face while being punished. Sometimes the contests of will were quiet and enjoyable, however. Once when her mother spoke of preferring washing dishes to any other household task, Gwendolyn laughed and asked why she didn't do it all the time, if she liked it so much. Her mother replied serenely that she would be a poor mother if she demanded nothing of Gwendolyn. In at least one other exchange in her preteen days, Gwendolyn thought that she did get the better of her mother. Keziah, after Christmas, engaged her in an argument about the correct clothes for dressing one of the dolls Santa had brought her for Christmas. Gwendolyn insisted that she had dressed the doll in the right clothes, but Keziah suddenly topped her by saying, "I ought to know because I bought those dolls, myself." After a brief interval of silence, Keziah, slightly flustered, tried to distract Gwendolyn's attention from the give-away comment. Gwendolyn, feeling a temporary sense of command, kept on smiling and did not tell Keziah that she was glad it was her parents who loved her enough to give such presents—and that they had not been delivered by "a busy flying fairy."

While Gwendolyn would perhaps never equal her mother's sense of certainty, she did know that she was a poet, a writer. In the ensuing years, while she changed from one school to another, or had this or that unsatisfying little adventure, Gwendolyn kept that firmly in mind and developed her will. She wrote a minimum of one poem each day, sometimes two poems, sometimes three, all because she *wanted* to. In school, she found particular challenges in Shakespeare, Latin, and the discovery of more and more romantic poets: Wordsworth and William Cullen Bryant on nature; Shelley and Keats on beauty; and eventually Lord Byron, in his postures of rebellion, world-weariness, sophisticated pain, and contained defiance of the emptiness of life. What she really got out of the poems was a love affair with language.

Looking back on this teenage period, Keziah was to say of Gwendolyn's poems: "The poetry she wrote during her early teens was the type that appealed to all rhyme-lovers, but it was not the kind the critics select when awarding prizes." Looking back herself, Gwendolyn affirmed this judgment. In *Negro Story*, she stated that she had known nothing of the "technical possibilities [of poetry] until she was 24."[7] That would have been in 1941, when she was participating in the writing workshop of Inez Stark Boulton—

an experience that contributed much to her writing progress. But when her comment about lack of technical knowledge before the 1940s is quoted to her today, she is puzzled, pointing out that she had read the *Winged Horse* anthology by 1932 and had by then begun to understand certain technical points from reading critics such as Louis Untermeyer. She had in 1933 written to James Weldon Johnson, the famous black writer of the Harlem Renaissance, and sent him some of her poems. In one of his two letters of response, he told her that she had talent but needed to read modern poetry. She had by then read Langston Hughes and Countee Cullen and other black writers in Cullen's anthology, *Caroling Dusk,* and in Robert Kerlin's *Negro Poets and Their Poems.* In Gwendolyn's notebook *Moods* (1935 and 1936 poems), she has a not well achieved poem in memory of another black poet, "A Picture of Joseph S. Cotter, Jr." She was moved by his death at the age of twenty-three, since he appeared to be a kindred soul: "All of his youthful brilliancy / Dead, at the age of twenty three! / part of my soul is with his in the skies, / Part of my heart is shut up where he lies; / Oh I could have loved those sensitive eyes. / Eyes that are dead."

Not until the late 1930s did Gwendolyn make a systematic and concentrated raid upon the storehouse of modern poetic techniques. And the raids were to increase under the influence of the Boulton workshop in 1941 and 1942 because it supplied what she had not had before: a systematic exposure of her faults and a coherent point of view regarding the assets of the modern poetry movement.

A reader who wanders into the juvenilia and the apprentice work by chance is likely to be startled. By 1931 there is a precocious body of work that predicts the early rise of a brilliant poet. The poet as delighted rhymester exists up to the latter part of 1935, during which period some development can be ascertained. The 1937–38 period shows a greater freedom of language, which the poet needed to get solidly into her own feelings. The progress became rapid in the 1940s.

Up through 1935, Gwendolyn's progress was mainly lateral. She entered into the experience of writing in several forms: the ballad (not new for her), variously metered quatrains, couplets, the sonnet, and occasional free verse. She worked with different possibilities in syntax: periodic and loose sentence structures and their combinations, short lines contrasting with long lines, end-stopped lines contrasting with run-overs. She used startling beginnings frequently, sharp comparisons and contrasts in descriptions, analogy, and color symbolism. Occasionally the imagery went beyond the atmospheric and ornamental, suggesting mind-states, and a distinctive

voice occasionally sounded forth from a poem. The thematic range increased: she involved herself somewhat with racial themes, although the
overwhelming concerns were love, love, love, along with world-weariness,
weariness of life, and world pain.

Outside her family, Gwendolyn knew almost no one to talk to about
writing, almost no one to take seriously a young, struggling, teenage black
writer. Most of black Chicago was overwhelmingly involved in the struggle
for survival. She would receive some encouragement in the last two years of
high school. But the kind of systematic discussion of writing that would have
accelerated—or perhaps stunted—her growth was missing until the late
1930s and early 1940s. She was also confronting the fact that the early
childhood universe could not have the momentousness or autonomy it had
once had. In her adolescent years, social maladjustment was even more
painful than earlier.

In the attempt to keep Gwendolyn in the better schools, her family used
the address of her Aunt Ella Myler to secure her enrollment in the Hyde
Park Branch High School. Here she moved from the shock of blacks against
blacks to that of whites against blacks. She and other blacks were frozen out
by a solid sheet of ice. By completely ignoring blacks, the whites let them
know that they were "not on their screen." It was Gwendolyn's first serious
encounter with interracial intolerance and was at first well-nigh shattering.
She was to recall: "It was my first experience with many whites around. I
wasn't much injured, just left alone. I realized that they were a society apart,
and they really made you feel it. None of them would have anything to do
with you, aside from some white boy if he 'fell in love' with you." Until her
experience at Hyde Park High, she hadn't thought "much about race
relations" because she saw whites only fleetingly, on the streetcar or at
certain movies. "There they were, just moving around. . . . I didn't see that
they had much to do with my life. I saw Blacks and reacted to them on a very
personal level."[8] Rising above the situation, she wrote "To the Hinderer,"
one of seventy-five of her poems that would be published in the *Chicago
Defender*'s Lights and Shadows column.

> Oh, who shall force the brave and brilliant down?
> There's not descent for him who treads the stars:
> What shall he care for mortal hate or frown?
> He shall not care, his bright soul knows no bars.

The second stanza acknowledged the oppressor's power to give pain but
asserted the indomitable power of the spirit to "rise and vanquish all." The
third invoked God's disapproval:

What thinks the Power buried in the skies
Of man's attempt to bruise and hinder man?
What pity has that Force for our poor cries,
When crude destruction is our foremost plan. [Dec. 1933]

By the time she composed the poem, she had already transferred to the all-black Wendell Phillips High School and begun a new set of adjustments. A girl who lived next door had told Gwendolyn that she would "have a ball" at Wendell Phillips High. Gwendolyn thought so, too, since it was all black and she was still smarting from her interracial experience at Hyde Park High. But by now she had really compounded the problems of grammar school, where she had found herself left out because of her lack of social and athletic skills and her dark skin. In high school, where the kids valued being "hip," she was not one of the girls who went to parties, danced the latest dances, or played Post Office and Kiss the Pilla—games on quite a different level than the games of the grammar school days. Inwardly, she yearned to be "popular," but she was not willing to try to change herself to become the "popular" girl. It seemed impossible. Given the reflexes now natural to her, which added up to a shyness that would be with her over many years to come, she was sure that she would fail as that type of girl. The intraracial prejudice against the girl with dark skin was also very strong. "A dark-skinned girl," she recalled, "just didn't have a chance if there was light-skinned competition." So she just "slumped through the halls, quiet, hugging my books. I had about two friends, if that many."

Using the address of a friend, she transferred again, this time to Englewood High. To a certain extent blacks were isolated there, but exceptions were sometimes made, and she made a few friends. When a white boy of affluent family flirted with her in a class, he was threatened by a black boy who had a hitherto-controlled "crush" on her. Meanwhile three teachers encouraged her writing: Ethel Hurn in history class, Margaret Harris in journalism, and Horace Williston in American poetry. She got along better at Englewood and remained until she finished high school in 1934.

At the age of "sweet sixteen" during the Englewood period, she went through a particularly painful social experience. Throughout high school she was not invited to the parties given by her schoolmates. She decided, then, to give one of her own and invite a large number of young people. Her mother, Aunt Beulah, Aunt Ella, and Aunt Gertrude all helped with the arrangements of the house and the refreshments. Their last-minute fixings carried them over the time at which the party was to begin. But that proved to be no problem since almost none of her schoolmates attended, and Gwendolyn was left to sit with hands folded among guests who were mainly

members of her own family. She knew that Aunt Gertrude and Aunt Ella
were making sympathetic comments, but she could not bring herself to look
at Aunt Beulah, who had made a career of not tolerating social or any other
kind of failure in her own life and was usually uneasy about failure in the
lives of others. But the misery of the party passed, and Gwendolyn steeled
herself once more.

The triumph of her sixteenth year was not to be social or coming to
terms with boys; it was to be in her writing and in the communications she
had with the black writer James Weldon Johnson. Johnson, a distinguished
writer and civil rights leader, was then serving as executive secretary of the
National Association for the Advancement of Colored People. His career,
which included service as educator, literary critic, poet and novelist, and
diplomat, took him to a variety of black community gatherings and organizations. Both Johnson and his assistant secretary, Walter White, had been
part of the black literary movement known as the Harlem Renaissance, and
they skillfully worked to help other writers and artists. Johnson believed in
art in both a practical and a sophisticated way. Art, he felt, on a practical
level, would show Americans that blacks had great creative powers and thus
deserved the better deal they were demanding.

In 1933 Gwendolyn wrote to ask Johnson what he thought of some of
her poems. Johnson replied that she was talented and that she must read the
best of modern poets, not to imitate them but to develop the highest
standards of self-criticism. The suggestion gave her a helpful push. She was
familiar with the work of Langston Hughes and Countee Cullen. Now she
began to read T.S. Eliot, Ezra Pound, and e.e. cummings, whose work she
did not like until she heard a record of him reading.

In 1937 she received further encouragement and criticism from Johnson. Of the poems she had recently sent him, he liked especially "Reunion"
and "Myself." "Reunion" was published in *Crisis* in November 1937:

> And when you come, how shall I courage gain
> To let you in the room! The silver pain
> Of seeing you, after so long a time!
> No verse at all, and surely not my rhyme,
> Can well enough express it; let it rest—
> But this I believe: reunion is a test.

Johnson was quite specific in criticizing sentimental diction, line inver-
sions, inaccurate diction, and the wrenching of a line to preserve the meter.
"Don't be afraid to put in an extra syllable," he stated—advice that Gwen-

dolyn would give to her own students later in writing classes. He underlined *phosphorescence* and declared: "This word is actually atrocious." On a poem entitled "Familiar," he noted: "starts out well but flickers out in the closing lines."

When Johnson spoke at the Carter Temple Church in Chicago, however, he proved to be distant and of forbidding presence. Gwendolyn was intimidated. But Keziah spoke up and told him that Gwendolyn was her daughter, "the one who sent you those poems, and you wrote to her." Johnson, who by that time had dealt with a multitude of aspiring artists, replied, "I get so many of them, you know." Gwendolyn and Keziah felt "chastised, properly put in our places," and "disgruntled."9

Fortunately, Langston Hughes provided an engaging contrast. He was warmly inspiring and carried himself as if he were "just folks." Gwendolyn and Keziah met him at the Metropolitan Church in Chicago and immediately felt his receptiveness. Not having written to him, Gwendolyn was hesitant, but her mother had brought "a little bunch of my stuff, and we showed it to him." He read the "work" on the spot, told her that she was "talented and must go on writing."10 During her adult years, Gwendolyn had a warm and generous contact with Hughes.

Although the surviving poems of 1933 are few, the evidence demonstrates that Gwendolyn was further motivated by the contact with "professional" writers. Her poems from this year deal with aspirations for freedom and the beautiful, and with death and prejudice ("To the Hinderer").

She began 1934 by making resolutions (*The Scratch Book*). The practice of making resolutions at the beginning of the new year, a habit acquired early, she continues to this day. The 1934 resolutions reveal firm purpose and determination:

New Year's Resolutions—1934

1. Write some poetry everyday.
2. Write some prose everyday.
3. Draw everyday.
4. Improvise at least ten pieces of music.
5. Invent several dances, including variations of the tap dance, and know them perfectly.
6. Sing persistently and improve voice by 1935.
7. Have at least seven stories accepted, and paid for by 1935.
8. Have at least fifteen poems accepted and published during the year.
9. Practice the piano continually.
10. Use correct English.

11. Become softer-mannered.
12. Become pleasanter.

Gwendolyn revised the resolutions later during 1934, reducing them to seven.

Revised New Year Resolutions
(Put into force, beginning April 1, 1934)

1. Have at least ten stories accepted and paid for by January 1st, 1935.

2. Have at least twenty-five poems (new poems) published by January 1st, 1935.

3. Become softer mannered.

4. Become pleasanter.

5. Found, "The Pioneer Star," monthly. To include 4, original, typewritten stories, 4, original, typed poems, 4 original drawings. Nine issues by January 1st, 1935.

6. Earn, during the year of 1938, from forty dollars to _____, by literary work. At any rate, not less than forty dollars.

7. Write and publish *good* book. 20 chapters, about 40,000 words. From $400 to $800, net results.

From *Writer's Digest*, Gwendolyn made a list of poetry and story markets, indicating where possible the amount paid for writings. Included in the "possible" poetry markets are *Independent Woman*, the *Chicago Herald Examiner*, *Kosmos*, *Universal Poetry Magazine*, Rose Company, *Wings*, and Buzza Company. Included in the possible story markets are *Sunday Magazine*, *Sweetheart Stories*, *Love Fiction Monthly*, *All Story*, *Romantic Confessions*, *True Confessions*, Northwestern Press, *Real Life Stories*, and Epsilon Press Service.

Two other pages of *Scratch Book* contain precise specifications of the contents for two publications she envisioned: "The Pioneer Star" monthly and "The Pioneer Star" weekly. She preferred the weekly and crossed out the outline of contents for the monthly. With something of a flourish, she added to the table of contents for the weekly: "Containing works of high quality only." Such plans were overambitious for a seventeen-year-old woman who was also finishing the last year of her high school work. But several poems of this period carry the notation: "Printed." Some poems and a rhymed story went into the Englewood High School paper.

Gwendolyn's surviving apprentice work for 1934 comprises close to a hundred poems and several stories. The majority are about a young woman experiencing the pains of unrequited love and, occasionally, world-weariness. The next largest category in quantity may generally be referred to as ethically concerned. Perhaps not surprisingly, the number of nature poems drops to a very few, and they sometimes express states of mind. Other categories: humor, friendship, current history (President Roosevelt), death, God or religion, domestic life, and school reading (a rhymed and a prose translation in March 1934 of Virgil's *Aeneid,* Book III, lines 1–444, a prose and lyric translation of lines 472–77).

Some poems are accompanied by notes revealing various moods: humorousness, wistfulness, disgust, despair. "Description" (December 17, 1933), a poem giving as her epitaph the sky as the best of friends to her, carries the note: "And here's hoping I go there." "Spring Tears" (January 11, 1934) speaks of being possessed by love for one who never knew of her love. Notation: "He's an old crabapple." In "Thoughts Straying" (February 17, 1934), she is in the painful throes of love for one who doesn't know and probably will never guess "that he's the cause of all the bitter gladness." Just below it: "Oh, yes he does." In "Oh, God, Art Thou Still With Me?" (February 22, 1934), Gwendolyn passionately appeals to God to be her Comrade, to help her brave the monstrous storm that batters her.

"Come, Springtime!" (February 22, 1934) is followed by a note quite understandable in light of the Chicago weather: "Come spring to me. Come, summer!" "Snow" (February 25, 1934), however, is followed by a note suggesting that the poem is written to relieve inner conflict: "Snow! What means it to me? Nothing means anything to me save warmly embracing arms, and love. Nothing." "Desires" (March 1, 1934) reworks the timeworn theme of love's whimsically making one person fall in love with another person who is passionately committed to someone else, who doesn't return the affections; the poem is followed by a realistic note: "It makes me sick. It does." "Pride" (February 27) pulls the persona back from an undignified grasping for a rejecting lover, but partly in vain.

> And, oh, he cut it clean, ["this fancy's root"]
> And, oh, he scraped it clear—
> But one small remnant, young and green,
> Clung to the soil, I fear.

The note to this states: "O pride!"

Gwendolyn was thus going through a literature-based storm of late adolescence, not unknown on other grounds to young men and women. Outwardly, she was quiet. Inwardly, she was seething. In the little booklet *Son-*

nets to Love, forty-one poems are devoted to love, though not all are sonnets. In these, the persona (often obviously Gwendolyn herself) goes through the various definitions and rituals of love. Love is most frequently suffering and pain, occasionally joy, in the guises of first love, absent lover, the heroine overcome by the image of another in her lover's heart, the deserting lover, the deceiving lover, the toying lover, secret love, despairing love, ecstatic love, and so on. In the forty-one poems of *Sonnets* and the numerous love poems among the fifty-two in *Poems,* Gwendolyn explores the roles of sufferer and enjoyer of love's pains and few ecstatic pleasures.

Despite so large a body of love poems, Gwendolyn's experience of love itself would remain imaginary until she left her teens behind. It is typical for the youthful writer to tend toward pathos and the tragic, to the imaginative exploration of the emotional universe, and even to the enjoyment of pain. Gwendolyn's poems are thus part of the usual development of adolescence and young poethood. In addition to the spillover tensions from real life, they partake of the romantic love of the movies and the romantic postures of other poets, with Byron and Sara Teasdale at the foreground.

The poems convey a sense of adventure at the move toward womanhood. The out-of-this-world etherealness of love imaginings gives place to the concrete: lips, arms clasping bodies, the breath of the lover upon the loved one. With this inner awareness of changes, Gwendolyn could also feel her mother's cold anxiety at recognizing the hazards of this stage of development. Rather than the "birds and bees" approach, Keziah had presented the facts of life directly, stating them simply and plainly and referring Gwendolyn to books on sexology, one being entitled *For Mothers of Teen Age Girls.* Keziah stressed the fact that mistaken steps by young girls brought on unwanted babies. Her mother was acknowledging her as no longer a child but as one confronting her destiny, though the complicated psychology of the situation was a matter for private musings and for her poems.

Gwendolyn's ethical posture is evidenced by a poem for her brother Raymond, "There Is No Spirit." The poem advised: "There is no spirit that can bring you down, / Except your own. / Your ruination shall be no man's frown / Except your own."

Poetry and writing were always fun, no matter what they involved. But Gwendolyn often had a direct kind of fun with both. She turned satirically upon the unrequited love theme in her story "Margy Is A Brilliant Girl." Margy, who had "a case on Jimmy Green," pursued him while he pursued learning and books. As a result, poor Margy flunked her classes and failed to graduate. The dramatic device is Margy going from room to room trying to get into a class with Jimmy Green, and Gwendolyn tells her fate in mock lament:

> Oh, Margy, Marge! Is this your fate: Oh, Marge,
>   you cannot graduate. And you've lost handsome
>   Jimmy—plague! He takes W.S. from Mr. Craig.
> Margy's head is in a whirl.
> Margy is a brilliant girl. [February 13, 1934]

Published in the Englewood High School newspaper, the piece was a great success.

Gwendolyn also wrote a mock lament that perhaps wasn't altogether mock regarding her difficulties with translating Virgil—"To Publius Vergilius Maro" (February 26, 1934).

> Oh, Virgil, dust and ashes in thy grave,
> Wherever that grave sepulchered may be,
> Forgive me this small speech, wherein I rave
> That thou didst ever live to harrass me.
>
> Oh, not that I do not appreciate
> The mild, concordant beauty of your lines—
> But I am puzzled by them: I translate,
> And every word seems but a set of signs.

Already she was anticipating graduation and a then uncertain future. She was not sure she would be able to go on to college, since the economic situation of her family in the midst of the Depression was not a comfortable one. Despite the uncertainty, she lost most of the pain of her experiences in the remembrance of pleasant things. In "Commencement" (February 28, 1934), she swung into the rolling Byronic lines:

> What ecstasy it is to graduate,
> And watch the dust pile on my books at last!
> But when I think of the uncertainties that wait,
> I glory in the brilliance of the past.
>
> What sheer transport has filled these final days!
> Now to my comrades I must say goodbye!
> And I foresee the deviation of our ways
> ~~My heart turns inside out and I could cry.~~
> Some courses wind to sea; some meet the sky;
> If I could join those buried in the core
> Of my heart, teeming with mixed joy and sorrow,

I'd give a hundred, happy, happy shouts and more—
But all alone I walk into the morrow.

Long have I planned, long contemplated leaping
Into the world's bright waters, swift and swirling.
Once they seemed only gleaming surface waters, sweeping
On to no end—but now I fear their whirling.

This is my prayer and ever shall it be—
That future days may sparkle with the light
And wholesomeness that my school life has held for me:
But can the future hope to be as bright?!!

A coded note follows: " 'The best laid plans o' mice and men / Gang aft agley,' " and after the Robert Burns quotation, "Oh; how true! How utterly true!"

Despite questions about the future, Gwendolyn recognized her positive achievements. She had made more friends at Englewood High than in any earlier school: Lula Battle, Cornell Kinnard, and others. Reflecting later in life, she would realize that more schoolmates had been kindly disposed toward her. As adults, they told her that they had thought she was nice, and then expected her to remember with them "the good old days." She had not made boyfriends. But there was some satisfaction that the approaches of a white boy had forced a black boy to recognize publicly her existence, and his own affection, by threatening the white.

Teachers and the school newspaper had recognized her existence and identity as poet. Ethel Hurn had given her an "A" for an extraordinary paper, a rhymed book review—a distinction indeed when very few children in Chicago were writing poetry of any kind. Margaret Harris had told Gwendolyn on the streetcar how much she liked her writing and that with her talent she must go on writing. Gwendolyn wrote of her embarrassment in being publicly singled out, but sitting in her room, a warm feeling later overtook her.

When she gave thanks for the support and kindliness of her parents, her feelings of uncertainty returned. Her father had managed to keep out of the pool of unemployed suffering the Chicago version of the 1930s Depression, when over half of the employable blacks in Chicago were out of work and 168,000 black families were on relief. [11] Gwendolyn would later learn more about such concrete matters. The fact that blacks comprised 40 percent of those receiving direct relief and nearly 33 percent of those employed by the WPA, while one-third of all Negroes in Chicago received some form of relief, was translated within the family into the general term "bad times."

The Brooks family did not experience unemployment or "relief." Gwendolyn's father and mother believed that welfare was only for the sick, the handicapped, or the elderly.[12] They insisted on their personal responsibility and, like many others, felt that relief was something of a disgrace for the able-bodied.

Gwendolyn shared such views or accepted them without question. Nonetheless, she and the rest of the family had suffered the effects of the Depression and had struggled to make ends meet. It was after sharp disagreements with her mother about his reduced salary at the McKinley Music Company that her father found part-time work at night painting stores and apartments.[13] Gwendolyn would remember seeing him trudge back out into the night after dinner. Keziah felt that they would have been better off without a tenant since the tenant's rent payments would not offset the increase in fuel bills. Keziah herself kept the tenant's apartment and her own comfortable by firing the old furnace during the winter. Gwendolyn's outgoing brother, who was well-liked because he had an easy and cheery word for everyone, worked part-time. Gwendolyn assumed more household duties. And resourceful though Keziah was in preparing varied meals, beans became a more frequent part of them.

How, then, could Gwendolyn expect to go to college? Fortunately for her, Wilson, the new two-year city college, opened in the fall following her high school graduation. Its tuition was low—about $6 per semester exclusive of book and equipment costs—and it had the support of the National Youth Administration.

She had by now experienced the delight of seeing her work in print, in minor publications, several times, and she was almost a weekly contributor of poems to the *Chicago Defender*. Besides the assurance of others, she had the writer's own evidence of identity: a considerable body of poetry, stories, and essays, mainly in notebooks—the concrete evidence of a writer's striving to express beauty in words. She would, of course, admit that her work was not all of high quality. Her drive to write one to three poems per day, she realized, meant that some efforts would be mere jingles, but some could be rescued by hard work. She had a sense of the struggle for effective language as the major problem, but did not yet feel all the ramifications of what the critics called poetic diction. Still, she was able to create some things that were truly good and to feel the excitement of catching, holding, controlling a universe of values.

By the time she left high school, Gwendolyn had worked with demanding forms and lines and was getting more of an instinctive feeling for form. What a pleasure it was to realize that, after quiet struggles behind the closed doors of her room, the piece was now right, or that a certain number of lines were right and needed no further touching. She struggled with tough traditional forms she had not yet quite conquered. She could frequently do, not perfect, but interesting things with, say, a pentameter quatrain, and she had struggled mightily with the sonnet, that most demanding of monsters and beauties. She could not yet draw the sonnet, as a critic was to say of her later, "tight as a bow string." She would realize later that at this point she was still violating sonnet form in a number of ways: using a refrain to do the job of the concluding couplet, repeating words and phrases that filled out the pentameter line but violated the principle of economy, not forcing each quatrain to clearly advance and complicate the argument of the preceding one, not placing the "turn" in the argument at just the right point. Yet she was at a point where the craftsman in her could take some pleasure in the truly good parts of an imperfect structural achievement. Take "Transformation," in which something of Byron and something of Wordsworth blend. It is not a sonnet but reveals the benefits of Gwendolyn's engagement with that tight form.

> Long have I felt a kinship with the cloud,
> And long a sweet alliance with the sea.
> Wild waters rolled, my soul rolled with them, proud
> To be in such majestic company.
> Nature's calm attitudes, or turbulence,
> All stirred me to the deepest exaltation!
> Sunshine or storm, it made no difference:
> Each drop, each beam but swelled a pure elation.
>
> The blossoming of flowers gave true pleasure—
> Twilight's pale mauve, and twilight's saffron hue—
> The cheery robin's merry, muted measure—
> Day's skyey stretch of cool, clear white and blue.
> . . . .
> But now a heavy feeling beats my heart,
> And every older ecstasy is gone—
> Gone, every chill that glimpse of moon could start,
> All dead, the rapturous delight of dawn. [October 26–27, 1934]

And so, as she left Englewood High School to face whatever the unknown morrow might bring, Gwendolyn could be aware of her identity as a poet, albeit at an apprenticeship level. In her notebooks and her already published work was clear evidence of her membership in the profession of letters.

2

Into the Morrow

A two-year program at a college goes rapidly, and later it blurs more easily than the all-encompassing environment of a four-year struggle to learn. Especially in her first year at Wilson Junior College, Gwendolyn made new friends. Over the whole period, names and faces were more distinct entities for her than before, among both close friends and those who might be called acquaintances. The old friends who now surrounded her included Lula Battle, Lucille Harris, Lavinia Olive Brascher, Myrtle Wilson, Kenyon Reid, and Theries Lindsay. Despite her habitual reticence, she had a deep feeling for people. She observed closely, wondered about destinies.

She wondered in one poem "What Will Become of Willie," who cut classes and did not study, whereas Larry, a class cutter, studied every night, while Johnny did no studying but assiduously took notes. She wrote warmly of Lavinia Olive Brascher and of Beatrice Abbott, a contributor to the Lights and Shadows column of the *Chicago Defender*. She also wrote admiringly of the friendly qualities of column contributor Lemuel H. Randolph, and of the poise and steadiness of Lula Battle. To Beatrice Abbott, she committed a series of consoling sonnets. To Myrtle Wilson, she devoted a poem asking to be remembered when Gwendolyn was rich and famous ("as I intend to be").

In the classroom, she responded to the humanity of the teachers. Something of the richness of Shakespeare came through Mr. Kaiser, he of the incisive "wit, soft cloaked," of "softness" in his "teacher-eyes." There were the "sharp, but dryer, harder, more congealed, and slyer quips" of Dr. Parsons. And she considered the "mild ways and bland / Expression that Miss Shipman has / Before, during, and after class" ("Teachers," January 1936).

Enjoying the literature courses most, Gwendolyn worked hard. She also maintained her pace as poet. A series of poems about her parents reveal her appreciation and love for them, as sometimes evident in the titles: "When

Mother and Daughters Are Friends" (October 1936), and "On the Future Loss, Through Death, of Parental Love" (April 7, 1936). The poem "To My Parents" (March 16, 1935), which carries the legend "printed," celebrates the qualities her parents revealed when free of their labors and quietly ᵥₐlking. Of her mother, Keziah:

> There is a sparkle in her eyes
> That effervesces with surprise,
> That softens with a tenderness
> And sharpens keenly with distress.

In the last lines of the verse she catches the other side of her mother: "That kind mouth can become severe— / Too docile meekness is not here." She celebrated her father's smiling patience and envied him such a gift.

Growing in her also was a racial pride for those who walked sturdily, and rebuke for those who did not appreciate blacks, including blacks themselves. Her pride is expressed in "A Brown Girl" (April 8, 1936), in which she is first sorrowful for those blacks who walk "hesitant, wonderingly, / Or cockily, with false nonchalance." But there is one tall brown girl: "How high and fine her head, / Her mouth, how firm; her eyes how cool; / How straight and strong her tread: / As if to say, 'I have no fear,' " coming down "one of their own broken streets." In her thoughts of the twenty-one-year-old heavyweight champion boxer Joe Louis, she found praise for his silence and seeming coldness, and she expressed contempt for men who were afraid to be silent. "Unspoken words are stronger, / Ungiven smiles are sweet; / Staid ice is the best cover / For strength's resourceful heat" ("Song for Joe Louis," June 28, 1935). She also, in a much lighter vein, celebrated Joe Louis's mother's pride, seeing Mrs. Louis as wanting no "slim Delilah" to teach her son to "sham and shim," wishing instead that her son keep up "your bam and bim."

On the other hand, Gwendolyn felt scorn for the woman who wrote on her job application, " 'I've Negroid features, but they're finely spaced.' " This truckling to Nordic concerns Gwendolyn found an outrage in the face of the achievements of Dumas, Pushkin, Frederick Douglass, Langston Hughes, Booker T. Washington, Duke Ellington, and Paul Robeson: "Oh, how much better if it had been phrased / "I've Negroid features—and they're finely spaced" ("Negroid," March 18, 1935). (A note to the poem states: "To be printed in *Opportunity, Journal of Negro Life*.")

Hearing blacks talk of prejudice gave her "grim amusement, and acute distress," since she felt that "the bronze youth" should be superior to false name-calling and be concerned instead with cleaning up their own prejudices. Thinking particularly of the skin color prejudice among blacks, she advised:

> But little men of Afric's swarthy shore,
> There is more prejudice within your race
> Than out beyond its shadowed bar; far more
> Within your tract than any other space.
> Why search for foreign dung, why seethe and foam
> When so much mucky filth lies loose at home?
> ["Thoughts of Prejudice," May 28, 1935]

In the last two lines here, the "quiet, reserved child" found outlet for her anger. During the next year, she would sardonically advise a "little brown girl" to cool out her love for a man attached to a "cream-hued one" who would get him first, but the grave would get him next ("Some Day," August 25, 1936).

Gwendolyn reacted sharply to Benito Mussolini's words "Dark men must learn to bow to bright." To refute him, she asked God for the "voice" and "speaking eyes" to trumpet some quick throbbing truth powerful enough to reach "the deeps of earth and skies." She wanted words "shining," hard, and "very cold," since her message is from the God who gave to blackness its "gold." Material nourishment comes from the soil of this "hated blackness" that "they despise," and "the rose whose sweets they cherish" ("Words for Mussolini," September 28, 1935).

In another vein, she attempted to register the pathos of a brown woman's temporary recapturing of her lost youth and illusions of bygone years through wearing a blue organdy dress that floats in the wind. As the breeze ceases, however, the woman is once more "merely brown / and fat and proud."

Looking back years later, Gwendolyn would see an irony in her persistent use of such terms as "brown girl," "brown boy," and "bronze youth." She had been paying unconscious tribute to blacks' evasiveness in the face of the color black.

Her poems registered her self-struggle, sometimes directly, sometimes through acquired postures of world-weariness and a worldly sense of pain. Her moods ran the gamut of youthful wonder about the future, from despair to moments of self-exultation and confidence—and sometimes defiance. In "One Thing Belongs to Me" (July 3, 1935), she sang of loneliness as her kingdom. In "Let Me Not Be Resigned" (March 6, 1936), she was weary of the monotony of work without prospect of happiness. Sometimes she saw no happiness in her future; at other times, she felt one must hold on until changed fortune brings happiness. "Another Girl" implies stoicism; the self-advice of the speaker is to not cry, since another girl has suffered "just as I." Perhaps for herself and humanity, Gwendolyn declared the isolation of all souls in "No Soul May See Another Soul," one of her better poems (August 6, 1936). She raised the question of identity, saw herself confined within four walls waiting for bright tomorrows, or found that happiness was not meant for her. Years later, when she was married and "still agonizing over "trifles," her father would say of her to her mother: "Gwendolyn wants something she'll never find—perfect happiness." On October 4, 1935, in "Plaint," she complained of God's hard, icy ears, of his failure to soothe her sufferings or to cool her tears. She pleaded that things not be as she feared, that "You, Lord, be there. / Be there, behind that enigma / Of clouds and changing air." In *A Street in Bronzeville*, Gwendolyn would carry on this dialogue with God in "God works in mysterious ways" and other sonnets of "Gay Chaps at the Bar." Throughout her work the "Enigma" harasses a universal little people who need definite answers, and finds some of its most explicit expression in *The Bean Eaters* (1966).

Returning to human beings, she warned those who neither spoke nor smiled to remember that the "caterpillars / You disclaim / When they are butterflies / May not remember your name" (May 6, 1935). In this same vein, she had written a prophetic little piece entitled "A Thousand Cheers," in which she saw herself overcoming those who strove to block her way: "A Thousand Cheers will ring for me some day / Showers of praise will fall." In the second stanza, the poet turned upon the unfriendly:

> The fools have thrown me down and bound me fast,
> But I shall break my chain;
> Is not the soul triumphant at the last?
> I'll rise again.

In still another mood, she would ignore the world and declare, in lines reminiscent of Emily Dickinson (whom she had taken to heart at Wilson Junior College after paying tribute to the delicate lines of Sara Teasdale), her complete self-sufficiency—"Myself," April 28, 1936:

> Myself is all I have,
> Myself is all I need;
> Should grain and blossoms be?
> Myself can plant the seed.
>
> Myself requires no other
> To help her better know

> Dawn splendour, gold of noon,
> Or ruddy sunset glow.
>
> Myself requires no teacher,
> Herself knows how to sing!
> She is full strong enough to be
> A lone and quiet thing.

The "Myself" realization was valuable in the midst of, at best, a seemingly indifferent universe. If it did not confer the grace of salvation nor the protection of powerful armor, it could still be summoned up for effecting truces with less confident moods. The truth is, Gwendolyn would not feel that it quite made up for a universe without love. The 1935–36 period is the one in which the surviving poems on love most abound. In her imagination, in response to inward yearnings, she became love's avatar. Now there were the throes of unrequited love. Now the lover not quite crediting her deepest emotions. Now a happy love. Now a love grown cold. Now a haughty lover returning as the beggar.

With an unconscious assist from Sara Teasdale, the poet spoke with a knowing composure of the vagaries of love and, in measured and contained tones, of love's power and love's pain:

> Two years now, and going on three,
> Sweet, you have been known to me.
> I remember every grave
> Glance, or merry, that you gave
> To me carelessly, and all
> Your mild smiles, the rise and fall
> Of your honey voice, your hand
> Hard and strong and steady, and
> The dark softness of your eyes.
> ["Two Years Now," December 5–6, 1935]

But Gwendolyn was not without humor or realism in her treatment of such an engrossing subject. "Spring" lightly points out that in the spring, while at school at least, a young man's fancy turns to thoughts of comprehensives (exams), and a young girl's "whimsy" to wispy summer clothes, bright seawater, rapturous handclasps, "warm eyes filled with admiration." The last line: "Two boos for comprehensives" (March 14, 1935). She paused in this torrent of love poems to ask herself a question: Why did she, who had not experienced love, sing of it? Her ironic and philosophical answer: "The artist is superb who knows no art." Gwendolyn's capacity for balancing sentiment (and dreams) appears in its maturity in "The Animal" (*Annie*

Allen, 1949), where the heroine is allowed to indulge in a riot of sentiment, although "reality" cannot sustain it.

Time in its swift passage effected her graduation and propulsion into the "big world" so quickly that she hardly had time to make assessments of her direction or to reflect much on Emerson's essay "Compensation," one of the pieces of literature that had most impressed her. In her universe of art, encounters with the works of Langston Hughes had made her more con-scious of the value of writing about ordinary life, so she observed life more closely and meticulously and listened to its sounds. A few poems were addressed to the general fate of human beings. At times people seemed stronger than they knew; at times, without purpose; at other times, beautiful simply as individuals. But she had not gotten down to the precise renderings that would characterize subsequent years. Her greatest triumph was a new sense of language provided by Langston Hughes and Emily Dickinson.

Now at graduation time, Gwendolyn would soon be facing a more personal relationship with the Great Depression. On March 16, 1937, in "A Brief Speech to a Graduating Class, By a Graduating Student," she spoke in the fine language of a thousand commencement addresses: "To those of us who have neither the prospect of a college education to look forward to, nor the definite assurance of a future job, all seems hazy. What is before *us*? We do not know. Perhaps fame. Perhaps obscurity. Perhaps wealth. Perhaps poverty. We do not know. But we can go determinedly forth, as steadily as possible, and with as much faith as can be mustered."

At first there was some reason for optimism. Since her seventeenth year, Gwendolyn had been publishing poems in the *Chicago Defender*. She could write a good precise story, and she had "published" a newspaper of her own at the age of 13—*The Champlain Weekly News*, which was handwritten and sold for 5 cents.[1] The news for this neighborhood paper was often born when neighborhood women told her mother stories regarding "their trou-bles and their tragedies, and I would 'accidentally' overhear them." She had also stood, without shame, in the "vestibule" of her home listening "to all of the life that went on" among the tenants of the second floor apartment. (Although Gwendolyn's reports caused some consternation in the neigh-borhood, the reason for closing down the paper was the pressure of her schoolwork.[2])

Dewey Jones, editor of the Lights and Shadows column of the *Chicago Defender*, thought that the black publisher Robert S. Abbott would give her a job as reporter. Abbott had achieved fame not only in Chicago but also internationally for his forthright reporting, his emphasis upon racial pride, and his championing of justice for blacks. He had created from zero a

million-dollar enterprise that gave to the black community powerful expression.

When Gwendolyn wrote to him, Abbott's reply setting up an appointment was cordial and obliging. At this prospect of a step upward in the
world, Gwendolyn and Keziah were excited. But their hopes were dashed at
the start of the interview, when Abbott's face changed expression upon sight
of Gwendolyn, attended by her mother Keziah. Gwendolyn remembers that
the interview was cold, perfunctory, almost hostile. Abbott said sternly, "If
we hire you, you will have to be on time every day," and after the interview
Gwendolyn did not hear from him again.

Since his letter had been so cordial, Gwendolyn felt that his change
arose from her old source of rejection: skin color. According to Abbott's
biographer, Roi Ottley (*The Lonely Warrior*), Abbott himself had been
warned not to try to practice law in Chicago because his skin was too black;
he also had an obsession about white-skinned black women. When he
divorced a wife who was light enough to pass for white, he was reported to
have instructed his lawyer to inform the judge that she was in fact not white,
lest such a mistake create for him a bad financial settlement.

For her personal satisfaction, Gwendolyn published her own mim-
eographed newspaper—the "News-Review," priced at 5 cents. A surviving
copy, dated October 6, 1937, reports on cultural matters, a speech by
Associate Justice of the U.S. Supreme Court Hugo L. Black, and a variety of
local happenings. She included an editorial, a short story, a poem, and a
cartoon of Justice Black contributed by her brother Raymond. The cartoon
shows a black hanging from a tree while a Ku Klux Klansman stands in the
foreground, rope in hand. Under the cartoon Justice Black, who had
confessed to having been a Klansman, is quoted: "I number among my
friends many members of the colored race."

The newspaper ran a series of brief biographies "to strengthen the
general regard for great Negroes and great Negro accomplishments of all
time." Under a brief life of Alexander Dumas on October 6 is a short
editorial:

If only those who are so prejudiced against Negroes would ponder on the true fact
that outer coverings are but the irrelevant wrappings of the Article, never genuine
indicators of its value.

Observe how carelessly the Ultimate Receiver disposes of those wrappings.
Watch you, how He drops them there, and leaves them to rot where they fall.

But the inner soul-gem He takes in His detergent hand, polishes and retains.

There are also quotations from Emily Dickinson ("Success is counted sweetest / By those who ne'er succeed"), Shakespeare on holding tightly one's friends, and the Reverend Harold Kingsley on the endurance of blacks. Then a quiz on black authors requiring the printed answers James Weldon Johnson, Countee Cullen, Claude McKay, and Langston Hughes. Gwendolyn's newspaper indicates the state of her racial consciousness—one shared by the progressive blacks of the period.

Results from her quest for jobs remained disappointing, though there were brief periods of employment. She put aside thoughts of the attainments that her education was supposed to provide, and took what jobs were at hand. She briefly held domestic jobs east of Chicago's Drexel Street, then a much guarded enclave, and on the North Shore. The terms of this domestic service, too humiliating to talk about at the time, stripped her of a sense of dignity. After long germination, Gwendolyn made slashing satirical portraits of the situations in Chapter 30 of Maud Martha, "At the Burns-Coopers," and in the poem "Bronzeville Woman in a Red Hat" (The Bean Eaters, 1968).

Her most haunting and humiliating work experience, however, was her employment by a spiritual advisor, E.N. French, in the huge deteriorating Mecca Building on Dearborn and State. French traded in dreams and frustrations and supplied "answers" to deeply troubled people. He sent his assistants, including Gwendolyn, through the several-storied building with "Holy Thunderbolts" and other fakeries. Meanwhile, all kinds of things were happening in the dreary, worn-out tenement building. Gwendolyn would later list contrasts: "murders, loves, lonelinesses, hates, jealousies. Hope occurred, and charity, sainthood, glory, shame, despair, fear, altruism."[3] The people represented the spread of black humanity.

Of her earnings of $8 per week, Gwendolyn gave one-fourth to her parents, about the only benefit of her job. Traveling all over the building, she felt involved in the fakery of the minister and the degradation and poverty of the inhabitants. Not wanting to go home empty-handed, she spent four months in this employment and left only when she was fired for refusing promotion to assistant minister, a position that would have required her to do some preaching. Periodically over the years she would struggle to write of the experience but would not succeed until the publication of In the Mecca in 1968.

Despite disappointments, Gwendolyn was on the verge of a transformation in her social and intellectual life. At the continued urging of her friend Lula Battle, she attended a meeting of the NAACP Youth Council—and joined. At that time, the Youth Council was the most militant organization for black youth except for organizations of the Left. Young black writers and intellectuals gathered there in a community of aspirers.[4] The Council had been established in 1936 by Jeanette Triplett Jones, civic leader and dean of girls at DuSable High School. By 1937 the advisorship passed to Mrs. Frances Matlock, then a young and energetic teacher just beginning her civic labors. Like Mrs. Jones, Mrs. Matlock gave to the organization physical, mental, and financial contributions.[5]

Gwendolyn found herself in sprightly company, some of whom would also accomplish their early ambitions: Margaret Taylor Burroughs, now a painter and founder-director of the DuSable Museum; George Coleman Moore, writer and teacher; Theries Lindsey, now an attorney; John H. Johnson, now head of Johnson's Publications; Sarah Merchant, now a teacher; Joseph Guinn, then the head of the Youth Council, now a California teacher.

Gwendolyn found herself immediately accepted as a valuable addition— someone who had definite skills to offer and, on those occasions when she spoke, something to say. On the purely social level of informal talk and dances, there was the usual pairing up of boy and girl friends, but not on the rather simple basis of who can dance, play kissing games, or display a light skin. Although they had the simple exuberance of youth at recreational pastimes, they were also self-consciously intellectual and were looking for another level of sophistication. In meetings and informally they were direct and, in terms of formal society, sometimes unconventional. But warm. Both Margaret Burroughs and Thelma Johnson, who also served as president, were dynamic young women who helped create a spirited atmosphere.

In this context, Gwendolyn felt a blossoming, although she often kept her mouth still while others were speaking up. She would not instantly get over the reserved and retiring mannerisms she had acquired. But she liked the people, and according to friends did not withdraw when she received friendly advice from some of the other young women. They felt that she dressed too conservatively, that she should wear clothing that gave a slightly bolder emphasis to the womanly appointments the Creator had conferred upon her. (Gwendolyn does not remember receiving this advice.) At any rate, their conversation was a far cry from the earlier nagging comments of teenage acquaintances who thought that because she stayed in her room and wrote while they attended parties and danced, she was asking to become an old maid. She was not totally committed to her mother's concept of the quiet, orderly, "front yard existence." But her younger contemporaries seemed to demand a command performance, a show. From that she would continue to shrink, but she was full of vitality and on the inside she was seething. Like others who had lived an ordered existence, she had her own yearnings for her share of the spontaneity of life. The Youth Council accorded better with the complex responses she felt within.

On the civic level, she found herself marching with the group about the streets of Chicago in protests against lynching—paper chains around the marchers' necks symbolizing blacks' lack of freedom. On the social level, there were dances, to one of which came worried union officials ready to close up if it looked as if the Youth Council would not take in enough money to pay the musicians. Mrs. Matlock boldly guaranteed payment so that the dance could go on—a matter that was eventually to get her on a list of those "unfair to labor" when the group defaulted and she could not make the payment.

Gwendolyn was also "receiving" young men at home and for long walking and talking dates. One day a dignified young man named Henry Blakely, who wrote poetry, stood in the doorway of the YWCA on Forty-Sixth and South Park (now Martin Luther King Drive). Sarah Merchant had suggested he come to the meeting of the Youth Council, where he would find a "girl who wrote." As a "fella who wrote," he was anxious to meet her. When she first saw him, Gwendolyn was sitting with Margaret Taylor (now Burroughs), then an aspiring painter. To Gwendolyn, Henry Blakely was a glorious man who stood with an obvious dignity—always to her an impressive trait in a man—looking the situation over. Suddenly, Gwendolyn heard herself saying with unaccustomed boldness, "There is the man I'm going to marry."

And Margaret, who was known for her spunk, called out, "Hey, boy, this girl wants to meet you."[6]

3

Struggles, Triumphs

On Sunday, September 17, 1939, two years after they had met at the YMCA on Forty-Sixth and South Park, Gwendolyn Brooks and Henry Lowington Blakely, Jr., were married in a simple 4 P.M. ceremony attended by relatives and old friends. The service proceeded smoothly, with the Reverend T.C. Lightfoot leading the ritual and Gwendolyn standing in a $7 red velvet dress, flanked by Henry in his new suit. When the minister asked, "Who giveth this man and woman in marriage?" there was a brief silence, although David Brooks was completely attentive. Keziah stepped forward and said, quietly but distinctly, "I do." The Reverend Lightfoot continued the ceremony without a break in rhythm.

Actually, the two mothers had all along played central roles in the courtship developments. Pearl Blakely had opposed the marriage on the grounds of Henry's needing more time to face hard realities. Even after the wedding invitations had been issued, she had resisted. Henry, she said, was a boy from a poor family, respectable and God-fearing but poor, something of a dreamy young man, still attending college and without the experience of a regular job. He had not had time to focus himself for confrontation with life, and was thus not ready for marriage. He did not even have the clothes for the ceremony, in fact. If he married now, he would marry in tatters. (Henry's Aunt Mary eventually bought his grayish-blue wedding suit.) Gwendolyn and Keziah thought over Pearl's speech. In his favor, Henry was obviously a good young man who had to struggle like everybody else. Gwendolyn cared for him, and he shared her interests, having written poetry since the age of eleven. Physically, he was above medium height, broad-shouldered, strong, and—she would even say under pressure of later tension between them—"a man of intellect, imagination, and dynamic 'constitution,' the old folks' name for a certain physical indomitableness, an on-going strength that resists, again and again, threats to its proud survival."[1] Henry had celebrated their future lives in a poem in which, today, trite diction and sentiment are equally noticeable—"soft voice / kindling to muted flame" and a love that could not fade with the years. The last two lines: "And our souls singing love's serenade / Till time is gone." Eventually, Keziah and Gwendolyn decided in favor of carrying out the wedding.

In the families of the lovers and in the lovers themselves, there were sharp contrasts to be dealt with. On the maternal side, Henry emerged from a closely knit extended family. They had followed Aunt Mary Telley's journey from Kentucky, where her grandmother had emerged from slavery as a child of seven. Seeking work, she soon became the leader, reared Pearl, and helped the others to become settled. But Henry's background also included a mixture of his parents' failed aspirations, the shock of his father's desertion when Henry was thirteen, and the love and severity of his mother in rearing children as a single parent. In contrast to Gwendolyn's relatively austere but stable material surroundings, Henry had moved nomadically with his family from apartment to apartment. His father's quest had brought him from Atlanta, Georgia, to Chicago, where he met Pearl at Wendell Phillips High School.

In his book *Windy Place* (1974), Henry portrayed something of the impact on him of his mother and father. Here his father is the ingenious technician and mechanic, the dreamer and adventurer who wouldn't be tied down, and a man who refused to give up his youth:

> Mother was earth
> and nourished us.
> But Daddy saw earth
> as mire
> trapping the feet and movement
> and promises of far journeys.

Henry Sr. was the source of the irregular financial support that often kept them moving into basement apartments and confronting lean table fare.

> Hunger I came to not care for,
> nor for Daddy,
> before I was old enough to see
> that dreams
> must be paid for,
> that it is as right
> to want fuel for flight
> as for boiling beans.

A man of dramatic successes as well as domestic failures, Henry's father had learned the steamfitting trade and at times held contracts on large buildings. But his dreams of inventing took time from more routine efforts to support the family. Pearl, feeling that they paid too much for his visionary ways, once smashed a hand laundry machine he had devised. When Henry Jr. and his two brothers were nearing adolescence, their father abandoned the family and began living with another woman. Of the children, young Henry seemed hurt most by his father's desertion. He was to remember his mother's upbringing as combining severe whippings—in her attempts to conquer his and his brother's mischievousness—with tenderness, which included reading poetry to them.

Although Henry could not acknowledge it then, he was the son of both the mother and the unacknowledging father. He had the technical abilities of his father, something of his dreaminess about life, and he would also reflect the more practical instincts of his mother. His work at Tilden High School fulfilled his technical bent; his work at Wilson Junior College fulfilled his desire to imagine and to know things simply for their own sake. Gwendolyn, on the other hand, had developed a will for the writing of poetry, having nourished it since her very early days. She retained a romanticism. The tales of knights and ladies had their place in a poetic imagination—even if their function was increasingly to drive home a certain kind of realism. Of direct influence also were American movies, which pictured existence above the daily tedium and upon which she and Henry would feed for important aspects of their own dream-life.

In the Tyson Apartments on Forty-Third and South Park, the newly wed couple looked out from their honeymoon kitchenette. Gwendolyn felt the cramped dreariness, the increep of bleakness into her earlier feeling of happiness. Yet the two would not be able to afford even the Tyson for very long.

The two years leading up to the marriage had somewhat eroded but not eliminated the "quiet, reserved child" by providing her a close citizenship within the Youth Council. Although she listened more than she talked, the group paid attention when she spoke and had made her its NAACP secretary. Margaret Taylor Burroughs drew her into helping organize the Cre-Lit Club, a group of artists and writers who shared artistic and social impulses, with emphasis on the social. Margaret remembers the young Gwendolyn as a person of quick wit and artistic commitment who participated in the heady social life of the group's parties. The group tended to assume a protective attitude toward her. With the women she gossiped about men—and about art, especially with the poet Margaret Danner, with whom there was intense discussion of men and metre.

Describing her relationship with men and groups during her adolescent period, Gwendolyn emphasizes herself as the "ugly duckling." But the autobiography *Report from Part One* points to dates with various young men, and she had more than one proposal of marriage—even after Henry's own proposal. She had very close friendships with other young men, who apparently took seriously her image as that of still waters running deep. Particularly, however, did William Couch excite the attention of all the young women in the circle, and Gwendolyn was no exception. He is remembered as dressing, talking, and gesturing with style, reaching for a world broader than that of the South Side.

Technically, the world of South Side blacks of that day was bounded on the east by Cottage Grove Avenue and on the west by Wentworth, but there were radical or liberal interracial enclaves, museums, and theaters. A goodly amount of "sophisticated" talk took flavor from the self-contained life of the South Side amidst specific institutions: the Regal Theater, the Club de Lisa, certain restaurants, shows (including vaudeville), and the greater world of events in art, literature, and politics. As it eroded, there would be nostalgia among those who had experienced this self-contained life of black institutions and the creativity evidenced. But Couch and other young men were also part of a break-through-your-provincialism thrust of the period. Attracted to the University of Chicago, he first attended lectures there and would eventually earn a Ph.D. in literature and become a college teacher. He and Gwendolyn's critic friend Edward Bland met after listening to a lecture on Schopenhauer and engaging in a fiery intellectual analysis.

Gwendolyn was surprised at the impact Couch had upon her. Plenty of imaginative encounters with men in her poetry portrayed the touch of the flesh, but the direct encounter was a different experience. Tall, handsome, of dark brown skin, and dressed in the hip manner of the period, Couch conveyed suavity. In a mixture of fascination and outrage at male boldness, repelled by its arrogance, Gwendolyn retreated. Perhaps the little girl of "A Song in the Front Yard" (*A Street in Bronzeville*, 1945), who was tired of the front yard roses and wanted a peek at the back where "hungry weed grows," had first been made aware of the disorderly impulses of the self. In her 1953 novel *Maud Martha*, Gwendolyn would use Couch as a model in the satirical chapters "first beau," "second beau," and "an encounter." He also appeared in one of the war sonnets, "Gay Chaps at the Bar" (*A Street in Bronzeville*), as the young man reporting on friends of shattered sophistication whom nothing had taught to face the lions of war.

Through her encounter with Couch, Gwendolyn was brought closer to Edward Bland, the young critic who assumed the group's role of protector. It was the beginning of a valuable friendship that would last until Bland was killed in World War II. He had been a member of the South Side Writers Group that Richard Wright organized in April 1936.[2] Later, his articles on poetry and fiction would show great promise, though he did not live to create a body of work.

Gwendolyn's extant notebooks of the 1937-39 period are fewer than in earlier periods, and some writing is in faded script and a difficult workshop handwriting. Still, the evidence is that Gwendolyn was filling notebooks with poems and stories and achieving publication. These poems are interesting for simple technical developments and for revelation of her state of consciousness. *Crisis Magazine* in June 1937 carried a poem of thirty-eight lines that protested lynching. In four-beat iambics, it graphically records the lynch scene, the dead black, and the lynchers. ("One lyncher goes / and twists the lips so tightly pressed. / Blood oozes from them.") At home, a young child waits for the dead and "loved father." ("Tardy, he! / Tardy forever are the dead. / Brown little baby, go to bed.")

In the notebooks of this period, the largest category of themes again concerns love: painful, satisfying, disillusioning, exulting. Fewer deal with world-weariness; several are involved with nature, the self, and friendships. There are also a few on moods and racial situations that reveal the poet's progress in consciousness. Often there are marked simplicity, restraint, a dramatic arrangement and pacing of lines, and images worked solely for functional impact. "Transfiguration," for example, celebrates the presence of the lover:

> My room is all aglow with light
> And fervid with a flame
> It never knew
> Until you came.

Such a poem, of course, is well within the tradition of such women poets as Sarah Teasdale and Elinor Wylie, though Wylie's cutting edge is usually sharper. In overall use of simple devices and structuring, the same may be said of "Gypsy Girl," which tells of the unhappiness of the poem's speaker, and "The Postman has passed," portraying disappointment over lack of a letter from the lover.

In "Wings" one hears an Emily Dickinson note in the second stanza.

> (So evident—
> His walking's nervous hopping—see?

> Indeed, a bird was meant
> To fly!"

An analogy is built up with the self, for whom the sky is also proper dominion. A note in parentheses states: "Addressed to myself, of course." This indirect method of approaching the self will frequently be found in the later poet.

Two poems may represent something of her racial consciousness: "To A Brown Butcher Boy" (February 1-4, 1937) and "Little Brown Boy" (January 26, 1938). The poem to the butcher boy advises the youth that he must rise by "measured difficult steps" and curb his excessive eagerness. It is interesting in terms of the conservative approach of the poet, although an argument could be made that it is a parable of the artist (or perhaps of any "rising"). But actually the poet seems to line up with Booker T. Washington.

> Your ascent shall be
> Significant of a race's gradual rise.
> Be not shame of puzzled feet that falter—
> Inevitable.

The boy is to retain the "dream-gold" in his soul-rich eyes and win by persistence. "Little Brown Boy" admonishes the boy for crying because a white child called him "darky" and argues that such worthy people as Paul Laurence Dunbar, Booker Washington, and Frederick Douglass ignored such nuisances and concentrated upon achievement. Thus he is called upon sternly to dry his eyes. Somewhat reminiscent of Langston Hughes's "Mother to Son," the poem achieves the illusion of presenting in the mother a wise and forceful personality.

The technical advance in other poems is in the poet's struggle with form, the Shakespearean sonnet, whose structure she still needs to tighten.

Several poems to friends are interesting for reflecting Gwendolyn's state of mind regarding herself. One example is the contrast between the inner peace and calmness of a friend ("For Lula V. Battle," August 7, 1937) and the speaker's "fierce unrest," "febrile furor," and "swirled confusion." An earlier first-person poem ("Then," March 20, 1937) speaks of personal confusion: "All is confusion within me now, / But this shall not always be so." In time, happiness would come, and forgotten would be "these waiting years."

Such conflicts appear frequently during youth. Perhaps of more significance for Gwendolyn was the conflict between becoming a woman and acquiring fame. In July 1937, she had created a speaker troubled by internal voices advising attention to her womanhood before attention to "hobbies" and other matters. "Dare you tell me this? No caution need I from your feeble tongue. I shall not heed your caution; twenty full Green springs have I seen burst to fruit. And Twenty amber summers: flowers of Golden autumns and white winters. I am now a woman: 'woman be' you cry! I am a woman even in this hour. But being woman simply simply 'woman,' nothing more— A meagre lot! Oh, glittering cloud rich height that waits upon my rise! Oh, sweet, bright renown: Up, up and out of my bright, sweet robin notes! Soon even to heaven—lush, wild, hysterical my voice shall charm the majesty of lands far across the sea."

> Faint voice, 'be still!
> 'First,
>   First,
>   A woman be, oh little maid!' [July 1937]

In the same month, the speaker overruled fame as the goal in a poem entitled simply "Girl" (July 5, 1937). She frankly stated her weariness with the quest for bright but evanescent fame, confessed desire to be loved, "touched," "kissed" and "held." She wanted "a man's heart / To race at my coming, / His eyes to glow softly— / I am only a girl / I am only a girl after all." Six months later, Gwendolyn returned to the theme in the poem "Since There is Always Poetry" (January 15, 1938). She questioned why she should not be satisfied with the creation of poetry, but decided that she would be dissatisfied: "But as for happiness, / That comes with Love alone, / I guess." Such poems strike the confessional note and suggest inner conflict and struggle. In terms of art, however, they reveal a movement away from a simple patness in which neatness of technique is the lasting impression. There is the definite impression that he who touches the poem may be touching also the flesh-and-blood woman. In her interviews and in letters of that period, the contradiction is unresolved. Certain statements insist that she is the ordinary wife and mother who writes; others, that writing has as high a priority as the domestic and is her only real interest.

Gwendolyn was also writing sketches and stories, as she had done in earlier periods. One of the undated stories, "Sixteen," about a young girl's romantic interest, evidences a skill that should have made it publishable in one of the popular magazines.

By 1939 Gwendolyn was ready to move out of the apprenticeship period. Earlier subject to unpredictable ambush by worn-out diction, she was now less caught by the conventions of the old masters. Her further development, however, awaited a catalyst that would arise partly from the ferment in her consciousness. The newly married state was causing her to look at the more Edenic life of her youth in new ways.

In facing the raw economics and brutally discriminatory housing of Chicago, Gwendolyn and Henry had naturally a certain innocence, optimism, and youth as their capital. *Report from Part One* recalls (amidst austerity) fun, company, mutual pleasure in reading. Still, the external Chicago pressures made this a period of great struggle. Housing was particularly troublesome. By 1940 the area where blacks lived in the city would nearly halt its expansion. Yet during World War II, 60,000 would migrate into the city—as had 40,000 during the Depression. Near the end of the war, the area would increase by one square mile. Gwendolyn and Henry went through a series of one-room kitchenette apartments, a device by which real estate operators were able to make good profits from the black community's pressure for living space. Whereas Gwendolyn's parents, by dint of savings and taking in a roomer, had soon moved into their own home on a quiet and idyllic street, Gwendolyn and Henry found themselves moving only to move again. At 6424 South Champlain, they increased their living space by renting a two-room apartment. There were, however, five apartments on their third floor location and only one bath, and Gwendolyn and Henry lived on the left side of the building with no view of the street. But Gwendolyn was more contented here than she had been in her last residence. She was also pregnant with their first child, a cause for domestic happiness but also for serious concern about money and the possibilities of another job.

Aside from housing difficulties, Gwendolyn and Henry were confronting what sociologists called "the job ceiling," which kept the masses of blacks confined to service jobs and to unskilled and semi-skilled labor. David Brooks, who had come to Chicago in 1908, had fitted himself into the service category and had held on there tenaciously over the years. White immigrants held most of the industrial jobs and they controlled the unions, facts that meant difficulties for blacks all along the way. The Blakelys' aspirations would naturally be above the job ceiling and challenge it at almost any level. Henry, having only high school technical training, was outside the recruitment areas for apprenticeship service and in-plant training. Such sectors as public utilities, electrical, manufacturing, banks, and offices had a whites-only employment policy. The government offered some escapes in the clerical area, but the competition for such jobs, even within the black community, was fierce indeed. As one person attempting to find work at the time stated, the black who did get the white-collar job displayed his symbol conspicuously—the closely clutched brief case. But in government the ceiling on technical work remained rigid; craft unions exercised considerable political power and were sometimes the ones to give the Civil Service examinations, in which case a highly qualified black who had passed state tests could find himself "failing" an examination prepared by the Chicago Civil Service Commission. The union administered the examination.[3]

Henry found work at a black insurance company, but it was dependent upon the unstable economic circumstances of its customers. After writing up a goodly number of new clients, Henry found them dropping the insurance because of family mishaps or the loss of their own employment. Whatever the calamity, insurance had to be the first expense to go among poor people, hopefully to be picked up as circumstances later improved. Since the company penalized losses of policies severely, Henry had difficulty predicting his own income from week to week. He also felt that the company's labor policies showed favoritism in assignments and opportunities.

At home, when Pearl Blakely was their guest, she sometimes peeved Gwendolyn by giving advice and instructions regarding housekeeping. But Pearl and other members of the family were most concerned about the amount of time Gwendolyn and Henry gave to poetry while they were facing one of the toughest and most discriminatory labor markets in the country. Finally, Pearl took Henry aside and told him bluntly, "Poetry ain't going to make you no living." Her dictum refused to be ignored, yet neither one of the couple could think of abandoning poetry. In time, the daily commitment to poetry gradually became Gwendolyn's to assume directly, and the hope was that she would make good for both of them. Henry wrote fewer poems and became more valuable for his critical suggestions to Gwendolyn regarding hers, while looking to his role of being the provider of material welfare.

These raw, realistic, no-nonsense confrontations combined with the thin stream of contacts from the Chicago Black Renaissance of the 1930s to push Gwendolyn's artistic sensibility further toward sophistication and poetic realism. Black music had had a renaissance during the 1920s in Chicago, with the entrance of blues and jazz. One Chicago writer who emerged from the 1920s with a very tough sensibility, beyond the exoticism affecting much of the Renaissance, was Fenton Johnson, who had published in *Poetry* magazine during the teens and had written very romantic poetry before being influenced by such realists as Edgar Lee Masters and Carl

Sandburg. Johnson's most famous poem, "Tired," was to be pessimistic and nihilistic. It stated that "I'm tired of building up somebody else's civilization" and concluded:

> Throw the children into the river; civilization has given us
> too many. It is better to die than to grow up and find that
> you are colored.
> Pluck the stars out of the heavens. The stars mark our des-
> tiny. The stars marked my destiny.
> I am tired of civilization.[4]

Fenton Johnson would probably not want to be remembered by "Tired" alone, but it shows the pressures in the climate on the individual consciousness. Later, such Harlem Renaissance writers as Langston Hughes and Arna Bontemps would be familiar personalities on the Chicago scene.

The Renaissance received a considerable push forward from the Left during the 1930s and the birthing of social ideals that opposed the old Renaissance feelings of uniqueness through exoticism. The Communist party had influenced the climate with its proliferation of John Reed writing clubs, thus providing a base for a large number of writers, including Richard Wright. By July 27, 1935, the Federal Writers Project was born, an agency that would subsidize and provide identity for many writers. Subsequent to the meeting of the Left-leaning National Negro Congress, Richard Wright brought the black writers' Renaissance to Chicago by organizing the South Side Writers Group in April 1936.

According to Michel Fabre, among the group's twenty members were Frank Marshall Davis, poet; Margaret Walker, poet and novelist; Marian Minus; Theodore Ward, who was then working on the famous drama "Big White Fog"; Robert Davis, poet; Edward Bland, poet and critic; and Russell Marshall, Fern Gayden, and Dorothy Sutton. Richard Wright and Claude Lightfoot, of the International Negro Youth, were the most radical, according to Fabre, but many considered themselves militant, and it was difficult not to be caught up in the social realism and proletarian literature of the time. Wright declared that his plan was to lead the group toward radicalism, although the group itself, said Fabre, may not have had such aspirations.[5]

Although she acknowledged that Wright had been her hero for years, Gwendolyn was not to meet him until the mid-1940s, and would not have read his manifesto, "Blueprint for Negro Writing." But Margaret Burroughs, the first person Gwendolyn had met with wide interests in ideas and the arts, brought Margaret Walker to see the young poet during the late 1930s.

She also provided Gwendolyn with her first experiences of racially integrated gatherings and had contacts across the board with social organizations, including the NAACP, the National Negro Congress, and the
National Labor Council.[6] Margaret would later find that the FBI had kept a
file on her beginning in 1937 and had labeled her as one of those attempting
to influence Gwendolyn politically.

Ted Ward, who had been part of Wright's 1930s workshop, eventually
moved into a storefront next door to the Blakelys' kitchenette on the second
floor of 623 East Sixty-Third and contributed to spirited discussions of art
and social issues. Gwendolyn apparently was retiring in the face of these
discussions, and they often boiled down to arguments between Henry and
Ted, since Ted held radical views. In one of Gwendolyn's major poems in *A
Street in Bronzeville*, "Negro Hero," he saw the issue of war not as idealism
but as a natural working out of the capitalistic system. Thus the poem in its
present form did not deal with the real issue. For a while his statement
cooled the friendship between him and Gwendolyn, since she felt he was
trying to tell her how to write.

Approaches from a simpler humanistic point of view were more influential. Edward Bland, it will be recalled, had been a part of the Wright group,
and his articles revealed a strong interest in the interaction between social
forces and literature. Gwendolyn speaks of the Bland brothers, Alden and
Edward, as people who "patiently helped teach Henry and me to *think.*"[7] As
Alden now reconstructs the sessions, they had to do with how the artist
conceived of his role and what values were to be stressed. The protest
against the distortions of institutionalized racism and painful oppression
were important, but so were the positive values reflected by the black
experience. Protest alone was not enough. Extremes to be avoided were
idealizing of the negative and excessive commitment to individualism. On
the other hand, the collectivist approach did not seem fully enough in touch
with the subtle springs of human motivation. The individual writer would
have to know what he deeply felt—the primal source of strength—and to
hope that the reader would discover a commonality. Thus arguments would
work themselves out in terms of technique—"how to say." Still today a
severe critic, Alden does not feel that he achieved such coherence in his
novel *Behold a Cry* (1947) nor that Gwendolyn fully worked out her role as a
member of an oppressed group.

Alden credits his brother Edward, who died during a dangerous volun-
teer mission in World War II, with having been the powerful influence.
Having written poetry and some fiction, he turned to criticism and worked
through writers' organizations and direct confrontations. According to

Alden, he was Socratic in his approach to another's writing, seizing the intention and, without laying down rules, demonstrating helpful parallels in the writings of others. Up to this point Edward's system seems similar to that of Richard Wright as described by Ralph Ellison in *Shadow and Act*. But it may have gone beyond the Wright of the highly political 1930s. Edward's way, according to Alden, created a voyage of self-discovery, so that a writer could consciously see the true feelings. The parallel readings then brought matters out more graphically.

Wright was drawn a further distance in his attempt to escape a simple middle-class consciousness imbedded in the ongoing system. In "Blueprint for Negro Writing,"[8] Wright gave a full development of his early radical point of view. In the individual writer's attempt to escape the harsh lot of the masses through individual achievement, he had been a part of a process which had created two cultures: an imitative Negro bourgeoisie, and the Negro masses who expressed their meanings and hopes in the powerful images of a spoken folklore. Folklore contained the beginning of a new culture in the shell of the old and a nationalism which the writer must possess in order to transcend. The task was to show blacks to themselves, to replace the waning authority of the Negro church, to create the values by which the group was to struggle, live, and die. The civilization is doomed "the moment a people begin to realize a meaning in their suffering." For many young writers, Marxism supplied the meaningful picture of the world as it is today. But Wright stopped short of saying that all writers must become Marxists. "No theory can take the place of life." But the writer must have "a theory about the structure, direction, and meaning of modern society" or be "a lost victim in a world he cannot understand or control." Other comments avoid yoking the writer to specific party platforms and expect him or her to respond to a deeply achieved consciousness. The necessity was to achieve in one's own life the feeling of the history of blacks, and the artistic heritage is equally that of Negro folklore and that of current great writers. The black writer should expect to absorb all human conscious thought.

Gwendolyn was, of course, too attached to the certainties of her upbringing, Christianity, and reformist middle-class democracy to be attracted to Wright's elaborate intellectual structure. Some of her mother's certainties can be gained both from Keziah's book and from Gwendolyn's formulations. Written when she was in her eighties, Keziah's "The Voice" is informational but perhaps suggests a personality more rigid than she actually was in earlier years. Gwendolyn spoke of her mother as "feeling firmly that you must pray, and that only good can come of it," when asked in the late 1960s about the difference between her own religious questionings and those of her mother.[9] In a later interview with Hoke Norris, Gwendolyn explained that her mother "brought me up to be a nice girl" and presented a simple set of certainties derived from concepts of duties held within the family.[10]

When Gwendolyn's conservative background met with the newer currents of her life, the changes seem to have been subtle, not radical. Ed Bland remained in close touch with Gwendolyn and other artists during the early 1940s, and he retained a warm personal interest in Gwendolyn's literary development, criticizing her poetry and recommending books for her to read. The correspondence reflects something of the evolution through which Gwendolyn was going. One misunderstanding seemingly occurred when Gwendolyn wrote that he had accused her of creating false notes in her poetry. Bland replied: "How intemperate! I do not accuse you of 'falseness' in your poetry. I speak of a 'contrary' or a 'new' or 'different' way of seeing an experience now that was evaluated—as I see it—in a totally altered fashion earlier. One grows and so does one's awareness. Why shouldn't the verse show such change as might take place. Not 'falseness,' my dear." He explained that the growth meant that she was living, that her "intake now is so rich and ample (of sensations, insights, observations . . .")."

Bland also sensed a change in Gwendolyn's racial consciousness from a news clipping she had sent him from the Negro Press. "The clipping on the Negro Press throws up a question in m mind. Yet I am fearful of wording it. But why not? Are you and have you been for some time interested in keeping up with Negro life via *our* newspapers? You seem to be so withdrawn from the onrush of things in general, that I was surprised by this bit of evidence to the contrary. I hope you mind not my naivete about you." In her memorial poem to Edward, the dedicatory poem of *Annie Allen*, Gwendolyn portrayed him as a man of unusual curiosity, excited by life, for whom nothing was simply a matter of categories. Her last stanza contrasts Bland and people in general. Unlike them, he refused the tidy answers and was a person in whom they would see either "insanity" or "saintliness."

Gwendolyn continued to reach out to her environment. Visiting public places, she often made her husband nervous by "looking briskly, examiningly, all around me, taking notes." Of the 411 Club which would appear later in her novel *Maud Martha* (1953), she could say that the walls and the waitresses, "are exact!" One feels this same confidence in exactness in several of the portraits in *A Street in Bronzeville* (1945).

On October 10, 1940, Gwendolyn gave birth to her first child, named Henry after his father. His existence soon rearranged their life. Being the first grandchild made him the center of the attention of grandparents on both sides. Still under economic pressure, the couple moved a few months after the birth of their baby to a little apartment, a converted garage on the edge of an Indiana alley. Movies provided a welcome escape from the grittiness of daily living, but a movie could also drop you back into the daily tedium with the abruptness of a drug. They enjoyed pictures with black actors—*Trader Horn* and *Sanders of the River*. The movies of Bette Davis absorbed Gwendolyn, and Nelson Eddy and Jeanette McDonald filled the theater with their own special setting—the magnificent lights, turns, music. Leaving such lush settings, Gwendolyn and Henry usually felt an afterglow that remained with them for hours.

But according to Henry, for Gwendolyn the aftermath of seeing *The Wizard of Oz* was depression. He felt that in light of their own circumstances, the movie's very magnificence caused discouragement to dominate her consciousness. They went home in almost complete silence. Henry observed that she was crying and felt that he had let her down. He felt defensive. Perhaps something of the situation of "The Anniad," a poem written much later, would seem to approach their universe.

> Sovereign [husband]
> Leaves the heaven she put him in
> For the path his pocket chooses;
> Leads her to a lowly room.

The heroine speaks of the attempts to recreate a universe through love. But the pressures of historical time and events (war, labor shortage, infidelity) overwhelm the timelessness of such a space.

Although her own parents' marriage had had its ups and downs, Gwendolyn lived with the certitudes of her mother: "In marriage everything is supposed to be orderly. You aren't untrue. You stay together. The man works, the man takes care of his family, and that's the kind of father I had—it was a duty, a pleasurable duty."[11] But under the pressure of circumstances, the couple separated for the first time. Henry wanted to solve their housing problem by sharing an apartment with his brother Julius, while Gwendolyn insisted upon a place of their own. They argued vigorously in the back yard of Henry's Aunt Mary Telley on the Fourth of July 1941. Gwendolyn recalls standing behind the screen of the back door, holding the baby, when Henry threw a firecracker in that direction, which exploded in the air. In high dudgeon, Gwendolyn went immediately to her parents' home with the baby and told them that she would never go back to Henry. But her father was able to persuade her to accept a reconciliation, and Keziah silently agreed.

Her philosophy, after all, was that a couple's adjustment to marriage required a period "from one year to a lifetime."[12] In more recent years, Gwendolyn and Henry are casual about their early separations but hold firm views as to their causes. Gwendolyn feels that Henry bent the knee too quickly to the assault of circumstance, that he made untenable compromises. Henry feels the marriage had required him to lose innocence and toughen up immediately, whereas Gwendolyn could retain a certain innocence. Since they had both gone early into poetry, he feels that he understood what she was doing in poetry far better than she could understand the realities he faced outside the home. Neither one will modify the viewpoint.

During 1941, changes in jobs and residences stabilized their home life. Henry worked first as a driver-salesman for the Zip soft-drink company and then in the defense industry. After moving again, the family settled in for seven years at 623 East Sixty-Third Street, where there were considerable changes in their artistic and social life. Gwendolyn, meanwhile, continued to produce work rapidly after a lapse caused by the birth of the baby and attendant adjustments. Unsuccessfully, she tried several approaches to money-making. One of them was secretarial services for businesses, professional people, churches, and other organizations. For $10 a month, she offered to do the work that would ordinarily cost $10 to $15 per week for a regularly employed secretary. She also approached the radio industry with a plan for broadcasting soliloquies that she would write. The first paragraph of a surviving soliloquy gives something of the flavor: "When he comes, now, I'll sit over on the right side of the sofa because I'll be in half shadow there. Half shadows make my face look *so* glamorous and seductive." The young woman ponders aloud other routines by which she thinks her caller might be impressed. (The radio industry did not react with appreciation to the script.)

Although Gwendolyn was unable to change her economic situation, she was still changing in sensibility. Her experiences were so distant from the idyllic ones of her parental home that she had to develop more ways of seeing the world. Her new sensibility would respond more rapidly to artistic possibilities and to the social world of artists.

A particularly notable influence was the Gold Coast socialite Inez Cunningham Stark, who was to conduct a poetry workshop for blacks at the South Side Community Center. Obtaining from the NAACP a list of blacks who wrote, she announced to them her writing workshop. Those who became members of the class, besides Gwendolyn and Henry, included Edward Bland, painter John Carlis, Margaret Burroughs, Margaret Danner, and others who had been associated with the Chicago NAACP Youth

Council. Stark's culture and sophistication impressed both Chicago blacks and those she later assembled in Washington, D.C. For most of them, she was the first contact with the rebel-aristocrat, whose tone and gestures and easy companionship seemed to proceed from being to the manor born. A more middle-class approach to the arts would soon be emphasized by her presence on the board of *Poetry* magazine. Her emphasis upon artistic form and approaches to language implied also an approach to audience that would affect Gwendolyn's artistic development.

Gwendolyn had read several of the foremost modern poets, but she had not looked closely at their techniques. Inez placed before her and the workshop her extensive knowledge of modern poetry. She emphasized fear of the cliché, the necessity to twist language and put it under strain in communicating meaning, and writing about the experience that is really known. Inez's procedure was to enter the workshop carrying books and copies of *Poetry* magazine, state a topic for the evening, and begin reading— often from *Poetry* but sometimes from Robert Hillyer's *First Principles of Verse*. Gwendolyn and the group then plunged in to criticize the work, praise it, or take it apart. Gwendolyn reports that they ferociously tore into their own work, and that most people said exactly what they felt. "We were all, those of us who remained after the first winnowing weeks, desperately earnest, and could not always be careful."[13] Inez's opinions, on the other hand, were expressed with coolness, objectivity, and frankness. Gwendolyn was now writing at an excited pace and breaking through into her own distinctive language. Langston Hughes visited the workshop and heard her present "The Ballad of Pearl May Lee," a poem that became a favorite of his and found its place later in *A Street in Bronzeville*. He was startled to find the group of young people already writing so well.

Certain poems show Gwendolyn's increasing commitment to ordinary life and to poetic realism. With elaborate irony, "The Ballad of Pearl May Lee" portrays the responses of a young black woman whose lover was lynched when he was falsely accused by his white woman lover. Stark's emphasis upon seeing and writing "uniquely based upon your experiences" encouraged Gwendolyn to come to terms with the life she was now seeing. Such works as "Matthew Speaking" show her struggle to maintain at will a conversational idiom, although it and the Matthew Cole of *A Street in Bronzeville* are not among her more sparkling poems. The Hattie Scott poems, also to appear in *A Street*, reveal conversational qualities, a reach for idiom, and the attempt to portray personalities. They were presented at the workshop and liked by Hughes and Stark. They represent events and speech Gwendolyn had heard in the kitchenette buildings. A further reach into technique and ballad form went into the elaborate work that brought forth "Queen of the Blues," a poem reminiscent of Langston Hughes's work with blues forms, but more sentimental. She wrote both poetic and prose versions of "Queen of the Blues" which show that Gwendolyn regarded the subject as a fallen woman who wished to recover her respectability. The prose version reveals the plot of a short story in the first sentence: "Ma'am Smith lounged against her work table in the ladies' dressing room of the Midnight Club, smoking while she waited for her cue, wondering if she would ever be able to get out of the mess and regain her self-respect." At 220 pounds, Ma'am Smith goes through the indignities of the nightclub scene, where she sings suggestively and the men slap her flesh and pinch her thighs. Hence "queen" is only an ironic title. As she leaves the nightclub she knocks down one man who assumes that the familiarities afforded by the entertainer are available outside the nightclub. At one point in the poetic version, she is resolved to quit her job, but the realistic ending is that she simply falls into bed in her little room. The poetic version thus has the more realistic ending but not the degree of realistic detail to be found in the prose.

"Queen of the Blues" recalled to Gwendolyn what she had seen of Chicago vaudeville and other shows on the South Side. In the blues, language is reshaped to express tough fiber, wit, contradictions of the self, salty humor, and often rituals of self-transcendence. Though overly sentimental in her concept of a downtrodden woman, Gwendolyn gets in the directness, pain, and something of the blues wit ("Found him a brown-skin chicken / What's gonna be / Black and blue") as well as a sense of blues rhythm.

Through a variety of parties, including huge ones that she and Henry gave, Gwendolyn knew practically every black artist of any significance in Chicago and numerous white ones. Inez encouraged the workshop group as a whole to reach out and enter competitions for prizes. In 1943 Alice Manning Dickey, director of the Midwest Writers Conference, suddenly appeared at Gwendolyn's residence to announce that Gwendolyn had won the conference's prize.

Gwendolyn also won prizes given by the Writers Conference in 1944 and 1945, with Paul Engle the creative writing teacher and poet. The system was not to inform the winner in advance. On one occasion when Engle announced that Gwendolyn was the winner, she sat as if transfixed, her mouth open. Engle shook her out of her daze by saying that she had better come up and accept the prize if she wanted it. At first the audience gasped to see that a black had won; then there was a swelling of applause. The winning poem was "Gay Chaps at the Bar."

Upon hearing of Gwendolyn's winning of the 1943 prize, Ed Bland wrote to tell her that she was breaking through into public recognition. He was right. Emily Morison, editor for Alfred A. Knopf Publishing Company, congratulated her and asked whether she had enough poems to fill a book. Of the roughly forty poems that Gwendolyn sent, embracing a wide range of topics, Emily especially liked the "Negro" poems, and asked that Gwendolyn approach Knopf again when she had a full collection in which the racial poems predominated. Fearing a second rejection from Knopf, Gwendolyn sent the next group of nineteen poems to Harper & Brothers, which accepted them and encouraged her to take a year or two, as long as necessary, to create the number of poems that would justify book publication. Elizabeth Lawrence, the Harper editor, sent along a letter of evaluation the company had sought from Richard Wright. This was a more direct contact with Wright than Gwendolyn had had before he moved from Chicago to New York. Wright's letter of response to the poems was addressed to his own Harper editor, Edward C. Aswell:

Thanks for letting me read Gwendolyn Brooks' poems. They are hard and real, right out of the central core of Black Belt Negro life in urban areas. I hope she can keep on saying what she is saying in many poems.

There is no self-pity here, not a striving for effects. She takes hold of reality as it is and renders it faithfully. There is not so much an exhibiting of Negro life to whites in these poems as there is an honest human reaction to the pain that lurks so colorfully in the Black Belt. A quiet but hidden malice runs through most of them. She easily catches the pathos of petty destinies; the whimper of the wounded; the tiny accidents that plague the lives of the desperately poor, and the problem of color prejudice among Negroes. There are times when open scorn leers through. Only one who has actually lived and suffered in a kitchenette could render the feeling of lonely frustration as well as she does:—of how dreams are drowned out by the noises, smells, and the frantic desire to grab one's chance to get a bath when the bathroom is empty. Miss Brooks is real and so are her poems. [14]

Wright registered the full impact of the poem "kitchenette," one of a series dealing with life in such close and depressing quarters, where Gwendolyn and her family had also lived. Of the six dwellings she and her husband had rented, one was a room, one a remodeled garage, and four were kitchenettes—one being the conventional five-families-per-bath type. Wright also cited such poems as "Negro Hero," "obituary for a living lady," and "when you have forgotten Sunday," the first dealing with the type of war hero represented by Dorie Miller and the second with aspects of courtship and marriage. The only poem he did not like was "the mother," in which a woman addressing her dead aborted children laments her sacrifice of them and declares her love. Wright did not feel that the poet had yet appeared who could "lift abortions to the poetic plane." On Gwendolyn's insistence that the woman's actions were based upon her poverty, the poem would remain and become a popular one in her readings. Wright also objected to the book's title, A *Street in Bronzeville*, as being obscure to anyone not familiar with Chicago, where the *Chicago Defender* had given the name to the black South Side section.

Wright's most serious reservation was that the book lacked a personal note. He observed that "most volumes of poems usually have one really long fine poem around which shorter ones are added or grouped." Although Gwendolyn need not follow such a model, she should either give us "twice as many poems of the kind she has, or . . . one real long good one, one that strikes a personal note and carries a good burden of personal feeling. Then I think she would have a book of poems."

Wright concluded his first letter: "But she is a real poet; she knows what to say and how to say it. I'd say that she ought to be helped at all costs. America needs a voice like hers and anything that can be done to help her to bring out a good volume should be done." Gwendolyn wrote Wright two letters of appreciation. The first, dated February 25, 1945, stated that many persons had encouraged her but few had gone out of their way to help her as he had, and she would work hard not to disappoint his faith in her. The second (April 9, 1945) stated that Wright had been a literary hero of hers for years and she was certain to be impressed by what he had to say, for or against her efforts. She was taking his advice about writing a long poem for the book, one that would express a little of her personal feelings about things and tie the other poems together. Apparently the poem emerged as the finished version of "The Sundays of Satin-Legs Smith." Thus the leader of the 1930s Renaissance exerted a strong influence upon the basis of acceptance accorded a work of the 1940s. Wright was attracted by qualities other than social realism in the writing, although Gwendolyn clearly identified deeply with a suffering community. As for Marxism, the bottom line for Wright seemed to be that the writer must have some theory that provides a coherent view of modern existence or become a lost victim in the modern world. Wright also insisted upon a deep consciousness and the autonomy of craft, in which a "complex" simplicity is achieved. From Wright's perspective, the pantheon of writers for absorbing modern consciousness and craft included T.S. Eliot, Gertrude Stein, James Joyce, Ernest Hemingway, Sherwood Anderson, Maxim Gorky, Henri Barbusse, and Jack London. While Wright's perspective went beyond Gwendolyn's, it also enabled him to see kinship with her deeper qualities.

Not until 1950 would Gwendolyn publish a work that concisely expressed her perspective on writing, "Poets Who Are Negroes," a work that would guide her over many years. Whether writing prose or verse, she wished "to prove to others (by implication, not by shouting) and to such among themselves as have yet to discover it, that they are merely human beings, not exotics," as she told her Harper editor, Elizabeth Lawrence.[15] She would sometimes use the word "curios" for exotics, but both terms seem to have been a reaction against the Harlem Renaissance. She resented "pure propaganda, and try (!) not to perpetrate it myself." She often enjoyed writing a thing that "can't be considered propaganda in *any* form, pure or alloyed." She felt that the turn of the times was toward relief for all "uncomfortables"—and that category included blacks. Thus she reflected the optimism of World War II.

Responding to Elizabeth Lawrence's requests for information as to how her personal life related to her writing, she described her domestic situation, which included a lively son who would soon be four years old. She often wrote while "scrubbing, sweeping, washing, ironing, cooking: dropping the mop, broom, soap, iron, or carrot grater to write down a line, or word." And "writing is the only *work* in which I'm interested." She also mentioned that she had written twenty-five loosely related poems about a family named Brown. (Later she would decide to tell the story of "The American Family Brown" in prose.)

Meanwhile, she set herself the task of doubling the number of poems she had already submitted to Harper & Brothers, as well as completing a long poem. Eliminating parties and movies, she examined rather good poems she had not sent, wrote in response to general stimuli, and planned to increase the number of war sonnets. She also enjoyed several successes. The Midwestern Writers Conference prize for poetry in June 1945 went to "the progress," and in August 1945 "Gay Chaps" and "And Still Do I Keep My Look, My Identity" would be accepted by *Poetry* magazine.

A good deal of exposure came from magazines. After unsuccessfully attempting to interest the Rosenwald Fund in making an award to Gwendolyn, Wright spoke on her behalf to Edwin Seaver of *Cross-section* and Dorothy Norman of *Twice a Year*. Margaret Anderson of *Common Ground* accepted "truth," a poem that would not appear until the publication of *Annie Allen*. Alice Browning chose five poems for *Negro Story*.

Good relations with Gwendolyn's editor at Harper had developed quickly, being somewhat maternal, since Elizabeth Lawrence was the older and more worldly. They had met on the last Tuesday in October 1944. Although Gwendolyn had been self-conscious and attacked by shyness, she had apparently not appeared the boring, stupid, stiff, "prim and impossible" person she thought herself to be. Elizabeth was accustomed to the fact that many highly articulate writers were in personal contact very quiet. Gwendolyn had had her first martini and had talked a good deal about literary technique, reacting against the clichés, worn-out language, and pure propaganda that black poetry often revealed. Poetry could be truth and beauty or merely beauty. But truth alone, no matter how noble or admirable, would not make a poem. These were rather demanding standards, and she realized that she herself had not yet met them to her own satisfaction.

Richard Wright's *Black Boy*, published on February 28, 1945, affected Gwendolyn extraordinarily. She had read Wright's *Native Son* (1940) in a single night "and finally went to bed almost blind and terribly scared of the dark." Gwendolyn found that *Black Boy* "pulls at you and you can hardly turn the pages fast enough—you want to read several pages at one time— and it *hurts* you when you realize you're getting to the end." She saw in the book "a sensitiveness, a pitiful search for peace and self-realization, a humanity that wants to spread but doesn't dare to." Critical of certain sections, she disagreed with those who thought that the discussion of "Beauty" on pages 7 and 8 meant improvement in style, and felt that certain sentences were too self-consciously struggled for: "There was the delight . . . . There was the faint, cool kiss . . . . There was the vague sense of the infinite . . . . " Wright was at his best "and most convincing when he is using the 'clear, clean, sweeping' type of sentence he himself says he admires." She reported that Negroes in Chicago were very upset about two paragraphs in parentheses on page 33 in chapter 2. Noting that "generalizations are always treacherous," Gwendolyn found that those passages were "so obviously, reports not on 'Negro' experience but on his personal experience, in spite of implications to the contrary, that I shouldn't think they'd trouble so many." The passages spoke of blacks' negative qualities being evaluated as positive, of their cultural barrenness, of their never having been allowed to catch the full spirit of Western civilization. Gwendolyn stated that she had never met Wright, but she had "about three friends here who belonged to a writing class with him years ago" who had said for a long time that "his confusions are more personal than general." She herself did not know about the confusions. She concluded that the book was nothing short of "valuable—necessary—and it will have a good influence on some of our current thinking."[16]

Soon afterward, on March 20, 1945, Edward Bland was killed in Germany after volunteering for a dangerous mission. A letter to him from Gwendolyn was returned, marked "deceased." His last critical work was an article entitled "Racial Bias and Negro Poetry" in *Poetry* magazine, in which he analyzed the impact of derogatory racial concepts on black poetry and expressed the hope "that the present war will create an environment more favorable to humanistic goals." Gwendolyn wrote to *Poetry* to express the writers' group's disturbance at his death, and took the initiative in establishing the group's Edward Bland Memorial Fellowship Prize, which was continued for three years and administered by the editors of *Poetry*.

The year 1945 was a momentous one for the poet. It was in that year that Gwendolyn began her adventure with the public, when *A Street in Bronzeville* was published. Although the claim of newness in art must always allow for relativity and exceptions, readers of *A Street in Bronzeville* during the 1940s were aware that it struck a new note in black poetry. Reviews reveal that white readers were impressed by the breadth of its humanistic concerns, while black readers were impressed by its refusal to be "obsessed" with race. Margaret Walker, poet, critic, and novelist, writing in *Phylon*, cited the newness of *A Street*'s global perspective and its sophistication of technique and form, which were to be revealed to a more marked degree in *Annie Allen*. In the tendency "toward internationalism rather than toward nationalism and racism," she saw a "basis for new conceptions that of necessity lead us in new directions."[17]

The poet had rejected the exotic vein of the Harlem Renaissance—the celebration of unique racial values, such as defiance of social proscription through emphasis upon joy and soul. A few poems in *A Street* work close to this vein, allowing the reader the enjoyment of the old colorful images, but use one device or another to bring them to the court of critical intelligence. Thus "patent leather" and other poems devalue the "hipness" that the Harlem Renaissance would have celebrated. Satire and realism invaded the roots of simple exoticism, with sardonic effect:

> That cool chick down on Calumet
> Has got herself a brand new cat,
> With patent-leather hair.
> And he is man enough for her.

The next two verses use the male point of view to ridicule the patent-haired lover's lack of masculine qualities, but the woman simply "strokes the patent leather hair / That makes him man enough for her." Thus a light subject is treated lightly and the woman lover simply expresses what fools we mortals be.

Poetry of this period was new in its manner of adapting the social consciousness inherited from the 1930s, turning upon the oppressor and protesting strongly on behalf of the group. Margaret Walker's most famous socially conscious poem, "For My People," calls for a new world and a new race of men to rise and take control—a call that would ring anew during the 1960s rebellion. Associated with the Harlem Renaissance period, Sterling A. Brown seems to fit more naturally into Margaret Walker's concept of the socially conscious 1930s. Gwendolyn's relationship to Langston Hughes, who represented both the exotic and the socially conscious veins, is more complex. On the one hand, she confesses to having learned from him the importance of representing ordinary life in poetry, but she presented his themes in a minor key, as in "patent leather," "a song in the front yard," and "Queen of the Blues."

Gwendolyn had reached poetic maturity during the years just before World War II, an extremely optimistic time in America's "democratic" and racial history. Barely concealed by the apparent simplicities of much of *A Street in Bronzeville* is the fact that she was a very ambitious poet determined to create a complexity of form equal to her responses to life in the city. The standard symbols of earlier authors had often been the stark ones of the rural South, whereas the interaction of people with the frequently anonymous forces of the North was another type of struggle.

Philosophically, according to Arthur P. Davis, Gwendolyn is the poet of the unheroic, a response to the cramped room in which modern man must gesture.[18] In an early unpublished poem, "After a Perusal of Ancient History," she portrayed a universe of little people with little minds engaged in minutiae as "their same little puzzled / Helpless hands / Pulled away at the Blinds." She saw this as human history past, present, and future. In the large city, one sees ordinary people muddling in ordinary settings, a common trait of all people. What the poet needs to dramatize is the tide that binds rather than the waves that separate.

The situation thus affects technique. Whatever else is in the poem, the existential must firmly reside beside it to show human commonality. The artist draws the unusual image or figure of speech from this stream of commonality or its experience. Or the writer's art makes it unusual or exercises a gift for seeing the unusual in modern life. Widely acquainted with traditional forms and the devices of modern poetry, Gwendolyn thus knew how to modify basic principles and to play conventions one against another. *A Street in Bronzeville* thus set the stage for the greater complexity of subsequent works.

"kitchenette building" is Gwendolyn's most famous short poem expressing social consciousness: in the modern tenement building, there is no human space for dreams and aspirations. It begins, "We are things of dry hours and the involuntary plan, / Grayed in and gray." The poem's language is basically prosaic but provides rhythmic pauses and strong beats. Contrasts in the rhetorical structure between the long question taking up stanzas two and three and the short declarative units give appropriate interest to the thought, while symbolic use of colors and contrasting imagery provide considerable drama: dreams, "white and violet, / fight with fried potatoes / and yesterday's garbage ripening in the hall" in order to try fluttering or singing "an aria down these rooms." Thus the reader confronts a very complex structure, although the poem reads simply and delivers its message directly. Because blacks were overwhelmingly the ones living in the five-families-to-a-bath kitchenette apartment, their involvement in the poem's protest was clear. On the other hand, the commonality of experience for them is the persistence of aspiration, just as they seek bodily comfort, the lukewarm bath. The simple bath reveals the oppressed not as pure victims but as actors in their own destiny.

"The Sundays of Satin-Legs Smith," the longest poem in the book, is also the most intricate in its social protest. On the one hand, it is a study of the futile response to life represented among blacks by wearing the zoot suit and being committed to hipness. In such shorter pieces appearing early in the book as "the soft man," and "the independent man," Gwendolyn's tone is sardonic amusement. In "Satin Legs" she exposes the sad roots of the style. On the other hand, the poem protests a society that deprives Satin-Legs of genuine material with which to express his art and his quest for beauty and gusto. The drama of the poem arises from the presence of a speaker and a white observer of conventional notions who is being indicted as a representative of the depriving society. The speaker and the white observer see Satin-Legs carry out his reign as "king" on a typical Sunday. His flower is a bright feather in his lapel, since he associates live flowers with death. His treasures are zoot suits ("Ballooning pants that taper off to ends / scheduled to choke precisely."), hats ("Like bright umbrellas"), and "hysterical ties / Like narrow banners for some gathering war." All his sculpture, art, and architectural design are displayed in his collection of treasures. Half of the poem presents Satin-Legs' treasures and kingly behavior as he prepares to go out, in images rich with his illusion of himself and his place in the world. As he moves into the streets, insulating illusions contrast sharply with the dreary environment in which he actually moves. Powerful images also unfold the new scene and frequently characterize Satin-Legs himself. The hip Satin-Legs is actually lost.

> The pasts of his ancestors lean against
> Him. Crowd him. Fog out his identity.
> Hundreds of voices advise so dexterously
> He quite considers his reactions his,
> Judges he walks most powerfully alone,
> That everything is—simply what it is.

Gwendolyn's attitude toward Satin-Legs is complex. Her love of art enables her to describe his artistic strivings with loving delight, a fact that creates further drama when she displays his thwarted and distorted aspirations. She can step aside from the immediate scene to protest and generalize on his condition. Unless he really wishes to disturb the world's social arrangements and recognize the equality and dignity of man by sternly dealing with the wealthy and the aristocratic, Gwendolyn tells the white observer, he might as well leave Satin-Legs to his own version of art. To be deduced is that Satin-Legs' art, though twisted, represents the indomitability of the human spirit in its quest for beauty. In addition, she satirizes his pretentions in his choice of women. ("Her affable extremes are like sweet bombs / About him, whom no middle grace or good / Could gratify.") Yet she recognizes that his affairs are also his kind of poetry and grants him the poetry in the last stanza.

> Her body is like new brown bread
> Under the Woolworth mignonette,
> Her body is a honey bowl
> Whose waiting honey is deep and hot.
> Her body is like summer earth,
> Receptive, soft, and absolute.

Early in the poem Gwendolyn's personal signature comes with regard and compassion for Satin-Legs and humanity in general.

> People are so in need of help.
> People want so much that they do not know.
>
> Below the tinkling trade of little coins
> The gold impulse not possible to show
> Or spend. Promise piled over and betrayed.

Thus the social concern is subtly woven into the poem. The hero is not simply victim but creatively active in his own destiny. The type had been celebrated by Sterling A. Brown ("Sporting Beaseley") and Margaret Walker ("Poppa Chicken"), in shorter poems and on a simpler level in which the protagonist could be viewed with admiration and humor alone. Gwendolyn sees the type on the big city scene, in the midst of the industrial economy where, theoretically, the possibility for achieving a rich life should have increased.

Gwendolyn also pays the respect of one artist to another by presenting the portrait in an elaborate art capable of communicating nuances. Structurally, the poem is dominated by unfoldings of the story, by contrasts between expectations and actuality, between illusions and actuality. The analyses of the speaker form part of the dramatic commentary. Imagery is often the vehicle of the contrasts. The reader is confronted with raw street imagery versus ruins of Satin-Legs' home environment, and an imagery musically delivered at the end of the poem announcing Satin's triumph as he would see and feel it. The white observer is nudged aside as a person only lately showing interest and unavailable at earlier moments when he was sorely needed.

Though the lines take some of the liberties of free verse, they have at their base a well-mastered, fluid blank verse. For special emphasis the poet occasionally breaks into rhyme, and the language has a flexible conversational idiom, a formal eloquence scattered with the vocabulary of the hipster. But for the most part the language is that of the poet-speaker and the white observer. The speaker's vocabulary and attitudes create sardonic tones of cool condescension and contempt in a number of messages addressed to the white observer. Gwendolyn thus elicits from a portrait of the hip life a group self-criticism that is also a serious criticism of life and society.

Rather noticeably, however, the cultural resources quoted in tones of approval are of white origin: the sounds of Saint-Saens, Grieg, and Tschaikovsky's "wayward eloquence." And there is the "tender drift of Brahms." Much of the black heritage to which Satin-Legs has been exposed carries an overtone of grossness. Most of the positive images from the black heritage hover a bit uncertainly in a stanza involving the church and do not seem to involve positive direction. Would a greater involvement in the reaches of black traditions have helped? In her interview with Ida Lewis, Gwendolyn stated that she "didn't even hear of [W.E.B. DuBois's] *The Souls of Black Folk* until I was well grown."[19] In addition, the drift of this optimistic war period was toward the resolution of problems through blacks' full and impending entry into American society, not in a separate cultural pattern. Hence the neglect of historic racial symbols and roots for those central to Euro-American culture. Nevertheless, "Satin-Legs" remains a poem of great power. With its sustained length and variety of poetic skills, it well fulfills its function as signature poem for the volume.

Other poems of protest include "Negro Hero," "Ballad of Pearl May Lee," "The ballad of chocolate Mabbie." Most notable, of course, is the famous "Negro Hero," whose real-life model, Dorie Miller, defied America's confinement of black sailors to the role of mess men, seized an anti-aircraft gun, and downed four attacking Japanese guns, an act for which he was eventually awarded the Navy Cross. Its protest is the most direct in A Street: "I had to kick their law into their teeth in order to save them." The speaker's ultimate motivation, however, is his love for a covertly hostile democracy that only smiled and stuttered its promises. The rest of the poem carries through a drama to resolution: Was it worth it? The answer worked through the protest is that it was worthwhile to help to save even a part of democracy, though it does not live up yet to its creed, and to do a good job. This despite the fact that the nation may prefer jim-crowism and racial hatred to its democratic creed. Thus Gwendolyn's old pre–World War II feelings press hard upon the current optimism as she gives her voice to the hero.

The hero's dignity and self-possession distinguish the poem. Since the 1920s, black poets had been moving toward a greater self-possession in their social criticism. The difference can be seen by a comparison with James David Corrothers's pre–World War I poem "At the Closed Gate of Justice." The first stanza declares:

> To be a Negro in a day like this
> Demands forgiveness. Bruised with blow on blow,
> Betrayed like him whose woe dimmed eyes gave bliss,
> Still must one succor those who brought one low,
> To be a Negro in a day like this.

Fenton Johnson, an early adherent of the twentieth century "new poetry" movement and a poet of pre-1920s origin, in "Tired" called for infanticide and cried out, "It is better to die than to grow up and find that you are colored." Gwendolyn's poem is a measure of blacks' new self-confidence and of the new, though cautious, optimism.

So much for patterns of protest. Actually, most poems in the book address general life issues arising from daily existence or from World War II. As Elizabeth Lawrence, Gwendolyn's editor, would later observe, the poems also have a certain news value. Gwendolyn's early plan for A Street, not entirely fulfilled, "was to take some personality or event, or idea from each (or many of) the approximately thirty houses on a street in this vicinity."[20] One of her goals was that the stories should appeal to a broader audience than that usually devoted to poetry. Whether the poem emerges from a first-, second-, or third-person point of view, a confident narrator speaks, moving from the apparently simple to the complex, from the neighborhood to the outer world. The narrator who carries readers through poems of day-to-day neighborhood life with such themes as frustration, exhaustion, reveries, death, foolishness, gusto, longings, and joys, turns easily to the war poems. The poet sees life through a variety of forms—ballads, quatrains, free verse, irregular stanzas, and sonnets. A *Street* shows a sophistication that would mature in her next book, *Annie Allen.*

In A *Street's* sonnets, Gwendolyn portrayed war as a shattering tragedy in a universe in which the presence of God seems uncertain. The opening sonnet, "Gay Chaps at the Bar," sets the tone for the sequence. Gwendolyn took its title from a war-front letter sent by her friend William Couch which spoke of sophisticated young officers who had learned to be poised in their social milieu but who lost command of themselves in the intense moral bewilderment of their military experience: " . . . and guys I knew in the States, young officers, return from the front crying and trembling. Gay chaps at the bar in Los Angeles, Chicago, New York . . . . " Other letters that she was receiving from soldiers, most of whom had been members of the writing group, provided the inspiration for the full sonnet sequence.

Central to the sequence is the struggle to sustain what is human in the face of ruthless slaughter, which seems to defy religion or humanism. As in Hemingway's Lost Generation, all values seem vulnerable, incapable of preservation, since those who survive the horrors physically will carry them in the mind. The speaker of "Gay Chaps" dwells longingly on the old days of sophisticated triumphs but complains that "nothing ever taught us to be islands."

> No stout
> Lesson showed how to chat with death. We brought
> No brass fortissimo, among our talents,
> To holler down the lions in this air.

The sonnets "piano after war" and "mentors" tell of the lost-generation feeling which will not allow survivors to enjoy the civilian life. "God works in a mysterious way" and "firstly inclined to take what it is told" tell of lost confidence in the divine. "love note I: surely" questions everything and the lover. Yet, among all these tensions which intensify each other, some values remain: identity, human memory, and the ability to assess life. "still do I keep my look, my identity . . . " tells us that despite death the art of the body survives in its insistence upon identity. In "love note II: flags," love celebration is given with such tenderness that its value survives in the imagination:

The blowing of clear wind in your gay hair;
Love changeful in you (like a music, or
Like a sweet mournfulness, or like a dance,
Or like the tender struggle of a fan).

In structure and technique, the sonnets in A *Street* have an extraordinary brilliance. Gone are the faults of the poet's apprenticeship years—
failures in diction, structure, economy of line, and in clear differentiation
between the sonnet and other forms. Instead, the poet experiments with
mixtures of traditional forms, breaks up syntactical structures, and frequently achieves sparkling diction—all of which give her great originality in
an old form with demanding conventions. The sonnets are given in off-
rhyme, reflecting the dissonance of war. A Shakespearean rhyme scheme
and structure mix with those of the Petrarchan. "Gay Chaps" effectively
mixes the syntax of the conversational with formal eloquence and creates
verbal surprises.

Structurally speaking, "firstly inclined to take what it is told," a questioning of God, is one of the most daring of the sonnet sequence. The
octave is the first part of a periodic sentence, with complex internal units of
truncated sentences and prepositional phrases. The sestet has one independent clause to complete the periodic movement. Elliptical structures then
fill out the nuances:

Thee sacrosanct, Thee sweet, Thee crystalline,
With the full jewel wile of mighty light—
With the narcotic milk of peace for men
Who find Thy beautiful center and relate
Thy round command, Thy grand, Thy mystic good—
Thee like the classic quality of a star:
A little way from warmth, a little sad,
Delicately lovely to adore—
I had been brightly ready to believe.

It is interesting that the second sonnet on God, "God works in a mysterious
way," not only responds to the statement of innocence of "firstly . . ." but
also carries the doubt expressed by "Plaint" on October 4, 1935. Gwendolyn
complained of "God's hard, icy ears," of his failure "to soothe her suffering or
to cool her tears." She pleaded that things not be as she had feared: that
". . .You, Lord, be there. / Be there, behind that enigma / Of clouds and
changing air."

Harper & Brothers published A *Street in Bronzeville* on August 15, 1945,
close to V-J Day. On August 3 Gwendolyn received ten copies of her thin

book, which she felt were like jewels, and sent thanks to all at Harper who had helped to create "such a wonderful piece of work." On August 26, as Gwendolyn and Henry left one of their almost weekly movies, they purchased the Sunday edition of the *Chicago Tribune,* in which Paul Engle, who had recently presented Gwendolyn with the 1945 Midwestern Writers Conference Award for poetry, had told them his review of *A Street* would appear. There, dominating the two right-hand columns of page 1 of the book review section, was "the review that initiated My Reputation,"[21] headlined "Chicago Can Take Pride in New, Young Voice in Poetry." Gwendolyn and Henry stopped under a streetlight at midnight to read the entire review.

"The publication of *A Street in Bronzeville,*" Engle began, "is an exceptional event in the literary life of Chicago, for it is the first book of a solidly Chicago person." So much for local significance. Then he moved uncomfortably close to William Dean Howells's rhetoric in launching the career of Paul Laurence Dunbar: "But it is also an event of national importance, for Miss Brooks is the first Negro poet to write wholly out of a deep and imaginative talent, without relying on the fact of color to draw sympathy and interest. Her poems would be finely lyrical and delightfully witty without the fact of color ever being mentioned. This is a remarkable thing which must be praised." The Howells approach used by Engle ignored the achievements of other black poets but was obviously sincere and deeply appreciative. It would also help in the marketplace of the city with the second-largest book sales in the country.

For Engle, Gwendolyn's poems were not "Negro poetry" any more than Robert Frost's poetry was "white poetry." "They are handsome and real and genuine poems by a civilized American citizen. They are poems for all men who left warmth and a softness and quick hand and slow voice. They come out of the pages of the book, as Miss Brooks says in another connection, 'like the tender struggles of a fan.' " Engle praised such poems as "The Sundays of Satin-Legs Smith," "obituary for a living lady," "hunchback girl," and the sonnet sequence "Gay Chaps," the latter being the most controlled and intense poems in the book. He had praise in general for her portraits of people and for her ability to go through Chicago with wide open eyes and artistically move the reader into its realities.

Mixing exhortation with his praise, Engle stated: "I hope that the people of Chicago who generously support genuine midwestern writing, will find in Miss Brooks exactly the kind of young but permanent talent they are looking for. The finest praise that can be given to the book is that it would be a superb volume of poetry in any year by any person of any color. This is the kind of writing we need in this time." Interestingly, his concluding remark is close to that of Richard Wright: "This [poem] is the real thing. So is Miss Brooks."

4

Bright Waters

During 1949 and 1950 Gwendolyn was most aware of the brightness of the challenging waters into which she was now moving. She was embarking upon several extraordinary adventures. Her adventure with the white liberal critical consensus would continue its present course for seventeen years and become the most extraordinary one experienced by a black American poet, with its mixture of brightness and ambiguity. Her adventure with life would continue to involve her in a struggle for basic survival, despite the achievement of a level of fame that usually opened up a fairly broad range of resources for earning money. It would also require redefinitions in her private life as well as facing up to the ordinary limitations on human existence. But the general brightness and forward motion of her voyage usually enabled her to recover, if not to sustain unremittingly, the balance she read into the life of the "light and diplomatic bird."

Gwendolyn's poetic thrust after publication of *A Street in Bronzeville* was focused on two projected works: "American Family Brown," which, after considerable metamorphosis, was to result in *Maud Martha*, and the collection of poems portraying a young black woman, published as *Annie Allen*. After being rejected by Harper in October 1947, "American Family Brown" was set aside for the time being, and *Annie Allen* saw the light of publication first.

The poet's relationship to her Harper editor, Elizabeth Lawrence, had now matured both personally and professionally, as revealed in the correspondence leading to publication of *Annie Allen*. Gwendolyn sent Elizabeth Lawrence the first group of poems for the collection on March 24, 1948, under the title "Hester Allen." Elizabeth, as usual, sought the response of her staff at Harper, but their reaction was so mixed that she sent the manuscript to the poet Genevieve Taggard on June 8, asking for guidance and noting that Gwendolyn was "undoubtedly in the process of evolving a new style."

Taggard's response was lengthy, more than eight hand-written pages, and generally negative. She found fault with many of the poems, beginning with "the birth in a narrow room," which she found "not quite written" and unclear as to whether someone is giving birth or being born. Of "The Hesteriad" (later "The Anniad") she complained that "nothing developes. . . . What is lacking finally is a real human story," and eventually the writing becomes "monotonous." She felt it was "a work-piece . . . good exercise, but no gift for the reader." Other poems were similarly faulted for obscurity, imitativeness, or incomprehensible diction.[1]

Elizabeth sent the full critique to Gwendolyn on July 14, noting that "for me it makes specific the generalized criticisms from the office staff." While attempting to soften the impact of Taggard's remarks, she essentially accepted their validity:

As I am sure you know, I regard you as a writer of rare talent and an authentic poet. Moreover, you have intelligence as well as talent, which means that you are capable of growing. It seems to me that this present collection shows you in transition. A *Street in Bronzeville* was clear, decisive writing with the emphasis on content rather than form. In many of these new poems, on the contrary, the form, the mannerisms, tend to intrude and obscure the content. There is a preciousness, an artificiality, about some of it that is foreign to you as I know you. Perhaps this is necessary to the process of development, and as you find your new direction the superficialities will be pruned away. But for the moment you often put a burden on the reader that is not commensurate with the rewards. You are too good a poet to have to resort to trick and shock devices.

Despite this generally negative response, Elizabeth found some poems in the collection "downright exciting" and assured Gwendolyn that Harper wanted to publish her next volume and would send her a contract at once.

The poet responded almost immediately, appreciating an end to the "long mailbox vigil" and "glad to be accepted, to see the word 'contract.' " But her feelings about the report were understandably mixed. She consented to the removal of "the egg boiler," the last sonnet group, and others, but vigorously defended several in the collection. While agreeing that she remained "curious about new and more effective ways of saying things," she insisted that "the quality of the 'things' is as important to me as ever. . . . I tried very hard, especially in 'Hesteriad' and 'the children of the poor,' to say exactly what I meant, instead of approximately. I'm surprised that this reaching toward a more careful language should strike anyone as 'a trick and shock device.' "[2]

A Harper contract was sent to Gwendolyn on August 11, with an advance on royalties of $100, only half what she had received for A Street in Bronzeville. Whether this reflected the hesitation of Harper editors or other factors is unclear. Gwendolyn continued to work on the poems during the remainder of 1948. On August 24 she suggested "Annie Allen" as a better title, a change enthusiastically accepted by Elizabeth.

The entire collection went to Harper on January 14, 1949. It included many new poems and a number of deletions from the earlier offerings, with other poems retained in revised form. In the accompanying letter, Gwendolyn offered her editor a panoramic view of the collection and her authorial intentions:

I now believe the manuscript has a cohesion it possibly lacked before. In the beginning we find the first, furtive or bold, graspings toward what is or might be real, and those "positive decisions" (as in "the ballad of late Annie" and "pygmies are pygmies still though percht on Alps") that, normally, only the quite young or the quite old can relax upon; in the middle, in the Anniad, although she is jumbled—first terribly certain, then terribly uncertain, then terribly though temporarily dead—she is most herself, hence the title made from her name. For it seems to me that a woman is never, before or after, so much and so beautifully her essential self as she is during her first intense love, when she is giving everything. In the end, the Womanhood, our funny and sad heroine speaks always in her mature voice (or thought). At least, here is as much maturity, in attitude and conviction, as we can plausibly expect her range to allow. Undertones of comedy and tragedy but never either to the extravagant degree of more youthful times.

In early March, Elizabeth could report that publication of Annie Allen was scheduled for August. She offered a number of marginal notes on the poems "which may not be worth calling to your attention, yet I feel that it is perhaps better to do so if you understand that they are no more than an invitation to re-examine the several passages." The editor objected to the third and last stanzas of "Maxie Allen," which were eventually omitted. Of "downtown vaudeville," she found she couldn't get out of it "what I feel I should get out of it," but Gwendolyn's subsequent explanation evidently satisfied her, and the poem remained. To Elizabeth's objection that "I love those little booths at Benvenuti's" had "something reportorial about it," the poet replied that she had "wanted it to be 'reportorial,' but of course 'poetically reportorial!' "[3] Again the poem was retained. Other objections were worked out in the now familiar give and take between editor and poet.

Harper sent the galleys for Annie Allen to Langston Hughes, among others, for comment early in the summer of 1949. Hughes promised to mention the book in his weekly column for the Chicago Defender and suggested that Elizabeth send a copy to Richard Wright in Paris with the suggestion that he review it for Hughes's journal, *Voices*.[4] Alfred Kreymborg, another poet who received galleys, found the book "fully as rewarding as her first book . . . . Though this volume weighs little in the hand, it weighs much in the heart and the mind." He admired the emotional range and found the technical range admirable, "with its many variations of form and an ear for colloquial language wedded to classical."[5]

Annie Allen was released in August, and reviews followed promptly. One of the earliest was that of J. Saunders Redding in the *Saturday Review* of September 17. His opening statement gave Harper a quotation for advertising the book: "*Annie Allen* . . . is as artistically sure, as emotionally firm, and as esthetically complex as a silver figure by Cellini." While his review was generally enthusiastic, he also raised questions of the sort the collection had met earlier in the evaluation at Harper. After expressing admiration for the second sonnet in "the children of the poor," Redding warned against the kind of particularism to be found in the following lines of "The Anniad" and in those of other poems:

> Stand off, daughter of the dusk,
> And do not wince when the bronzy lads
> Hurry to cream-yellow shining.
> It is plausible. The sun is a lode.
>
> True, there is silver under
> The veils of the darkness.
> But few care to dig in the night
> For the possible treasure of the stars.

Responded Redding: "Who but another Negro can get the intimate feeling, the racially-particular acceptance and rejection, and the oblique bitterness of this?" He then "universalized" the principle: "The question is . . . whether it is not this penchant for coterie stuff—the special allusions, the highly special feeling derived from an even more special experience—that has brought poetry from the most highly regarded form of communication to the least regarded."[6] One wishes Redding had named what he regarded as the other offending poems. Should the following two lines from the poem "shampoo-press-hot-oil-&-croquignole (the smoking iron)" be avoided? "Lay it on lightly, lay it on with heed. / Because it took that stuff so long to grow." In different terms, such approaches to black literature would appear in critical statements stemming from the media and from a succession of writers' conferences until the late 1960s and, after a few years of quiescence, resurge in the mid- and late 1970s.

Actually, *Annie Allen* challenges not so much by its particularism as by its craft and its universality—further developments of the resources and approaches present in *A Street in Bronzeville*. The poems in *A Street* offer a deceptively full realistic surface and make use of well-known devices from the conventions and techniques of poetic realism. There are abrupt beginnings in *A Street* and some elliptical syntax, which demand that the reader drop everything and attend closely, but neither is developed to the extent manifested in *Annie Allen*.

One major difference between the two works is that the reader of *Annie Allen* is more openly confronted with the necessity to read actively. Although people and their life stories appear in plots sharply outlined, presenting easily recognized issues from the daily round of existence, and move to definite climaxes and decisive conclusions, there are frequent signals of the presence of more than one perspective—additional comments upon the human condition available beneath the poems' realistic surface, representing engagement with the contradictoriness and complexity of experience.

The opening poems of the two works illustrate the difference. *A Street* opens with "the old-marrieds": "But in the crowding darkness not a word did they say. / Though the pretty-coated birds had piped so lightly all the day." Except for the abrupt beginning with "but," there is nothing to discomfit the reader. The syntax is regular except for punctuation of a clause as a full sentence in the second line—certainly no radical break with established practice.

Annie Allen, proper, on the other hand, opens with "the birth in a narrow room": "Weeps out of Western country something new. / Blurred and stupendous. Wanted and unplanned." Whereas in "the old-marrieds" the issue and perhaps the mystery of the story are almost immediately suggested, "the birth" requires careful and repeated readings to grasp the theme: the slow absorption of "reality" by infant life and the creative experiences awaiting the infant between the stages of unreflecting confrontation with existence and realization of its limitations. The poem demands greater reader participation and creativity: an acceptance of the elliptical syntax in the first stanza and a grasp of images with mythic functions—not merely of day-to-day "reality." The infant's first movement into time is an almost passive survey of artifacts, with the last image foreshadowing something of the magic of the childhood world: "the milk-glass fruit bowl, iron pot, / The bashful china child tipping forever / Yellow apron and spilling pretty cherries." The second stanza mixes images of reality with expressions and gestures connoting the transforming power of early childhood imagination:

But prances nevertheless with gods and fairies
Blithely about the pump and then beneath
The elms and grapevines, then in darling endeavor
By privy foyer, where the screenings stand
And where the bugs buzz by in private cars
Across old peach cans and old jelly jars.

"Downtown vaudeville," a portrait of whites subjecting blacks to silent, dehumanizing ridicule, has one of the more unusual patterns of syntax and is marked also by unusual twists of diction and imagery operating almost entirely on the symbolic level. But the poem's major challenge is the elaborate use of synecdoche and the substitution in the last line of the demonstrative pronoun "that" for the relative pronoun "who." The almost conventional beginning makes the sudden appearance of grammatical substitutions all the more startling:

What was not pleasant was the hush that coughed
When the Negro clown came on the stage and doffed
His broken hat. The hush, first. Then the soft

Concatenation of delight and lift,
And loud. The decked dismissal of his gift,
The sugared hoot and hauteur. Then the rift

Where is magnificent, heirloom, and deft
Leer at a Negro to the right, or left—
So joined to personal bleach, and so bereft:

Finding if that is locked, is bowed, or proud.
And what that is at all, spotting the crowd.

Much of the difficulty in reading the poem disappears when one realizes that key qualities of the audience are standing for the whole. In the structurally conventional first line, "the hush that coughed" is at first confusing. But the third line's repetition of "hush" makes clear that the word describes expressionistically the audience's sudden antagonistic silence. From the "hush" action through that of the last line, only the gestures of the audience are presented when we would expect a human agent to be named; the device underlines the audience's inhumanity. Since the clown is identified as a Negro and the rapid put-downs are aimed only at the clown and other blacks, the reader can identify the audience as white. The expression "personal bleach" not only identifies the color of the audience but seems to suggest that it is acting *very* white, white white. The blacks dotting this sea of whiteness are bereft of qualities that the audience feels they should have gained from contact with this superior whiteness. Conjunctions are a key device: "decked dismissal," "sugared hoot and hauteur," for example. But individual words also carry heavy burdens: "rift," in which the white members of the audience separate themselves from the blacks among them; "magnificent," as the audience begins to display its consciousness of its own richness; "heirloom," which adds to the audience a tradition of richness and mastery.

Subtlety of technique and forthrightness of attack make "downtown vaudeville" a strong statement. In it Gwendolyn eliminated the old protest rhetoric and launched a savage attack simply through a sharp description of the audience's behavior. Claude McKay, black poet of 1920s fame, had tried to eliminate protest rhetoric by creating as persona a romantic rebel who spoke in broad symbols about persecution, and by describing his becoming—in the process of rising above his tormentors—a superior person. His poem is more easily accessible but his broad symbols sacrifice force and his romantic rebel seems inadequately separated from nineteenth-century Byronism.

Gwendolyn took a greater risk, since the process of understanding her poem requires that the reader reconstruct the scene in order to experience it completely. For the white reader-creator, there is a booby-trapped assault in understanding the poem. Without the reader's achievement of complete apprehension, the poem's basic impact is likely to be lost.

One of Gwendolyn's favorite devices during the *Annie Allen* period was to play conventional and unconventional structures against each other, and sometimes to work apparently conventional structures for very special effects. Once the reader's creative participation was invoked by simple or complex devices, the momentum might be sustained by various linguistic means: figurative language, challenging twists of diction, unusual conjunctions of words, shifts in pace or rhythm, or creation of special tones. The poem "the parents: people like our marriage, Maxie and Andrew" illustrates the symbiotic function of conventional and unconventional structures:

> Clogged and soft and sloppy eyes
> Have lost the light that bites or terrifies.
>
> There are no swans and swallows any more
> The people settled for chicken and shut the door.
>
> But one by one
> They got things done:

Watch for porches as you pass
And prim low fencing pinching in the grass.

Pleasant custards sit behind
The white Venetian blind.

Again, the reader enters the structure by way of a synecdoche which, though vivid, requires complete attention for comprehension. The end of the second stanza makes clear that "eyes," a part, stands for "people," the whole. The "swans" and "swallows" of the third line tease the reader into associating the images with the painful choices of people. Images and movement strive to express the exact quality of the people's subsequent actions and achievement. The sound system, diction, and imagery suggest the satiric but compassionate view of the speaker-witness. The last two lines of the third stanza, with the assistance of internal rhyme, alliteration, and assonance, suggest the rhythms of a careful and prudent ordering of existence. And the final couplet moves without more than brief pauses to register neatly the quality of the "people's" achievement. The unconventional opening is soon replaced by a series of seemingly very conventional declarative sentences, whose explicitness functions to increase the feeling of precise measurement.

Several poems make varying degrees of alterations in the conventional system of reference, though other devices may provide the major means of communication ("the birth," "do not be afraid of no," "Beverly Hills, Chicago," "I love those little booths at Benvenuti's," and others). Obviously, a series of devices work in conjunction to create overall effects, but imagery can often be singled out as the most striking. A good deal beyond realistic, representative, or pictorial functions was already to be found in *A Street*. Gwendolyn modified the realistic image on some occasions merely by attaching to it a striking descriptive term ("crowding darkness"), by combining a figurative gesture with it ("could a dream send up through onion fumes / Its white and violet"), by contrasting realistic and symbolic functions (crooked and straight in "hunchback girl"), by presenting expressionistic description ("Mabbie on Mabbie with hush in the heart"), and by emphasizing the figurative role of the basically realistic term ("wear the brave stockings of night-black lace" and "temperate holiness arranged / Ably on asking faces").

The imagery system of *Annie Allen* moves still further away from the simple representational into the symbolic in the range of its functions, although the range of *A Street* is included within its broadening circle. In

"Sunday chicken," the range includes vivid realism and a surrealistic flash to emphasize the savagery retained by "civilized" meat eaters. In "Beverly Hills, Chicago," a poem rendering the complex response of the poor to the graces afforded the rich, Gwendolyn combines her synecdoche system with images her reader will experience as part of the common fate. In the yards of the wealthy, she presents the brutal threat of decay that affects us all through the image of the leaves as "The dry brown coughing beneath their feet" which the handyman is on his way to remove. In their golden gardens, the leaves fall in "lovelier patterns" and "the refuse is a neat brilliancy." The wealthy "flow sweetly into their houses" to tea, whereas for the poor tea will be merely the result of throwing "some little black dots into some water" in crowded and unprivate surroundings. The contrasts are moulded into complexity by the reflections of a worldy wise narrator.

The sonnet sequence "the children of the poor" succeeds by dint of numerous graces, not least among them Gwendolyn's skill in eliminating from her use of imagery the distance between the representational and metaphorical modes. She tends to work here almost entirely in the latter. The first sonnet of the series provides a striking example while contrasting the hardness sometimes expressed by people without children with the perplexity and love of those who must care for them: "People . . . / Attain a mail of ice and insolence"; "through a throttling dark"; and "makes a sugar of / The malocclusions, the inconditions of love."

A further range in the use of imagery derives from Gwendolyn's exploration of imagery within romantic, expressionistic, and surreal categories. The romantic is particularly noticeable in the ballad, but in "do not be afraid of no," a poem sternly lecturing the self regarding the path to integrity, the surreal reaches into Poe-like patterns. The old pliable self is "like a street / That beats into a dead end and dies there." And like

> . . . a candle fixed
> Against dismay and countershine of mixed
> Wild moon and sun. And like
> A flying furniture, or bird with lattice wing; or gaunt thing,
>   a-stammer down a nightmare neon peopled with condor,
>   hawk and shrike.

Such a series of images, however, seems to overdramatize the self's revulsion.

Among the shorter poems, "do not be afraid of no" is singular for its experimental imagery. A more elaborate and interesting example is the long poem "The Anniad." As her longest poem prior to the publication of "In the

Mecca," it was in a class by itself. Its closest runner-up from *A Street* is "The Sundays of Satin-Legs Smith," which extends its realistic imagery by various means but retains—as it should for its kind of satiric purposes—the very strong impact of the realistic. But with "The Anniad" come allegory, an extremely universalizing form, and a black particularism—seemingly somewhat overwhelmed by and not quite meshed with the allegorical lines. Very simply, "The Anniad" is the story of Annie Allen's young womanhood and married life, an experience that forces her to accept disillusionment and the narrowness of the areas in which life's small satisfactions can be seized. Annie Allen matures by moving from the epic universe of her dreams to the more prosaic one in which her best laid plans often go astray.

The imagery tends to respond to the ritualistic. And to the extent that the loving and mating of the young woman are overweighed by dreams, the imagery must move away from ordinary versions of realism to encompass incongruities. Having inherited the love lore of her country and the disabilities imposed upon her black identity, she is, at the beginning, at once the would-be epic heroine of song and story who moves in fairyland and the black woman vulnerable to special experiences fraught with disillusion. Forgotten by "the higher gods" and berated by the lower ones, she must negotiate, nonetheless, with what she has inherited. A few stanzas reflect the range of imagery. The dreamer and the flesh-and-blood woman provide the romantic and the realistic, the former being the more emphasized after the stanza's opening lines:

> Think of ripe and romp about
> All her harvest buttoned in,
> All her ornaments untried;
> Waiting for the paladin
> Prosperous and ocean-eyed
> Who shall rub her secrets out
> And behold the hinted bride.

Following the images of the heroic knight are the most realistic images of the poem.

> Think of thaumaturgic lass
> Looking in her looking glass
> At the unembroidered brown;
> Printing bastard roses there;
> Then emotionally aware
> Of the black and boisterous hair,
> Taming all that anger down.

In expressing the climax of the accumulated problems, storms, and confusions of Annie's young life, Gwendolyn turns entirely to expressionistic imagery:

> In the indignant dark there ride
> Roughnesses and spiny things
> On infallible hundred heels.
> And a bodiless bee stings.
> Cyclone concentration reels.
> Harried sods dilate, divide,
> Suck her sorrowfully inside.

Gwendolyn would comment upon "The Anniad" in her 1969 interview with George Stavros. She warmly and affectionately remembered the process of creating the poem and the pleasure it afforded, although it was "labored, a poem that's very interested in the mysteries and magic of technique." Closely textured was "every stanza in that poem; every one was worked on and revised, tenderly cared for. More so than anything else I've written, and it is not a wild success; some of it just doesn't come off. But it was enjoyable."[7]

Although Annie's dream of happiness is shattered, the images of the last stanza suggest that she salvaged something from her experiences: "Stroking swallows from the sweat. / Fingering faint violet. / Hugging / gold and Sunday sun. / Kissing in her kitchenette / The minuets of memory." Thus "The Anniad" promises that Annie will face life with greater maturity.

"Appendix to the Anniad, leaves from a loose-leaf war diary" portrays an Annie much less preoccupied with herself and her fortunes. She thinks about war's general and personal impact. Imagery is not, however, a very striking feature of the three poems. In particular, the imagery of the second poem suffers from the reader's excessive exposure to those on television purporting to present the gusto life: "we two are worshipers of life / Being masters of the long-legged stride / Gypsy arm swing." "the sonnet-ballad" loses itself in self-consciously insistent romantic imagery and labels: "empty heart-cut," "coquettish death."

But "Appendix . . . " functions as a transition to the mature Annie of the section entitled "The Womanhood." The imagery and other devices in the sonnets of "the children of the poor" suggest a person who takes a tough-minded look at the difficulties of life, meets them courageously, and reveals, in the process, a richly reflective mind. Life is to be fought for and its unchangeable conditions rigorously faced. Romance seems to allow Annie to feel out her capacities and to assert important values, whether or not they can be fully realized in this life. Other poems reveal humor, courage, and angry and reflective stances regarding racism.

The responses to publication of *Annie Allen* brought Gwendolyn a number of experiences that stirred varied and often contradictory emotions. One such was the portrayal of her life aired on September 18, 1949, in the radio series "Destination Freedom." Two weeks before the broadcast, Gwendolyn wrote Elizabeth about the coming presentation of her life, noting that " 'My life' has had very little drama in it, and I'll be interested to see what manipulations they make with so little material."[8]

Despite its errors, the radio play "Poet in Bronzeville" can be seen as foreshadowing her impact on the popular consciousness as the poet who continued to belong to people in general rather than to critics and other poets only. Using the raw, broad contrasts often favored by radio drama of the time, the story portrayed Gwendolyn struggling unwaveringly through misunderstandings and hardships to become the outstanding poet who absorbs and expresses the true rhythms of community experience. As she writes in her small apartment, the El train interrupts with its noise, and the neighbors knock with requests for favors, but they are able to halt Gwendolyn's typewriter only temporarily. It clacks forth poetry triumphantly after each pause. Her experience with discrimination in employment is also dramatically portrayed, but the play errs outright by placing Gwendolyn's mother, Keziah, James Weldon Johnson, and her teachers among those who misunderstand.

Written by Richard Durham and directed by Homer Heck, the play had roles for various talented black actors: Oscar Brown, Jr., Fred Pinkard, Dionne Crist, Hope Summers, Janice Kingslow, Dorothy Pate, and Wezlyn Tildon, who portrayed Gwendolyn. Gwendolyn herself read the last poem from *Annie Allen*, "Men of careful turns, haters of forks in the road." She gave an excellent reading, but hearing the tape today she is concerned about the play's false spots and shudders at the vulnerability and innocence evidenced by the high, sweet tones of her thirty-two-year-old womanhood.

Another area of ambiguity in Gwendolyn's life was her continued association with Inez Stark Boulton of the 1940s workshops, who arranged for her to read her poetry at Howard University on October 29, 1949. The reception was good and Gwendolyn met several of the black intellectuals and artists of Washington, D.C., among them the poet May Miller, a member of the writing workshop Inez had now formed in Washington. After the reading and a party, Gwendolyn enjoyed four restful days in Inez's Washington home. Inez would later report to Karl Shapiro that Gwendolyn's stay with her was without "strain" or the necessity for thawing, and that Gwendolyn's attitude toward her "white friends and friends of white friends" was "free of any race's taint." She felt that Gwendolyn had a large nature and suggested to Karl Shapiro that he and his wife Evalyn would enjoy becoming more closely acquainted with the young poet. Shapiro would later extend an invitation and Gwendolyn would accept, unaware of the prompting of Inez or her patronizing regality.

A more unfortunate experience was a trip to New York in November 1949. Gwendolyn introduced Inez to Elizabeth Lawrence, but Inez's effort to publish a book of poetry with Harper would not be successful. Inez and Gwendolyn first stopped at the Barbizon Plaza Hotel, where Inez was to stay and where Gwendolyn expected to change clothes and temporarily leave her baggage. The clerk registered Inez but announced that Gwendolyn "is not going to stay here" and "can't even go to the room." As they left the hotel, Inez said, "I guess I should have refused to stay there." But Gwendolyn noted that her tone seemed more a question than a conclusion.

But many things were going well during this period. By mid-March 1949, Gwendolyn thanked the editors at *Poetry* for presenting some of her poetry from the forthcoming *Annie Allen*, particularly for selecting the first three sonnets from the section "the children of the poor" and "a light and diplomatic bird." A week later she and a friend met the staff of *Poetry*, a pleasant encounter during which she invited the group to a Langston Hughes gathering at the George Hall Library at Forty-Eighth and Michigan on the evening of March 28. And on November 23, Hayden Carruth wrote to tell her that the editorial staff at *Poetry* had voted to award her the Eunice Tietjens Memorial Prize for the poems in the March 1949 issue. Finally, in April 1950 came *Poetry's* five-page, discriminating review of *Annie Allen* by Stanley Kunitz. Though Kunitz carefully identified weaknesses, he placed Gwendolyn's talents among the best of those possessed by twentieth-century writers, and the amount of space given to her was itself a tribute of a very high order.

The round of autograph parties and public appearances and the pleasures and pains of private life kept the poet stepping lively even before May 1, 1950, when she received the announcement that she had won the Pulitzer Prize. "Am sick with happiness and know how glad you are for me," she telegraphed Elizabeth Lawrence the next day. And two weeks later she wrote to thank Elizabeth for flowers. "The card made me want to cry. I have been wanting for years to make you proud. Because always you have gone out of your way to help me and to please me." She reported "many telegrams, letters, long distance calls, interviews, invitations!"[9] Among the mail were letters from friends she had not heard from for a time and invitations to read her poetry and speak on race relations. She declined the public speaking requests, feeling that she was not good at expressing herself orally. She was also still shy among strangers, though not nearly so shy as in early womanhood. Other letter writers wanted her to criticize their poems, and she had to refuse one person who wanted to send eighty poems. People dropped by her residence at 9134 South Wentworth to see what she looked like— some from the neighborhood but also two white women of considerable social pretensions from the North Shore, who Gwendolyn felt conducted themselves rather sniffingly. Out of the experience she made "The Lovers of the Poor," which would appear in the next volume of poetry.

Even the *Saturday Review's* publication, on May 13, 1950, of its "feeler" poll, listing those whom outstanding editors would have chosen for the Pulitzer prizes, couldn't dampen things, though it pointedly contrasted the qualifications of the *Review's* nominees with those of the actual winners and spoke of Gwendolyn, among others, as still being a "writer of promise." On the other hand, it also called her a writer of "remarkable talent," quoted J. Saunders Redding's commendation of *Annie Allen*, and revealed Van Allen Bradley's influential vote for her in the feeler poll. Robert Frost's *Complete Poems* was overwhelmingly first choice in the poll, and William Carlos Williams's *Paterson III* was second. Others nominated for the poetry award were Conrad Aiken's *The Divine Pilgrim*, Harry Behn's *Little Hill*, Lloyd Frankenberg's *Pleasure Dome*, and Robert P. Tristram Coffin's *One Horse Farm*. The writer of the article, an R. W., attacked the Pulitzer selections over the years and thus scattered his fire: "Indeed, in looking over this and previous Pulitzer lists, one is disheartened by the qualities that characterize them. Promise rather than accomplishment, conscientious but commonplace scholarship, long belated recognition for meritorious work done in the past are garlanded far more than the actual distinction of performance." R. W. seems not to have noticed that it would have been difficult to settle upon Frost as winner without suggesting that the nation's poets were bankrupt of talent, since Frost had already been awarded the prize in 1923 and 1936.

Meanwhile, Gwendolyn was experiencing some of the rewards of accomplishment. In a bookstore on May 12, she found Pulitzer Prize bands draped around her own books. Early in June the Society of Midland Authors, "the 'grandest' literary organization here," gave her an "exquisite tea." The guests included representatives from all of Chicago's daily newspapers and other literary editors. Here she met, among others, Karl Shapiro, "who had just arrived in town, John Frederick Nims, Clara Ingram Judson,

Alice Gerstenberg, playwright, Clare Jaynes (Clara Spiegel and Jane Mayer). Mary Jane Ward, who wrote *The Snake Pit*, helped receive." Though the Society had not heretofore shown much awareness of her existence, they now invited her to join the group. "So now they say I am a member of that austere body," Gwendolyn reported drily to Elizabeth Lawrence on June 12, 1950.

Gwendolyn and Henry seemed to thrive on all the activity, and Henry Jr. enjoyed taking over his parents' guests and friends upon their arrival at the Blakelys' residence. The home routines were pretty well set, since they allowed for independent operations. Henry Sr. was occupied during the day as an estimator of job costs in the automobile repair business in which he held a partnership. But he was usually ready for an evening's outing, whether a literary occasion or personal entertainment or recreation. Frequently, Gwendolyn wrote from 9:00 A.M., intermittently, until Henry Jr.'s return from school. He would later remember being awestruck by her furious and concentrated activity at the dining room table on the few times he surprised her.

The child's mischievousness often prompted his grandmother Keziah to counsel teachers on methods of getting more work out of him. At his grandfather David's insistence, he was frequently brought to 4332 Champlain Avenue when his parents took an evening out. There he delighted in games and storytelling sessions with his grandfather, and his devoted grandmother helped to keep order.[10] At home he entertained and exasperated his family with elaborate goodnights. Goodnight to each of his parents. Goodnight to Cocoa, his puppy. Good night to Water Boy, his fish—then simply goodnight as a refrain until the lights went out.

Periodically, Henry Jr. was for Gwendolyn the source of a poem. For a dead pigeon he had found, he and Gwendolyn held a funeral, and she promised to make a poem from the event. Changing the characters, she created "the ballad of the light-eyed little girl," a piece in a seriocomic vein included in *Annie Allen:*

> She has taken her passive pigeon poor,
> She has buried him down and down.
> He never shall sally to Sally
> Nor soil any roofs of the town.

In "Life for my child is simple, and is good," she celebrated, in the womanhood section of *Annie Allen*, Henry Jr.'s life-drive, spontaneity, fearlessness, and reach. The woman speaker identifies with the child's tendencies and seems also to be giving herself a lesson on persistence and continued aspiration in the face of life's discouragements.

> Not that success, for him, is sure, infallible.
> But never has he been afraid to reach.
> His lesions are legion.
> But reaching is his rule.

The three opening sonnets of the section of *Annie Allen* entitled "the children of the poor" resulted from her thinking of him and of her motherhood. They are among her best.

Henry Jr. wrote his own poems and stories, although he also spoke of becoming a painter. In late 1949, he wrote:

> It seems like clouds hold hands
> And go about the skies in glossy ways
> And look at me while I wash the pans
> I have not seen them in days.

Despite such "swallows" arising out of the routine paths of daily life, Gwendolyn would soon be thinking of her affairs as being like "scrambled eggs" and her mind as "either a blur or a blast." Writing, the participation in public life now exacted by her fame, and managing the tensions of personal life were not giving her an easy way to go. When the various elements of her life maintained proportion, she contained the tension and turned to matters in which she could lose herself. Other than her usual writing, she enjoyed book reviewing, a critical activity she began in 1948 under Van Allen Bradley, then literary editor of the *Chicago Daily News*, and continued until 1967 with various other editors: Herman Kogan, Hoke Norris, and Jack McPhaul of the *Chicago Sun-Times*; Bob Cromie of the *Chicago Tribune*; Richard Kluger of the *New York Herald Tribune*; and Hoyt Fuller of the magazine *Negro Digest* (later renamed *Black World*). Her reviews also appeared in the *New York Times*. For her review in the *Herald-Tribune*, she had an entire page.

Any reader who had previously encountered Gwendolyn's reviews would anticipate a pithy, informal style, full of contrasts, imagery, wit, and sudden sharp focus. Her subjects encompassed various genres: poetry, fiction, autobiography, biography, and criticism, from international sources. She reviewed the outstanding writers of the day. Of Wallace Stevens's *The Auroras of Autumn*, she wrote:

Almost three decades ago Wallace Stevens, with the color, sensitive music and careful manufacture of such poems as "Sunday Morning," "Domination of Black," "To the One of Fictive Music," and the famous "Peter Quince at the Clavier," startled the more royal provinces of poetry; and doubtless there are few young poets writing today who have been able to ignore his influence.

Stevens has always been wide awake to his world and goes about sniffing, stretching his eyes and hating his ears for not being more faithful reporters (although many a better-known poet wonders at their quality).

The Auroras of Autumn, Stevens' sixth volume of verse, provides his customary luxuriance. It seems, however, more distinctly drawn and more certain.

Her review of Robert Frost's In the Clearing opens with a quotation from his first book of poetry:

"They would not find me changed from him they knew— / Only more sure of all I thought was true."

Thus spoke Robert Frost in the first poem of his first book. So steady has been the integrity of this man and so unchallengeable were his early clarities and rightness that 'In the Clearing,' published now on his 88th birthday . . . , seems an italicized confirmation of news offered half a century ago.

Still uncrushed are the Frost conviction, the mania for stripped truth, the reliance on the infallible validity of life. Still limber is the old unhaughtiness and still lively is the amiable salt.

Again with Frost's Letters to Louis Untermeyer, she exploits the incisive phrase: "Often he [Untermeyer] served as a sort of literary, and golden spittoon for the giant who aimed in his direction giant-secrets galore." Frost cared not "overmuch for any human being as a huggable item, held back in his emotional transactions with one-and-all." She quoted liberally from Frost, frequently illustrating unfavorable qualities, but emphasizing that the rich essential wisdom remained.

After books of poetry, the largest number of books Gwendolyn reviewed seem to have been novels. About poetry, she was frequently concerned with language (favoring boldness and risk), vision, and form. About the novel, her emphasis was most often on richness of perception, presentation of character, and development of story.

Gwendolyn's rapt focus upon creative work, both reviews and her own poetry, soon came into conflict with the more basic problems of her life and turned her affairs into "scrambled eggs." Opportunity to relieve some of the financial pressure upon the family appeared when Henry arranged to share an apartment with his partner, Ernest Price, who needed less space because he had recently separated from his wife. Mrs. Price told Gwendolyn that the arrangement would be agreeable to her, and the Blakely family moved in. Gwendolyn found it a difficult situation. As a woman whose work was confined entirely to the home, she was out of step with many of her near neighbors. She knew that the other women thought of her as one who did no work at all and was thus, at best, strange. She felt the sharp dislike of some. Mrs. Price had been respected, it seemed, partly because she had a job outside the home. Gwendolyn's next-door neighbor made the point clear by saying loudly enough for Gwendolyn to overhear: "Like I say, if you worked for it, you could have it."

Increasingly miserable in this hostile atmosphere and fearing that their temporary housing would become permanent, Gwendolyn pressed for moving, and when Henry seemed unwilling to try for another arrangement, she left for the house in Kalamazoo, Michigan, that had been purchased for rental a few years previously, where there were still two vacant rooms. But this new arrangement too proved unworkable. The Kalamazoo school staff wanted to put Henry Jr. back a grade, as a matter of course, and Gwendolyn's tenants were not comfortable with the owner residing in the same house. The townspeople talked much of possessions and seemed to the poet "thing-minded," conservative. Possibly part of the problem was that previously she had been able to choose what she would commit herself to, given Chicago's size and variety.

Gwendolyn eventually returned to Chicago, and she and Henry resolved their differences, but their housing situation would worsen before it improved. They were unable to find a residence where all three could live. Gwendolyn and Henry Jr. took an apartment in the 6800 block of South Evans, where there were rough-spoken neighbors. One rather wild young woman with a spiteful daughter lived with a light-skinned man in a common-law arrangement, the source of some sort of sick pride: "And light, too, honey," she said of her man. "And you know *they* kind of particular." Having grown up in a more ordered world, Gwendolyn felt considerable shock at this experience. She would remember this housing situation as the downest part of her married life. Meanwhile, Henry Sr. was sleeping in the downtown garage he helped to manage.

Finally, in April 1951, the family were reunited at 32 West Seventieth Street at $100 per month rental, after paying $300 in advance. Even after their painful experiences, they could not celebrate at such terms, but there was no way around them. The housing noose that maintained a strangling grip upon the Blakelys was a systematic force poised to pounce upon any blacks in the city of Chicago. At the end of World War II, job discrimination against blacks increased and the business community pressed to block legislation for fair employment practices. But housing was the major cause of racial conflict. Between 1940 and 1950, the black population increased from 277,731 to 492,265, yet Chicago and its institutions refused to extend the area to which blacks were, by and large, confined. Between 1945 and 1954, at least nine major race riots occurred in Chicago.[11]

Something of Gwendolyn's consciousness of institutionalized discrimination in housing appears in her essay "They Call It Bronzeville" (*Holiday*, October 1951), an assignment secured for her by novelist Nelson Algren. Primarily a tour of black South Side Chicago and a demonstration that blacks are simply like other people struggling for life's limited rewards, the essay first states that this area, "set aside for the halting use of a single race," should not exist. "Because of its cramped housing conditions, Bronzeville keeps stretching, stretching—leaning, cutting farther north, farther south, farther east, farther west. When this happens, violence follows; for a while there are beatings, window smashing, crowd gatherings. In time the active violence subsides (though not the regret) chiefly because it is found that the new, unwanted neighbors maintain their yards, their houses, their children and themselves as well as, if not better than, the Old Guard had been wont to do."

Gwendolyn was thus hardly unaware that her family's housing dilemma owed much to the existence of systematic and institutionalized racist forces. But it would be about seventeen years before she and most other blacks recoiled at the extent to which racism rolled forth in waves as part of the natural function of American institutions. In the essay, she describes the attitude of a "Bronzeville" black toward whites as "one of wary friendliness; he likes them when they let him." For now she and other progressive blacks confronted racism through personal courage and Christian faith. Perhaps her state of consciousness for that time is represented, at its outer limit, by "The Ballad of Rudolph Reed"—a poem that would appear ten years later in her next book of adult poetry, *The Bean Eaters*. The doughty, courageous Rudolph Reed lays down his life in defense of home and family. Breaking through the area in which the black community had been confined, Rudolph establishes himself and his family in a formerly all-white area and is goaded to violence when a white mob wounds his daughter. "Then up did rise our Rudolph Reed / And pressed the hand of his wife, / And went to the door with a thirty-four / And a beastly butcher knife." But Reed's gesture and glory are personal, since he is "oakener / Than others in the nation."

Despite continuing discrimination, the freedom talk of World War II seemed to keep hopes aloft. General Dwight D. Eisenhower, in an article entitled "The Future of the Negro" in the pages of *Negro Digest*, praised blacks for their patriotism, loyalty, sacrifices, and progress, and predicted all the rights of American citizenship by the year 2000.[12] Gwendolyn maintained her belief that relief for the "uncomfortables" of this world was yet high on America's agenda and that a moderator with a properly stiffened back stood by to see that the issue got proper deliberation and disposition. When the balance was threatened in her own mind, she gained some relief by allowing situations to feed her ironic vision in her poetry. Some of the poems would create a sense of uneasiness in whites, who feared her slipping from the universal into social commentary: "downtown vaudeville," "I love those little booths at Benvenuti's," "The Lovers of the Poor," and others.

But beyond the fact of racial discrimination was Gwendolyn's philosophy of life: goodness begins simply with the fact of life itself. It is good to be alive, and life is to be lived for its own sake. This conviction enabled her to march forth unhesitantly as outstanding artist, citizen, and, for blacks, exemplar. She was particularly pleased by the strong reception she had gained from the black community, though she still did not receive invitations from black organizations with the status of, say, the National Council of Negro Women. Yet the *Chicago Defender* favorably reviewed her work, and in its June 10, 1950, issue she appeared on the front page as one of the distinguished judges of a $10,000 popularity contest it was sponsoring. It pictured her with several blacks of acknowledged prominence: Ashby B. Carter, Mrs. Irene McCoy Gaines, Bishop William J. Walls, Mrs. Etta Moten Barnett, Judge Fred Duke Slater, and Dr. Henry Allen Boyd.

She had already read her works at Howard University, the black institution that saw itself as the "capstone" of Negro education. Forthcoming were two adventures with the intellectual community of Atlanta University, an institution with a status similar to Howard's and that numbered W.E.B. DuBois among its scholars: a reading on October 28, 1950, at a big book fair, and an essay in Atlanta University's *Phylon* as one of a group assessing the state and direction of black literature.

The journey to Atlanta was Gwendolyn and Henry's first encounter with the Deep South. They were given a tour of the general Atlanta area, with startling views of the elaborate property acquisitions of some of the upper-class blacks. Most memorable for Gwendolyn was her meeting with the celebrated Mrs. Mary McLeod Bethune, founder of Bethune-Cookman College, founder of the National Council of Negro Women (1935), member of Franklin Delano Roosevelt's "Kitchen Cabinet," friend of Eleanor Roosevelt, politician extraordinary, and an unusually commanding personality.

To her attempt to engage Mrs. Bethune in conversation, Gwendolyn at first felt a cold response—an uncomfortable situation since they were sitting side by side. It seemed clear to her that Mrs. Bethune did not want to be bothered. This was certainly different from the warm response and hospitality she had afforded Langston Hughes. When Gwendolyn got up to speak, "I suddenly decided that to 'speak' was irrelevant. I was a poet, and, as my Aunt Beulah once told me, 'a poet *poets.*' " So instead, she read a few poems and felt the cold eyes of Mrs. Bethune casting upon her an increasingly warm glow. When Gwendolyn returned to her seat, Mrs. Bethune applauded her more enthusiastically than she had anyone else, congratulated her effusively, and pumped her hand. During her own speech, she was generous in her praise of Gwendolyn and her poetry.[13] At the end of the luncheon, Gwendolyn and Mrs. Bethune stood for picture-taking, flanked by Dr. Bell I. Wiley, Emory University historian, and the black historian Dr. L.D. Reddick.

The responses of the two leading black universities and of the more popular media were signs that the slow process through which the artist is absorbed by her own people had begun. The special issue of *Phylon,* a scholarly journal based at Atlanta University and founded by W.E.B. DuBois, to which Gwendolyn contributed, also marked something of this progress, but it was equally conscious of her in the role of exemplar. The special issue reflected an urgency about developing greater universalism in black literature.

Mosell C. Hill and M. Carl Holman, editors for the special issue, "The Negro in Literature: The Current Scene," had assumed that a standard mid-century appraisal would blur the focus by summoning up too many names and that the 1930s and 1940s in black literature had obviously been more fruitful than any prior period. Hoping that their respondents would simply take the series of questions posed as instruments for getting to the heart of the matter, they queried several black critics and creative writers:

What are the promising and unpromising aspects of the Negro's present position in American literature? Are there any aspects of the life of the Negro in America which seem deserving of franker, or deeper, or more objective treatment? Does current literature by and about Negroes seem more or less propagandistic than before? Would you agree with those who feel that the Negro writer, the Negro as subject, and the Negro critic and scholar are moving toward an "unlabeled" future in which they will be measured without regard to racial origin and conditioning?[14]

The contributors, however, were given freedom to ignore the editors' questions and explore the theme of the current scene in their own way. The poet-critic-scholar Sterling A. Brown simply presented a solid analysis of folk literature, which would be frequently quoted and reprinted. The satirist

George S. Schuyler celebrated the work of the white novelist Carl Van Vechten in creating a more enlightened climate for the reception of black writers. Others gave more consideration to the editors' questions "but treated issues of much greater pertinency and complexity than those we [the editors] had provisionally indicated."

The creative writers, who were given the lead-off position, spoke of the creative process and of practical opportunities. William Gardner Smith, a bright star on the horizon of fiction (*The Last of the Conquerors* and *Anger at Innocence*), and Gwendolyn were to some degree in agreement. In "The Negro Writer: Pitfalls and Compensations," Smith pointed out the pitfalls of polemics, excessive idealization or excessive condemnation, lack of humor in serious works, and failure to universalize. The black writer's compensations: basic emotional contact with the people of his society, a grasp of individual and social truth, and the emotional depth endowed by the automatic pressures of the environment.

Gwendolyn did not address the political as directly as Smith did. Her title would have pleased the white liberal critical consensus and was in line with the thematic emphasis of the black literati: "Poets Who Are Negroes." She began: "The Negro poet has impressive advantages. Ready-made sub-jects—which he may twist as he wills. Great drives. And that inspiring emotion, like tied hysteria, found only in the general territory of great drives." White poets would envy these advantages of the black poet, but the black poet cannot afford to yield to the temptation to rest upon such advantages, an act that would be like throwing raw dough to "the not-so-hungry mob." The one-page essay then moves rapidly to its climax as poem:

You have got to cook that dough, alter it, until it is unrecognizable. Then the mob will not know it is accepting something that will be good for it. Then it will eat, enjoy, and prosper.

Every Negro poet has "something to say." Simply because he is a Negro; he cannot escape having important things to say. His mere body, for that matter, is an eloquence. His quiet walk down the street is a speech to the people. Is a rebuke, is a plea, is a school.

But no real artist is going to be content offering raw materials. The Negro poet's most urgent duty, at present, is to polish his technique, his way of presenting his truths and beauties, that these may be more insinuating, and, therefore, over-whelming.[15]

Gwendolyn thus threw considerable emphasis upon craft. She had been very impatient with those black poets who she felt "just put down anything off the tops of their heads and left it there."[16]

In tone and frequently in specific comments, other critics in the special issue of *Phylon* tended to recognize Gwendolyn as the exemplar of a new wave of emancipated black writers with great interest in form and craft, universalism—whether devoted to blacks or not—elimination of propaganda or its subordination to artistic concerns, exploration of non-racial themes, and global thinking. In the coming-of-age psychology after World War II, which would continue well into the 1950s, the critics looked with some disdain upon black writing marred by agonized and self-conscious protest.

One of the more searing indictments, Hugh Gloster's "Race and the Negro Writer," called for the black writer to break out of an area of entrapment. Because of discrimination and oppression, the black writer had naturally focused upon "themes of race defense, protest, and glorification," but propaganda, Gloster felt, had handicapped the artist by preventing a cosmic grasp of varied experiences, tragic and comic, by arresting the growth of philosophical perspective, by limiting the literary range to race in America, with the threat of Jim-Crow esthetics, and by assisting critics in consigning the writer to cultural isolation.

In various ways, many of these concerns had been expressed earlier, though not with the emphasis given by Gloster. Two articles in the March 1949 issue of *Phylon* could serve almost as blueprints for the negative and positive characteristics that critics saw in blacks' writing: Charles Glicksberg's "The Alienation of Negro Literature," which vigorously censured narrowness, and Alain Locke's, "Wisdom de Profundis: The Literature of the Negro, 1949," which allowed more room for racial themes but praised the younger poets for "the rise of the universal theme supplementing but not completely displacing the poetry of racial mood and substance."

Locke's ease in juxtaposing such terms as "universal theme" and "poetry of racial mood and substance" leaves the reader the job of fleshing out the distinctions. Taking a cue from the fact that he quotes a poem expounding the theme of war, it seems safe to assume that he sees such themes as obviously universal, while the "poetry of racial substance and mood" is not universal. However, he also sees *Annie Allen*'s "the children of the poor" and "the rites for Cousin Vit" as reflecting near-success in Gwendolyn's attempts to "discover the universal in the particulars of a modern woman's experiences of love, motherhood, struggle, frustration." Yet, of the poems he mentions, the second sonnet of "the children of the poor" is the only one that summons up the racial situation; it does so not by direct labels, but by picturing the extremity of society's rejection of the children. Is that approach representative of the bottom line for universality? Here Locke seems to say so. He seems also to juxtapose the roles of the black poet: as "basically a modern poet and an American poet" who expresses the universal, "but conversely, too . . . at the proper time and in the proper way a Negro poet, a spokesman for his innermost experiences." What Locke seems to be saying is that the universal elements of black experiences can be pushed to the foreground, with race being implicit. "Such instances of successfully universalized expression as 'the birth in a narrow room' by Gwendolyn Brooks, Helen Johnson Collins' 'To an Avenue Sport,' and 'Two Lean Cats' by Myron O'Higgins amply attest to this. With basic human denominators of experience discovered, the racial overtones are all the more poignant and meaningful through being left implicit."

Responding in the December issue of *Phylon* to the commentators for the special issue on the Negro in literature, however, Locke is still clearer, and his words are essential for pinning down some of the commentators' use of terms:

Beginning with the broader social identifications of *Native Son*, and the social discoveries of common-denominator human universals between Negro situations and others, these critics rightly claim, artistic expression with Negroes has become increasingly sounder, more objective and less racialistic—in the limiting sense of chauvinism—but withal even more racial in the better sense of being more deeply felt and projected. This third dimension of *objective universality*, they feel, is the ultimate desideratum for a literature that seeks universal appeal and acceptance. I agree. In fact, have always agreed.

Locke also stated that in "universalized particularity" there has always resided the world's "greatest and most enduring art," and he found it necessary to remind the critics that this quality had appeared as early as 1923 in a work that, surprisingly, none of them had referred to, Jean Toomer's *Cane*. "Here was something admirably removed from what [the critic] Mr. Chandler calls very aptly 'promotional literature,' but it is Negro through and through as well as deeply and movingly human." Near the end of his essay he gave his concept, perhaps oversimplified, of the mandate which the critics were presenting to the black creative writer: "Give us Negro life and experience in all the arts but with a third dimension of universalized common-denominator humanity."

Locke went on to cite Russia's greatest writers, each of whom "produced great writing and universal understanding for Russian experience." In short, the universal can be reached either by the intense awareness of the relatedness of human experience, of its common denominators, or by the intensity and depth with which the particular is approached. More immediately applicable to criticism are the following approaches: universalism through common denominators of racial experience without mentioning race; universalism through materials, where race remains as overtone and implicit; and (for Locke, the best source) universalism with great emphasis upon racial particularity but without chauvinism (as in Jean Toomer's *Cane*).

One must admit, however, that the attempt to achieve some coherence in Locke's use of the term "universal" among several of his statements demonstrates the shiftiness of the term. Other writers for the *Phylon* special issue increased the feeling of shiftiness through generalized attempts to establish universality not by a sufficient examination of the internalities of a work but by stating another level of abstraction for the work (a character as an example of the diminution of the romantic spirit) or by relating it to other externals. Concealed within this shiftiness are the critics' negotiations for the acceptance of a black literature with a skeptical and remote white audience that, despite its ethnocentrism, will give all the final examination grades and rewards. Two of the critics directly acknowledged the audience situation, but one of them announced the end of that audience's resistance. White critics would increase the confusion by adding terms to an already unstable rhetoric: One "transcends" racial experience. The "human experience" is opposed to that of being "Negro." For both blacks and whites, a "protest" element becomes a propaganda novel and transforms the writer into a protest writer. A Negro writer is a protest writer; a writer is one who addresses the "human condition," and so forth. Thus Gwendolyn would be carefully watched for universalism, bitterness, and propagandistic tendencies. The *Phylon* critics, while esteeming her highly, were negotiating for the literature's entry into the "mainstream" without challenging the vagaries of the entry terms laid down by white society.

Audience situation could not help but be a part of Gwendolyn's consciousness. She had been urged by her editor to move, in her next book, to a more universal base than that of *A Street in Bronzeville*. Since many of the poems in that book were universal, the admonition seems to have been a request to remove or reduce the particularism implied by the focus on the term Bronzeville. And Gwendolyn seems to accede to this universalist emphasis in rejecting Genevieve Taggard's charge that "a light and diplomatic bird" is "imitative." The poem, Gwendolyn wrote her editor, "imitates no one. I remember thinking, as I finished, that it especially would please you. It seemed, to me, to have an element of that universality which you hoped, long ago, I'd get on more familiar terms with."[17] The poem portraying a woman's desire for the poise of a bird with which to confront the pain of life's confusions does not particularize race, an identity the reader gets only from the fact that Annie Allen's heroine is a black woman. Despite the reservations expressed by Saunders Redding in his review of Annie Allen, it should be clear that in its poems Gwendolyn achieved the universalism that coincided with the viewpoint of much of the post–World War II audience. In comparison with A Street in Bronzeville, Annie Allen registers a drop in racial particularism. Besides possessing what Alain Locke called "common denominator humanity," few of the poems individually identify the race of the protagonist. The "common denominator" clearly supersedes particularism. Thirteen of the pieces in A Street individually emphasize racial identity, if one does not include "kitchenette building" (though I think most readers would include it). Seven poems indirectly point to the racial by tone, speech rhythms, and cultural associations. Twenty-three poems do not, individually, suggest racial identity.

In contrast, seven poems in Annie Allen (eight if "old laughter" is included) emphasize race but do so far less forcefully than those in A Street. The physical violence of racial conflict and conspicuous black cultural styles are almost unrepresented. What poems indirectly point to race? "Men of Careful Turns," with its emphasis upon the form of modern prejudice, would seem to fit, but little else. Perhaps more important, the life of Annie, the heroine, reveals few cultural points peculiar to blacks, though it unfolds the crucial impact of racial conflict and situation.

To justify a work's universality through a count of the racial references has the unfortunate suggestion of using mechanical skills as a gauge. As indicated earlier, however, Gwendolyn was herself a member of the universalist party as the common property of black literati and white, and this universalism would have no basis without the power infused into it by her poetry. Her move toward greater universality was perhaps also facilitated by the obsessive interest in technique that Annie Allen reflects.

But two matters are still more important. Gwendolyn had very early recoiled from the exotic image of blacks sometimes encountered in the writings of black artists of the 1920s and 1930s and had struggled for an art that would present blacks simply as people. This situation provided a range of approach, from realistic presentation, with some excursions into the cultural, to exploitation of humanness without identifying tags. She had pointed out to her editor during the conflict over Genevieve Taggard's evaluation that she was no longer interested in doing such a poem as "the date" but that she respected "obituary for a living lady" (also part of A Street) as much as she did when she wrote it.[18] It is significant that the woman protagonist of "a date" falls within very simple categories of conflicts: the servant woman recoiling from the foolishness of her woman employer and going out to have a ball with her man. Victory was available on a simple level. Only the protagonist of "obituary for a living lady," among her women characters, enters those complex rhythms of existence in which winning is also losing. The lady seems to win her struggles with the bald sexism of men by aggressively absorbing religion in "the country of God," but is soon in a situation in which the minister will confront her anew on the sexual terms she thinks she has escaped.

In *Annie Allen* Gwendolyn was intent upon exploring minutely the complex rhythms of existence and upon making coherent the psychology of a young woman similar to herself and experiencing the world in a similar way. In poetry she could use analogies and nonrealistic imagery to escape confessional detail, a method that keeps the reader at some distance throughout the book, while exploring intimately the inwardness of a modern young black woman's experience. The character she created had not been, heretofore, the focus of a work of art. Obviously the work has strong autobiographical overtones, and its universalism is partly the result not merely of the new black optimism but also of the work of putting into order deep and obsessive personal drives and confusions.

With the publication of *Annie Allen* and the receipt of the Pulitzer Prize, Gwendolyn achieved rank both as an artist and as a citizen of the world. Van Allen Bradley was sending her poems to T.S. Eliot. And she was invited to be one of the judges for the National Book Award. For both whites and blacks, Gwendolyn would from now on be tagged "the first Negro to win a Pulitzer Prize," and with that label would come the roles of spokeswoman and arbiter in the upper realms of her city's and her nation's cultural affairs.

5

A Complicated Universe

Early in 1951, Gwendolyn experienced a personal triumph in her second pregnancy and was temporarily disengaged from the making of books, though she was fulfilling briefer writing assignments and reading poetry with Peter Viereck and others. In February, she managed a trip to New York to assist in the National Book Award selection. She stayed at a dismal hotel but enjoyed dinner with her editor, Elizabeth Lawrence. Elizabeth found Gwendolyn in wonderful spirits and looking fit, convinced that she was pregnant. On her return to Chicago, her condition was "certified, confirmed, entered." She experienced a little discomfort now and then but felt that "that can often be expected when a woman is of my great age" (she was now thirty-four). Meanwhile, she learned that a royalty check for $169.00 was due, for which she already had a use.[1]

She completed book reviews and worked on three articles. In March, *Negro Digest*, which had earlier reprinted her poetry and published an article on her life, presented her essay "Why Negro Women Leave Home," an attack on husbands' dollar "dole-outs" and failure to approach their wives with "dignity and respect." Her last paragraphs reflected some of the heat of the situation:

A wife whose husband respects her as a person, instead of "humoring" her as though she were a chattel or a slightly idiotic child, is not likely to leave him, despite his poverty, possible infidelity, or stupidity in other areas of their relationship.

Women who cannot obtain such regard will increasingly prefer to live alone.

In June, *Negro Digest* published "How I Told My Child about Race," in which Gwendolyn relived both the pain of having to explain the unexplainable and the pleasure of Henry Jr.'s optimistic openness toward all races. Her major effort was work on the essay assignment that novelist Nelson Algren had obtained for her from *Holiday Magazine*, "They Call It Bronzeville." The article required research, renewal of acquaintance with old familiar sites, and numerous pictures of high life, cultural activities, and the struggles of ordinary people. The editors liked her first version and, after calling for additions that they thought would make it even better, published it in October.

On September 8, at Provident Hospital, her daughter was born and promptly named Nora. Gwendolyn had been convinced that she was bearing a girl baby, and the family looked forward to her arrival. Henry Jr., now eleven, was eager for either brother or sister and showed no symptoms then or later of sibling rivalry. Asked by his grandmother what he wanted the baby to be, he replied: "I don't care what it is as long as it's something. All my friends at school talk about their brother or sisters and I haven't got anything. I know it will be cute."[2] Henry Sr. would soon classify the arrival of the second child as a case of reliving the experience with the firstborn, since the years that separated the two children caused the family to respond as excitedly to the second child as it had to the first.

Nora cried all night for the first two nights at home and then, abruptly, became the perfect baby and the center of the family.

As the situation settled, Gwendolyn and Henry discussed the possibility of purchasing their own home. The idea became a goal for Gwendolyn, and they kept looking at houses. The endless moving about went against the grain of her desire to feel rooted—in place. Growing up in her parents' home had convinced her that "living in your own house" was the way to live. She had a habit of building expansive daydreams about expensive homes she saw while she and her family took long drives in the countryside. For the purpose of daydreaming, the bigger and more elaborate the home the better, except when some painful recollection of her actual circumstances entered the scene. But most often she contented herself with imagining the lives lived in such houses. In her actual quest, she was more practical.

One of the homes that appealed to her, for example, was not one with fancy trimmings but a well-kept residence of "six rooms, two-story, firm brick: tight, ceilinged basement: gas heat: bargain price for Chicago." A careful white-haired couple had owned it for twenty years. Gwendolyn found it just right for her family "except that we are blocked by our lack of sufficient down-payment."[3]

Nonetheless, the ownership of the right house remained an insistent theme. She planned to sell the house she owned in Kalamazoo for at least part of the money needed for a down payment on the new home. Mindful of the housing goal, she turned again to writing fiction. Was it possible that the right amount of money might arrive from such a source? Elizabeth

Lawrence had earlier pointed out that there was more money for both author and publisher in fiction, and that among several of Gwendolyn's incomplete manuscripts was material from the old "American Family Brown." Gwendolyn began to recreate the individual pieces.

On January 16, 1952, she sent Elizabeth Lawrence her revisions and recreations, which the editor had seen long ago in their original form—but now "hacked or snipped, or embellished, or extended, or re-modeled, etc." Gwendolyn called the work "Bronzevillians," seeing it as a collection of short fiction that would be warmer than *Annie Allen*. She thus took the first major step toward what would eventually be the very original novel *Maud Martha*. Elizabeth, replying on February 26, found the manuscript quite interesting, an "unorthodox novel," but one more moving than the old manuscript "American Family Brown." "In general, what this manuscript needs is more of the people and the currents and cross-currents of their lives." She did not think that photographs, a suggestion of Gwendolyn's, would be suitable, nor that Gwendolyn had yet found an appropriate title. She returned the manuscript for further work.

During subsequent revisions Gwendolyn discovered several ways to improve the work. Instead of a loose series of short stories, she would present the development of one person in a family, with the other members seen "chiefly in relationship to her." Since Maud Martha (formerly known as Evelina) was the most interesting, she would be the central character. Changing the name to Maud Martha seemed to clear up Gwendolyn's conception of the story and the outlook she would want Maud Martha to project. She moved with a good deal of excitement, which was dampened only by the fact that Henry Jr. had to go to the hospital for what had seemed to be bronchitis but required observation for the possibility of polio. The tests turned out negative, however, and by September 15 Gwendolyn's revised manuscript was on its way to her editor.

Elizabeth was both encouraging and critical in her October 17 response. She found it dramatic, expressive of elemental emotions, and of some originality. The opening pieces were "superb, lovely in a universal way and touched with heartbreak too." A contract would soon be on the way stipulating a $500 advance against royalties. The rest of the letter turned to the matter of improving the manuscript. Although she did not emphasize the fact, Elizabeth sensed that Gwendolyn was working rather close to the autobiographical vein. Consistency in the makeup of her characters was one question that arose. Elizabeth and her staff recognized Maud Martha as "intelligent, her mind active, her sympathies wide and warm," but the manuscript had not prepared the reader to find her with a taste for Henry James. Would Gwendolyn make sure that Maud was not, in this circumstance, becoming an extension of the author?

In the chapter on the pretentious "second beau," the reader could see reasons for rejecting him, but since Maud soon afterward reveals a fondness for some of these very aspects of his background, why does she reject him? There were problems in making Maud's marriage relationship probable, partly because the point of view shifted from Maud to her husband, Paul. What was there that attracted them to each other, Elizabeth asked. It was confusing to have Paul suddenly pushing Maud away when, only recently, she was the one pushing him away. Other criticisms: the literary club group did not come off well; nothing prepared the reader to find Paul interested in John Ruskin; it was very difficult to make literary people interesting on paper. The editor suggested that Gwendolyn might want to explore the marriage in relationship to a philosophical passage about the search for someone to lean on. Was the marriage a case of both parties seeking this? Such a possibility might be useful to the development of the novel, since most intimate arrangements don't stand up under the pressure of such quests. Could there be a development that would offset to some degree the experiences with the prejudiced white Santa and the white cosmetic saleswoman, to give substance to the optimism about the world expressed at the end of the story?

Gwendolyn retained her excitement, even in the face of the work suggested by requests for revisions.[4] Regardless of revisions, her first book of fiction was about to come to birth. She liked her heroine, found her editor's criticisms clear and sometimes a "revelation," and always found the "making of a book . . . such a grand experience." With the contract came a few more suggestions from Elizabeth. Although the manuscript hinted strongly of a more pleasant outcome ("rewards and humors"), it currently emphasized Maud Martha's fears, dissatisfactions, and frustrations. More diversity of mood and more depiction of Maud's relationship to her original family would add to the novel. At present, the story seemed to suggest that all relationships with her prior family ended with Maud Martha's marriage.

On December 31, Gwendolyn returned to Elizabeth the revised manuscript and a report of the changes made. She had solved the point of view problem by having everything seen through Maud Martha's eyes; eliminated "Maud Martha's literary club"; increased the length of a chapter she had called "Oberto. Eugena. Clement" and renamed it "kitchenette folks," and added two chapters, entitled "an encounter" and "a crowded street car." Of the additions, "an encounter" survives in the published version, but she agreed in February that "a crowded street car" could be dropped, since it "does not push the story and does not furnish especial lights for later parts of the book." (The content of the eliminated chapter is not known.) In the chapter entitled "love and gorillas," she gave to Maud Martha the experiences that she had formerly assigned to Maud's young daughter Paulette. They were an "exact" reconstruction of a dream of her own. At the opening of the story, she changed Maud's age from ten to seven and addressed the problem of presenting an image of hopefulness at the conclusion to counter the impact of so many of Maud's unsatisfactory experiences: "She is going to have a second baby, and feels optimistic, although many of her little problems remain standing." The published version also adds the impact of Maud's brother's return from the wars.

Gwendolyn also resisted some suggested changes. She wanted to arouse and intrigue, rather than to satisfy by being fully explicit. The reader should gain some understanding from silences. Thus, she felt that the reader, recalling experiences of compromise, should realize that Maud's settling for Paul as a husband was just such a compromise, a step away from her earlier dreams, at eighteen, of the good life. She also felt that compromises were more easily managed by the poor and near-poor because they could afford neither escapes nor psychiatrists, and because "sometimes it is a simple matter of 'compromise or be cold.' " She resisted making the desire to lean the central conflict of the marriage. "In the New-York-fine-stuff stage, she [Maud] does not feel the need of a 'post' in the form of some*one* to lean upon, and she would have laughed at the idea of becoming interested in a Paul," the poet wrote to Elizabeth.[5]

Gwendolyn then revealed her concern about her other goal, a house of her own. Should she try to sell individual chapters of *Maud Martha* prior to book publication? Would *Harper's* magazine be interested in any of them? Elsewhere, was there opportunity for a digest (condensation) or serialization? Remembering that *Omnibook* had published a digest of Ann Petry's novel *The Street*, she asked whether the publication still existed. Since Elizabeth was better informed, she might feel that none of these approaches was feasible, but "if it is possible to make extra money from the material, . . . I am eager to do that, for I am still passionately devoted to the idea of getting enough pennies together for a down payment on a house."

Elizabeth's reaction to the revised manuscript was that Gwendolyn had done excellent work on the Maud Martha story, "and as a result the whole thing has greater unity and body—it is a thing!" The editor's preference would have been for more elaboration—the relationship between Maud Martha and Paul for example. "But it is your book and no one else's."[6]

Elizabeth and the staff had further suggestions for Gwendolyn to consider, since all concerned wanted the complete realization of the story's potential. For a title, *Maud Martha* would seem better than the current *The Maud Martha Story*, although perhaps too similar to *Annie Allen*. Elizabeth had only been able to come up with *Daughter of the Dusk*, a phrase lifted from *Annie Allen*. If unsatisfactory, could Gwendolyn think of something better? A reader had felt that the white wife (appearing in the revised, published version of "kitchenette folks") was an overfamiliar type; if she was not to be removed, perhaps giving her a different treatment would eliminate the "curse of overfamiliarity." In the current manuscript version, the dice seemed loaded against the (white) Miss Ingram in the beauty shop episode from the start, and the effect was faintly trite, contrived. So important a point deserved the fresh, unhackneyed treatment Gwendolyn was capable of. The chapters "crowded streetcar" and "on thirty-fourth street" felt strained and forced and failed to make their point with dramatic effectiveness. Netta Cooper of the Chicago Concord Book Store would soon be coming to New York and had asked about the novel's progress. There was still time for revisions, as publication was not planned before fall. But Elizabeth was anxious to get the book into proof and read by those whose word would be useful in promoting it.

Exchanges between Gwendolyn and Elizabeth increased in frankness and directness as they approached the end of the bookmaking process characterizing the efforts of the modern editor and writer. Gwendolyn was pleased that the book had been improved and delighted with the descriptive copy for its jacket, and wanted to change the chapter title "The Elementary School" back to "Spring Landscape: Detail" (the title of the second chapter of the published work). However, *Daughter of the Dusk* as the title "sounds so cutely-grand." (She had used the expression in *Annie Allen* in "in light sarcasm".) What about *The Natural History of the Dandelion* (the flower with which Maud Martha identifies herself in the first chapter) or *Little Landscape*? Elizabeth would object to both titles as being too suggestive of a still life, while the book "is people." At Harper there was still support for, but not insistence upon, *Daughter of the Dusk*.

Gwendolyn said that rewritten versions of "The Self-Solace" chapter (the beauty parlor–Miss Ingram episode) had proved wooden. She was prepared to substitute another chapter, "At the Byrne-Coopers'." She was afraid that the dice might be loaded against the "new little lady, too, but the chapter does supply Maud Martha with a new understanding of one of Paul's workaday itches." In the published version of the chapter, the white woman treats her black maid as an object devoid of human dignity. (The reference to Maud's understanding Paul's "workaday itches" may have some reference to Gwendolyn's memory of Henry Senior's feelings of dehumanization in his employment with an industrial company.) Gwendolyn also seemed reluctant to give up the episode of the white wife, since she felt that she had pointed up the white wife's dilemma "with suggested sympathy as well as humor." She asked whether Elizabeth thought the episode would give unnecessary offense.[7]

Elizabeth expressed appreciation for Gwendolyn's willingness to listen and to weigh matters, but pointed out that her role and that of her staff could only be "to suggest spots where communication is blurred between author and reader—where the author has put in more than the reader gets out." She would accept the substitution of the Byrne-Cooper piece because of its extension of Maud's understanding of Paul, but the hyphenated name seemed unnecessarily pointed. Elizabeth then confessed: Yes, the dice were loaded in the Byrne-Cooper chapter. She recognized that Gwendolyn was reporting accurately in the pieces where the Byrne-Coopers and the white wife appeared, yet the sections rang false to her and the staff. Why? Elizabeth had thought about the situation "in many odd moments the past few days." It was certainly not a matter of giving offense.

I believe that the trouble lies deeper, and that it will disappear as you grow into a more secure personal freedom. When you are dealing exclusively with Negroes and their relationships, you are wholly the creative artist; your observations, your reactions are your own and as fresh as if no one had experienced them before. But with the entrance of a white person into your writing you suspend your function as creative artist and become a Negro. Your reactions are group or class reactions, no longer individual and so no longer truly fresh. It is understandable that this should be so, but it is not inevitable with a person as potentially big as you are. Someday you will know for a certainty what you now tell yourself is true—that Negroes are as much God's children as white people, neither superior nor inferior. When you can laugh at us and pity us to the same degree you laugh at and pity your own people, you'll command the show.[8]

Elizabeth then offered an analysis of Maud Martha's own insecurities. The editor suspected that Mrs. B-C was not more particular about her housekeeping than Maud was about her own. Thus Maud's problem had not been that the work was too much, and, as for the money, Gwendolyn had said it was "good." Maud's real problem was that deep down inside she accepted Mrs. B-C's belief that housework was "a demeaning occupation suited only to lesser people than the Byrne-Coopers of the world." Only Gwendolyn as the creator of the character could know whether this analysis was sound, but if it was, then she should carefully distinguish herself, as author, from Maud Martha and thus not become caught "in her confusions or distortions."

Gwendolyn replied that Elizabeth's letter was one to keep and study, for there was much in it requiring serious reflection: "The new chapter drives down to the explanation at the end that what scrambled her up inside was the fact that her employer could not see her as a human being, but only as a tool and a performing bear. Her disturbance had nothing to do with the kind of work she was doing, although admittedly her preference is for office work. Her feelings would have been the same if she had been, to the same *sort* of employer, a secretary in a bank."

Gwendolyn proposed retaining the hyphenated name, but to spell "Byrne" as "Burns." She did not want to use "Cooper" alone; that would make her think of "*Netta* Cooper!—and for her I have affection." Thus Gwendolyn made it clear that she did not consider her character at all confused, that she would not resort to any device to separate herself, as author, from Maud, and that she shared Maud's dislike for the Byrne-Coopers of the world.

Apparently the poet had had no response from her editor about the possibility of sending individual chapters to magazines, since she renewed her query: Was it too late or inadvisable to try for such sales? There was a house near her apartment at 32 West Seventieth Street that she and her family were "all on fire about."[9] In response, Elizabeth sent Harper & Brothers' copy of the manuscript to *Harper's* magazine and asked Gwendolyn for another copy to send to the company's agent, who would try it out on other editors. She explained that digest sales to such publications as *Omnibook* and *Reader's Digest*—with any luck—would come after the book was published. She felt that *Maud Martha* would be special fare for a discriminating minority, and warned Gwendolyn not to get her hopes up for its being a money-maker although "greater miracles have happened."[10]

Gwendolyn agreed to keep calm about possible sales, adopting the protective attitude of expecting nothing. But she was soon excited by another possibility when she heard the rumor that *Life* magazine had paid either $38,000 or $55,000 prepublication rights to Ernest Hemingway's *The Old Man and the Sea*. Perhaps Harper could manage such a sale of her book to *Ebony* magazine. She understood that, in the Hemingway case, Scribner's had profited from publication in *Life* by an increased volume of sales. She pictured the story "accompanied by wonderful shots supplied by *Ebony's* excellent staff of photographers."[11] "(*Life* had illustrated *The Old Man and the Sea*.)

The reason for Gwendolyn's focus on the returns from her book, of course, was the desire for a home of her own. She had even set aside the $500 advance against royalties without cashing the check until Elizabeth explained that, uncashed, it was a strain on the company's bookkeeping system. She had put her Michigan house up for sale; she was looking at houses in various neighborhoods and learning about loans. Her income from reviews, royalties, and readings came in handy, but it was not Pulitzer Prize dramatic. Henry Sr. had ventured into a new business, a consumer consultant buying corporation, but it needed time to grow.

Elizabeth thought well of sending the *Maud Martha* manuscript to *Ebony* and other magazines, but warned that while the drama of *The Old Man and the Sea* was direct and singular, that of *Maud Martha* was underplayed. Gwendolyn's work, she felt, depended more upon "'literary' values." Over a period of several months, Helen Strauss of the William Morris Agency sent the *Maud Martha* manuscript to *Life*, *Ebony*, *Harper's Bazaar*, and *Mademoiselle*, but there were no takers, although *Mademoiselle* held on to it for a long time.

Meanwhile, Gwendolyn was able to sell the Michigan house, and the family found a suitable residence in Chicago to buy, on South Evans. The down payment exceeded the Michigan equity, but with the assistance of a friend and a $500 loan that Gwendolyn's parents volunteered (repaid in $15, $20, and $50 installments over the years), the home was theirs. There was no lump-sum payment from sales of *Maud Martha*, unfortunately. Gwendolyn was all too familiar with the pain of mortgage payments out of slim resources.

After *Maud Martha*, Elizabeth advised Gwendolyn, "In the next novel I long to have you get out of the skin of a person who might be Gwen, perhaps out of a woman's skin entirely, and present this very complicated world you know from a different angle."[12] The statement impressed Gwendolyn greatly because she had been thinking along similar lines. She promised in future to think as deeply as possible and "to write only when my people are walking and breathing in the room with me."[13]

Other matters related to her writing were less sobering. The poem introducing *A Street in Bronzeville*, "the old-marrieds," had been translated into Serbian by the Yugoslavian Dragoslav Andric and was included in his anthology of modern Negro poetry.[14] Gwendolyn found it exciting to look at her work in a foreign language and to consider "that an idea of mine has traveled to 'another world.' "[15] By this time responses to the galley proofs of *Maud Martha* were coming in from a distinguished group of writers and critics. Robert Hillyer, the poet, reported that he had been deeply moved by the book, which he had read in a single sitting, finding it tender without sentimentality; he commended a technique that was realistic and yet poetic in its economy. After commenting that it made available characters who would ordinarily be unfamiliar to the reader, he stated a reservation: "Just between ourselves, I wish the conclusion had not been left quite so up in the air; the events and characters deserved a little more rounding out; it seems to me that they had gained a momentum which the author stopped abruptly by laying down her pen. I suppose I noticed this the more because I was so profoundly touched by the book."[16]

Worth Tuttle Hedden's view was that Gwendolyn had "epitomized the lives of countless sensitive young women" and produced "an aesthetically satisfying novel" telling "a story essentially human while it reveals, almost incidentally, those non-essential, traumatic conflicts no white American knows anything about."[17] Others sent in quite favorable opinions.

But Gwendolyn's greatest pleasure came from reading the comments of Ann Petry, author of *The Street* (1946), in which she too had portrayed the life of a struggling young black woman. Petry wrote to Elizabeth Lawrence:

I read Maud Martha with absolute delight from start to finish, delight in the beautiful structure of the book, delight in the way Maud Martha comes alive as a person caught up in timeless elemental situations.

It was sheer reading pleasure to follow her development from childhood to adolescence, from courtship and marriage to the birth of her child—all of her experiences seemingly directed towards those final pages when she emerges as a full-grown adult viewing the world with a philosophy of her own—compassionate, tender, brooding. All of it wonderful, all of it perfect![18]

Gwendolyn read the comments with astonishment. To her editor, she said, "As you know, this is my first book of fiction, and I could not imagine what people were going to think and say. But in my wildest dreams I wouldn't have expected anything so favorable."[19]

Elizabeth sent a telegram on September 29: "Happy publication day, Gwen. The *New York Times* next Sunday finds *Maud Martha* fresh and cheerful, having insight and rhythm and depth of implication, a novel alone of its kind. Congratulations." By October 9, Gwendolyn was reporting "grand reviews" in the *Chicago Tribune, Chicago Daily News, Chicago Sun-Times,* "and, I hear in some great California paper!" Langston Hughes sent her his enthusiastic *Chicago Defender* review. Van Allen Bradley and Herman Kogan, literary editors of the *Daily News* and the *Sun-Times,* respectively, called her with the highest praise.

"We were both hopeful, of course," Gwendolyn wrote Elizabeth, "but I am really amazed, at the response the book is getting. How I thank you for urging me to 'novelize' my material." A further boost was that someone "involved in motion pictures" wanted to talk with her about getting the book "into movie form." One part of her letter perhaps referred to some of the editor's earlier reservations: "Oh, aren't you *surprised*, Elizabeth? And you must be as happy as I am."[20] A bit later Gwendolyn would learn that Johanna Lodge No. 9, United Order of True Sisters, had secured permission to publish *Maud Martha* in Braille.

Elizabeth was happy with the reception, though she cautioned against expecting great sales. She also felt still that the book had not been worked up to its potential, as she expressed in an exchange of letters with Gwendolyn's mentor from the old workshop period, Inez Stark Boulton. The latter had written to Elizabeth to express appreciation for a copy of *Maud Martha*. She admired the book in many ways and thanked the editor for "remembering me and my interest, which shall be everlasting in anything she [Gwendolyn] does." But Inez also had objections, not based entirely on literary grounds. She felt that "from the point of view of most white readers it will be just another story of a Negro overcoming the tendency to have the chip knocked off her shoulder." She had had the pleasure of recognizing the autobiographical parts, but the public would not be able to appreciate the verisimilitude. "We are at the turning point, don't you think, where racial segregation should not be stressed, since so many advantages have been accorded Negroes in the last two years. My Negro friends in Washington, particularly the learned ones, are all vocal on this subject and agree that now is the time for negating any stories, poems or other propaganda showing ill treatment of Negroes." A friend in the diplomatic service, now back from Germany, had told her of the good that had resulted from marriages between black GIs and German girls: "In what is there called the American ghettoes, in Munich and Berlin, these couples live unquestioned among their white associates, and are accorded equal friendship as well as rights."

Inez was sure that Elizabeth was Gwendolyn's inspiration and thought the criticism offered would be of interest for orienting Gwendolyn in the future. The negative comments should be kept confidential: "Eyes only Elizabeth Lawrence," as high-ranking government officials use those words.[21]

Her letter expresses a concept that so frequently infuriated blacks: two enlightened whites conspiring to put a well-meaning but somewhat benighted black in line. Ironically, the letter carried something of the arrogance Gwendolyn had portrayed in the chapter Elizabeth had objected to, "At the Burns-Coopers." Elizabeth, however, was on the firm ground of having stated her objections directly to Gwendolyn. She agreed with Inez that the book did not have the full stature that Gwendolyn could have given it. The critics, she felt, had been too kind, but their encouragement might contribute to Gwen's development of the confidence needed for her next book. Gwendolyn was already aware that Elizabeth felt her work suffered when she brought a white person into it. "She has not yet learned to see us individually and until she can do that her people will be stock figures, her drama stereotyped. So deep those fears lie."22

Elizabeth's last comment is ironic, for in American writing rarely has either the white or the black writer portrayed members of another race as individuals. One must include William Faulkner in such a category, although some years back critics of the white liberal consensus tried to lift him above it. Writers' performances seem to reflect the fact that in American democracy, members of the black and white races compulsively relate to each other through historic pressures that make roles, rather than individuality, the point of contact.

The satire and racial typing worked into Gwendolyn's portraits of most of the white characters are part of the overall system of *Maud Martha*, which turns satiric shots upon any corrupt and pretentious ways of confronting existence. In the published *Maud Martha*, a character first gives clear evidence of asking for the satiric thrust, as a rule. In the chapter "the self solace," for example, Sonia's response to the white saleswoman's use of a racial epithet is an insistent stupidity, which is treated with withering contempt. Mrs. Burns-Cooper also expresses arrogance in the casual way in which she commands the servant to scrub the floor on her knees. The racist white wife of a black man in "kitchenette folks" also reveals arrogance in approaching the black women in her building to learn how to deal with a black man as a special type of man. Where the book's approach does not work is in cases where the evidence of arrogance does not emerge sufficiently from the subjective responses of Maude Martha, as in "millinery," in which the reader is too aware of Maud's rage to accept her authority in rendering the portrait. In subsequent works, Gwendolyn will present kinder portraits of whites but reserve the right to present also the devastating images.

Maud Martha would prove to be an enduring work of art, and its form, a startling departure from the conventional novel, established itself as part of the originality. Comprised of thirty-four short chapters covering only 180 pages, the novel provided the reader with the images needed for understanding Maud's life and evolution from childhood into mature young womanhood, against terrifying obstacles to be overcome in reaching security in love and home life, producing and developing a family, warding off attacks upon her dignity, and maintaining her integrity. The universe is one in which there will rarely be more than temporary triumphs, and most things to be cherished are possessed momentarily only. In such an arena, Maud emerges as a persistent and very tough contender.

A major triumph in this small novel is the imposing portrait of a black woman without recourse to the exotic, the violent, or the sensational, as so frequently had been part of the portrayal of black characters. To keep the reader attending a portrait unfolding from the daily round of existence is, of course, a feat not often achieved in any novel.

The novel does run a danger course and is not without some problems. The intent is to persuade the reader that, despite what the novel refers to as grayness, life for Maud Martha is fundamentally promising. But the power in the images of frustration threatens to make any optimism seem willed and somewhat strained. The annoyances of the kitchenette, the marriage blighted at the roots, the disintegration of so many graces of tradition that had made poverty bearable, the putdown of her child by the white "Santa Claus" must, somehow, not pile up enough negativity to overwhelm such positives as Maud's happiness with her parents, her capacity for laughter at herself and others, the swellings of rich inner life, the miracle of human birth, and the capacity of man to be glorious and brave. The end feeling is that of some shakiness in the balance, which Maud's commitment to her second child may right. There is also a lack of anything to command the reader's understanding of the coming together of Maud and her husband Paul. As the person who is decisive in Maud's life, he requires projection a bit beyond Maud's subjective perceptions.

The sources of both the strength and some of the weaknesses of *Maud Martha* may be the work's autobiographical character. Gwendolyn feels that Maud is "a nicer and a better coordinated creature than I am," and points out that much in the story is not autobiographical, but she also concedes that much of the book was drawn from her own life, turned about, muted, or heightened. The portrait of the children at the elementary school mixed memories of Henry Jr.'s early school days with those of her own. "Death of Grandmother" follows closely the death of one of Gwendolyn's aunts. In "Tim," she used her Uncle Ernest Myler, but only as a point of departure. In "Helen," the title character is mainly imaginary, Gwendolyn never having had a sister, but Emmanuel was the real name of the little boy who had been cruel because of her darkness. The chapter "low yellow" was based not upon her husband but upon a youth who lived with his grandmother on the second floor of her original family home. The chapters "first beau," "second beau," "Maud Martha and New York," "a birth," "kitchenette folks," "self solace," "Paul in the Oll Club," "brotherly love," and "at the Burns-Coopers' " are described in Gwendolyn's autobiography as containing varying amounts of significant autobiography.[23]

In Maud Martha, Gwendolyn was trying out her wings in fiction by bringing to coherence materials she had to a large degree explored in A Street in Bronzeville and Annie Allen. Combining sharp, realistic images with an overall poetic approach, Maud Martha has more detail, more flesh and blood and warmth, more intimate encounters than did the more poetic symbolic structures of Annie Allen. Interactions with others are given in close-up scenes in which they carry a good deal of the symbolic freight. Both works are ultimately positive in their approaches to existence, although Annie Allen escapes the hint of strained optimism.

The deficiencies of Annie Allen can be seen in episodes that seem to have their origin in whimsy rather than necessity, and in the remoteness of the male character. In Maud Martha, the deficiencies can again be seen in the remoteness of Paul and in such a scene as that involving the saleswoman of "millinery" in which we are too dependent, in the beginning, on Maud's omniscient entry into the saleswoman's mind. As noted, the portrait of the heroine is a triumph in both works. In addition, in such episodes as "first beau," "second beau," and "an encounter," Maud Martha's sensibility seems unthreatened, especially fitted, therefore, to present fully the satirized portrait.

Although the old period of Gwendolyn's life would continue at intervals to impose some of the old questions and their magnetism, the coming decade would provide much to push her beyond the immediacies of those rhythms marking the encounter of self with the world. On winning the Pulitzer Prize, she could still feel the urgency for a particular cycle of her life to complete itself, and she could lose herself in bits of wonder. She could recall that as a child she had thought that she would write better if she lived in the country. She had seen movies showing children running in the bright countryside and picking flowers, and she had met people who knew the names of flowers, trees, and birds. But the intensity of her commitment to her surroundings had made her realize the value of growing up in the city, of confronting humanity in the mass and in its infinite variety.

She had had, on the occasion of winning the Pulitzer Prize, the pleasure of momentarily feeling her distinctiveness in all that mass. After being informed that she had won, she and Henry took their already planned outing to the movies, feeling ebullient and knowing that the people she passed on the street didn't recognize her at all—or at least did not realize her "specialness."

6

Reachings

The decade of the 1950s was a good time, but a different movement of the life cycle seemed to impend. On October 10, 1953, Henry Jr.'s thirteenth birthday, Gwendolyn and the family moved into their new house on South Evans. She would think of their having moved in on a wing (tattered) and a prayer. Nevertheless, she had achieved the move with a husband and two children—a baby girl and a somewhat turbulent teenage boy who would begin to disturb her world in a new way as he discovered the larger world from his private adolescent point of view. Amid the flux, she was rooted—though swayable and uprootable—not simply a shifting element in the gray mass. Their tight little house sat snug and distinct upon its pillars. In it, her own life and her family's, if not snug, was distinct—they had won ground that had not been available to her Maud Martha.

Through getting more desirable apartments, Gwendolyn had, of course, long fled the worst afflictions of Maud Martha. The slick-looking, undefeatable roaches had long since ceased to make their sudden appearances on the mirror as she brushed her hair. Long gone also was the crowding upon her of tarnished lives barely maintaining their spiritual existence and immersing her, by sound or odor, in their mortality and their arrested movements toward transcendence. Long gone was Maud Martha's dreaded return from the silvery scenes of the movies to hear the unnerving sound of little animal feet scratching through the garbage thrown out from crowded lives. Gwendolyn had long been rid of them, except in memory, and that had at least been subjected to the exorcism of creating an autobiographical work of art. There was now something of the illusion of holding again that more inviting space of her childhood days.

For her own children, it was a fairly easygoing atmosphere. Whereas Henry Jr. had always been bright with curiosity, he had required nudging from family and teachers to step up his application to schoolwork. He began, however, to become very interested in science, an area in which he would more and more excel as he advanced through high school. He would remember being encouraged to think, to question, and to hold patly accepted matters under suspicion. The home was not especially religious but encouraged church-going. When he visited his maternal grandmother's, a more restrained environment, his grandfather afforded spontaneity and permissiveness. For Nora, reading and writing came naturally. Among the first reading instruments she used were signs on the street, and she occasionally startled the family by enunciating clearly such words as Budweiser and Schlitz, though the family did not keep beer on hand. Elizabeth Lawrence, Gwendolyn's editor, was impressed with the easygoing but joyful environment when she visited the Blakely family in March 1954, and felt that Gwendolyn must find in it a "great measure of contentment." Although form might sometimes suggest itself as more important than content in Gwendolyn's writing, Elizabeth stated, her "jolly family and . . . so-pleasant home" contradicted any such assumption: "These are products of more than manners and technique."[1] Henry Jr.'s recollection of one of the disturbances he caused reveals the extent to which Gwendolyn had invested in this stability. At the age of fourteen, he went one day to the movies and stayed to see the film a second time, arriving home late at night. Although he had anticipated reactions from the family, he was surprised to find his mother, usually self-contained, crying almost uncontrollably from worry.

Gwendolyn was seeing the world in a new way. In the summer of 1955, Emmett ("Bobo") Till, a Chicago youth visiting relatives in Mississippi, was brutally beaten, slain, and dumped into a river because he allegedly made sexual advances to a young white woman in a Mississippi crossroads store. The case gained national attention and received very dramatic emphasis in Chicago. Those accused of the deed were acquitted. Gwendolyn thought of her own son and his vulnerability and gained little relief from recurrent thoughts of what the world might do to him, until she had written a poem about the trial that dealt with the situations of the white and black mothers, "A Bronzeville Mother Loiters in Mississippi . . . " (The Bean Eaters).

After the U.S. Supreme Court decision against school segregation on May 17, 1954, the poet was gradually absorbed into the national black consciousness of rising expectations. Chicago itself was slowly changing in the 1950s. The uncertainty of service in public places in Chicago's central district gradually diminished, so that the discovery, in the Maud Martha vein, that "we're the only colored people here" was less frequent, and when it occurred less dismaying. Economically speaking, there were no dramatic changes in the picture during the 1950s,[2] and there would be no fundamental change until the 1960s, under the pressure of the national civil rights movement, the executive orders of Presidents John F. Kennedy and Lyndon Johnson, and the Illinois Fair Employment Practices statute. But public agitation was in the air, and housing was an insistent matter in the public consciousness because of the notorious bombings after blacks moved into Chicago's Trumbull Park housing project, among them Gwendolyn's friends the Frank London Brown family. On the national scene, the civil rights movement gained impetus as the May 17, 1954, Supreme Court decision became a source of struggle, friction, and violence. Gwendolyn's consciousness was also in a process of change: although the poet had always looked at developments in the outer world, beyond the neighborhood, her awareness would begin to respond strongly to external pressures.

There would be struggles for a goodly interval, however, and some aborted works before clear evidence of her new consciousness was forthcoming. By March 10, 1954, she was discussing with her editor a plan to write a novel entitled "The Life of Lincoln West" and to revise other works, all of which were going slowly. Elizabeth, interested in the proposed novel, asked Gwendolyn to define West's nature. What to Gwendolyn was the meaning of his life? Its significance in relationship to Negro life? On the racial level, Gwendolyn tended to hold to her simple formulation that blacks were like other people. After thinking over their conversation, Elizabeth suggested moving beyond the idea of likeness to other people, since " 'other people' are the people we do not know, except as spectators." She asked whether Gwendolyn did not really mean that "all people have an essential dignity worthy of understanding and respect." Her point in asking Gwendolyn to define West was to help establish a principle which she felt would form a central line for unfolding the drama of the story and stand in response to the fact that everyone searched out by the eye of the artist loses typicality and becomes special.[3]

Gwendolyn felt that she had not yet organized her thoughts about the book, but the idea of all people having essential dignity was a beautiful way of bringing together what she had been groping to say. Still remaining somewhat vague, she stated that she wished to write a good "*solid* book" and "two juveniles."

Actually, the thinking would go on for a while, since she and Henry were finding that keeping the mortgage going required regular sources of income. Gwendolyn toyed with plans to study to become a teacher but also allowed her mind to rove over other possibilities. After reading an article by Florence Jane Soman about working as an outside reader for a major motion picture studio, summarizing the story line of books, plays, radio scripts, and other writing that might be turned into movies, Gwendolyn became interested in such work. She felt that her tendency toward precision and conciseness might make her good at it, and she asked Elizabeth about it.[4]

Elizabeth's understanding of outside reader work was that the pressure was great and the pay bad. She put Gwendolyn in touch with a man in Chicago who taught and, with his wife, did some writing for a junior encyclopedia. Unsuccessfully he made inquiries on Gwendolyn's behalf and made several suggestions that afforded Gwendolyn hope but did not bear fruit, although she appreciated his efforts. Meanwhile, prospects improved. Recommended by Frank London Brown, the poet applied for a position teaching a poetry writing class at Roosevelt University. Although she did not hold a college degree, she felt she might get the job, since a member of the staff of the education department had told her that that was not a requirement. Unfortunately, she was not accepted, but Henry reduced his work in his consulting business to mornings and found a job with Diamond T Trucks, where he began as an assembly worker and would eventually be promoted to foreman.[5]

Gwendolyn was writing, however, during this period of great struggle—not the Lincoln West fiction but juvenile poetry, which had proved easier to handle. Ursula Nordstrom of the juvenile department at Harper had responded to twenty-five children's poems Gwendolyn had sent and requested more during early 1955. Encouraged, Gwendolyn maintained a schedule of creating one poem per day until fifteen stood before her. Actually, the children's poetry was a pleasure to work with. "Mexie and Bridie," the first of the collection *Bronzeville Boys and Girls* (1956), was also the first one composed. In it Gwendolyn relived her own experiences as a child playing at having a tea party with a friend. In "Ella," she found that a poem written during her early teens could be worked up to her current standards for publication. It tells of a girl who leaves a meal to run out into the winter to see the clouds. The first stanza reveals the poem's tight economy:

> Beauty has a coldness
> That keeps you very warm.
> "If I run out to see the clouds,
> That will be no harm!"

What emerges from the poems is childhood's sheer drive for joy, beauty, companionship, freedom, and imaginative flights. Mirthine is somewhat envied by the other girls at a party, but it turns out that without her giggles, beads, and bangles, she is no prettier than the others. Materially rich Elnora is a democratized citizen of this universe because of her desire for jolly companionship and play. Luther and Breck play out the old knightly tales and thus transform the limitations of the city setting. But various moods enter the picture and various notes are struck. Rudolph is tired of the city and wishes to escape into the country, and Michael is afraid of storms. Rather interesting language, comporting with the verbal resources of the childhood world, emerges.

> Lightning is angry in the night.
> Thunder spanks our house.
> Rain is hating our old elm—
> It punishes the boughs.

At church, Beulah is surprised by joy while harnessed in by extreme cleanliness and adults.

> only hold your song-book—so!—
> With the big people closing you in,
> And the organ-sound and the sermon
> Washing you clean of sin.
>
> I do not want to stay away.
> I do not think I should.
> Something there surprises me:
> It feels good to be good.

And there is wonder. Robert learns that one may look into a mirror and discover a stranger—"A child you know and do not know." Lyle wishes to escape moving from house to house and to enjoy the permanence of a tree. DeKoven loves the ungraspable stars. But poverty also tinctures in its smears. Otto hides from his father his disappointment in the Christmas presents he receives. And there is John, desperately poor, who lives "so lone and alone" and is not to be bothered with questions concerning the beginning or ending of his hunger.

Gwendolyn's poetic skills are well used in accurately gauging the ways poetry can describe for the very young child the world of his or her experiences. Poems with bouncy rhymes are intermixed with those of more subtle and varied sound patterns. "Ella" is notable for varying its sounds and pacing by use of trochees and iambs. Emphasis on the monosyllabic word at the end of the end-stopped line, variation in the length of the lines, use of repetition, and other devices maintain an interesting poetics that does not patronize the childhood world.

Reviewers tended to emphasize the universality of the poems. The *New York Herald-Tribune* stated: "Because Miss Brooks is a Negro poet she has called these *Bronzeville Boys and Girls*, but they are universal and will make

friends anywhere, among grown-ups or among children from eight to ten."
Race is not mentioned in the poems but is clearly represented by the
sensitive and lively illustrations of Ronni Solbert, all of which, however,
have white faces—a fact that Gwendolyn found disturbing. The responses
common to all children, presumably, are placed in the foreground, and
there are no conflicts carrying a racial tone or overtone. Obviously,
Bronzeville Boys and Girls represents the more Edenic side of Gwendolyn's
own childhood.

   While working on *Bronzeville Boys and Girls,* the poet postponed work
on the proposed novel "The Life of Lincoln West." In March 1955 she had
written to Elizabeth Lawrence of a return of excitement within her about
that project and hoped she would be able to send a "decent sized portion" by
May. She also hoped Elizabeth would "see some possibilities in it."[6] The
novel apparently was to represent the very opposite of the Edenic. It was
Lincoln's fate to reach the printed page only as a short story in Herbert Hill's
anthology *Soon, One Morning* (1963) and as a poem in Gwendolyn's collection *Family Pictures* (1970). The poem is based on the first chapter of the
proposed novel; the remainder of the novel never got beyond the stage of an
outline.

   As the work stands, it is clearly not concerned with the conventional
idea of universality; it is a statement on black identity, a subject that would
be received by audiences during the sixties, seventies, and subsequently
with great enthusiasm. Lincoln West's pronounced African features call
forth repulsion from those familiar with him and from the public at large, a
response that has greatly confused him in his quest for acceptance. Ironically, his solace comes from a white man who is quite explicit regarding the
basis of Lincoln's encounters with rejection. When Lincoln was seven he
heard a white man whispering loudly to his companion at the movies:
"There! That's the kind I've been wanting to show you! One of the best
examples of the species. Not like those *diluted* Negroes you see so much of on
the streets these days, but the real thing. Black, ugly and odd. You can see
the savagery. The blunt blankness. *That is the real thing.*" Lincoln did not
understand all the opprobrious terms. But he understood and liked the
expression "the real thing." "He didn't know why, but he liked that. He
liked that very much." Afterwards, when he felt hurt, stared at excessively,
or left too much alone, he told himself, "After all, I'm the real thing." The
manuscript states that the expression comforted him and meant a lot to him
for "almost four years." In other versions the time limit is deleted. The
manuscript version thus suggests that, in the novel, Lincoln would have his

earlier resolution of his condition further challenged—at school and in the world generally.

In her youth, it will be recalled, Gwendolyn had lived both the Edenic life of the juvenile poems and the rejected one outside her neighborhood and at parties. The unfinished "Life of Lincoln West" illustrates the kinds of tensions that may be left out to please white audiences and those black audiences of a compulsively integration-oriented mind. In a sense, the omission thus chops off the negativities through which blacks strive in order to get to the positive, veiling essential tensions of the black experience.

Had Gwendolyn been able to describe to Elizabeth the full significance of Lincoln West, it is difficult to guess what the editor's reactions would have been, since she wished for clear universalism. One difficulty in the first chapter is that it runs so quickly into the form of a parable and seems so complete in itself. It would seem to make a rising sort of development difficult.

In the foreign market for Gwendolyn's work, there was a new development in 1954, when Janheinz Jahn, who was compiling a German anthology of modern black poetry, secured permission to use the poems "the preacher: ruminates behind the sermon," "a song in the front yard," and "Negro Hero"—all from Gwendolyn's first book, A Street in Bronzeville. In May of 1955, S.D. Clouts of the International Press Agency, having heard of A Street, wondered whether she had other works suitable for serial publication in South Africa and requested a copy of whatever work Gwendolyn would like the agency's editors to consider. He was sent a copy each of A Street in Bronzeville, Annie Allen, and Maud Martha. Clouts himself read the works with excitement and immediately offered them to one of his clients, to make selections for serial publication. But by late 1955 it had become clear that the poetry was "too sophisticated" for such use, although Maud Martha was to remain in limbo until October 1956.

As was her custom, Gwendolyn had drawn up among her New Year's resolutions for 1956 several writing projects: a book of poems, "Another Coming of Christ"; a book of stories, "Bronzeville Men and Women"; and several stories for magazines about a "whimsical maid, entitled 'Big Bessie.' " By early January she had done some work on all three projects. Haunting her mind, periodically, was the long-ago experience of working in the huge apartment building known as the Mecca for a "spiritual advisor" who was eventually murdered. She would see herself toiling up the stairs to various ones of the 176 apartments to deliver "Holy Thunderbolts" and "Liquid Love Charms" to people whose lives were so often steeped in misery and violence; then there would be the stark images of the people them-selves.

She had also become concerned about having more of her poetry appear on phonograph records, after Glory Record Company at 2 West Forty-seventh Street in New York, included "when you have forgotten Sunday" in a group of poems read by Sidney Poitier and Doris Belack. Gwendolyn had received a $25 advance against royalties and a complimentary copy of the record. She and the family went to her parents' home to listen to it and had "a delightful time."[7] She would have liked a group of her poems on record, possibly "the old-marrieds," "kitchenette building," "the soft man," "when Mrs. Martin's Booker T.," "the preacher: ruminates behind the sermon," "of De Witt Williams," "Negro Hero," "Ballad of Pearl May Lee," and "the white troops had their orders but the Negroes looked like men"—all from *A Street in Bronzeville*. They had a sense of drama, and she felt they would quickly be appreciated by the general public. But her adventure with recordings would not begin until the late 1960s, under the auspices of Caedmon.

Her writing continued to be slowly fruitful, and other matters were productive. By dint of careful planning, she and Henry were able to envision the elimination of the second mortgage by January 1957 ("Hallelu-jah"), making way for a lot more "brightness." They postponed responding to Elizabeth's urging that they take a trip to New York, despite the advice of Gwendolyn's friend Era Bell Thompson: "Go now. You may drop dead in January."[8] Instead, they made plans to paint the house.

Gwendolyn's writing efforts received a shot in the arm early in 1957 from a request by Ursula Nordstrom of Harper's Juvenile Books Department that she seriously consider writing a novel for teenage readers, possibly about a Negro girl's growing up in Chicago. Miss Nordstrom asked for a paragraph outlining the proposed contents and a sample chapter. She felt that there were no "absolutely good" novels about Negro girls although there was clearly a need for one.[9]

Gwendolyn decided that for the novel she would make use of the lives in the Mecca Building; the main character would be an ambitious girl sharing the hardships of a beleaguered family and still seeking fulfillment. By late May the poet was able to send a couple of chapters, but in June she was made aware of difficulties in the treatment of the material. Miss Nordstrom was enthusiastic about the content of the novel. The setting, the house, and the characters "are all rich and fascinating and absolutely the sort of thing I hoped you would put into a book." But the material was presented too obliquely for teenage readers, though the treatment would be fascinating for the mature reader.[10]

On receiving a letter from Gwendolyn evidencing discouragement, Miss Nordstrom begged her not to give up. But Gwendolyn soon decided that she would have to try to tell the story in poetry. Two chapters of Gwendolyn's work have survived. They reveal both the interesting quality and slight difficulties.

In chapter one, Giovanna, the main character, is shown to have temporarily risen above the limitations of her surroundings in the ceremonies marking her graduation from high school. The story begins:

Giovanna was Commencing. High School days were over. And at last she was a Something. At last. The aunts and uncles and cousins and great-aunts and the soon-graduating friends.

She had her height, too, in the Mecca, that sick four-story hulk in which she lived among balconies and tincans and fire escapes and chitterlings and little darling mice and big self-possessed rats and swaggering, seeking youth—and puzzled-eyed middle age and shut-eyed old age and the smells of thousands of meals—and children children children.

Some of the population of the Mecca hung about the halls, or leaned against the balconies, watching her descent from the fourth floor, the last floor—down, down, down, and on into glory, queenly in the voluminous silk-net it had taken two aunts, two great-aunts, one cousin and a mother, combining their dimes, to buy. Queenly, yes, and tense, and wondering, and hot-hearted and oh-so-sixteen-going-on-seventeen.

She is "drawn, in her Cinderella coach [a taxi]" to the high school for the ceremonies. The focus shifts to "The Speaker from City Hall," who ruminates on his dilemma. At the Steinmetz High School, a more affluent institution, he had been able to advise that the students "Assail! Find the big things! Approach only the things with fruit and challenge!" But he now confronts students who are about to enter a world of blight. "He sighed, and looked at this dark vague sea. He began his Speech—Choice Number Three. 'Graduates! This is not an ending—but a beginning.' "

The ceremonies end the Cinderella rituals for Giovanna. She gathers with her family: Pepita, John, Kathleen, Eileen, Curtis, Casey, Mo, Aunt Dill. "She received her flowers. A transient queen, with courtiers, she began Life. She walked back to the Mecca."

In the next chapter, Giovanna's art teacher, Miss Ward, comes to discover from Giovanna's mother, Mrs. Hunt, what is to be Giovanna's next step now that she has finished high school. It becomes apparent that Miss

Ward has introduced Giovanna to the great world of art: Cezanne, Botticelli, and others—a world which most Meccans would not understand and not want to understand though their experiences could be seen in such works as Cezanne's "The Card Players" and Botticelli's "Adoration of the Magi." But more important, Miss Ward recognizes Giovanna as having the potential to become a great artist. Miss Ward is taking a sketching trip to France, Italy, England, and Holland, and wishes Giovanna to accompany her, an act which Mrs. Hunt must consent to because she owes it to her "nice daughter." The mother, with great and pained dignity, acknowledges owing much to Giovanna *and* to her other daughters and her sons, but replies she is a woman deserted by her husband and possibly on her way to dying of cancer within two years, who must meanwhile eke out a living for her family. Giovanna's help in earning extra money by selling cakes on Saturdays will be her only contribution. Disappointed but impressed, Miss Ward promises to become a regular cake buyer and requests that Giovanna not be allowed to marry the "first buck that looks at her."

Chapter 3 does not survive. But Chapter 4 portrays Giovanna with her immediate tasks, making the cakes, washing, caring for the children, frustratedly trying to dream of the future. So burdened, she realizes that if she were a mother with children she would probably never get a chance to pick up the brush and paint again. As things are, she has, for painting, only stolen moments. She dreams of the leisure afforded by the life of a debutante as she has derived it from the society pages of the newspapers. She rejects the silly things that are reported to occupy the time of debutantes but recognizes that such a life would give her a chance to succeed as an artist. We see her fearing to face the fate of her cancer-stricken mother, caring ambivalently for the children, making the cakes, and confronting the sour-dispositioned women of the Mecca as she waits for an opportunity to use the washing facilities.

The manuscript clearly needed considerable revision if it was to be fitted into the conventional concept of a novel appealing to large numbers of teenagers. Achieving a light touch and, at the same time, pursuing the documentary approach of the surviving chapters would be difficult. But the characters, certain images, and the story's basic mythology are memorable. Giovanna, her mother, and the art teacher appear to be caught in a tragic realization of the limitations of their existence. The brief images of the Mecca, with its smells of "thousands of meals," its proliferation of children, and its resistance to dreams and aspirations, seem to represent a vastly larger kitchenette building and to multiply the capacity to concentrate human misery. The sketches achieve the necessary depth to express the power of the

Mecca Building and its people, which was to haunt Gwendolyn over so great a number of years.

In the midst of her writing efforts, Gwendolyn encountered an advertisement that gave her some hope that *Maud Martha* might be republished in paperback. Bantam Books editor Saul David had advertised in the 1957 *Writer's Yearbook:* "Publish reprints only. Probably the only pure reprinter in the business. Your published hardcover titles may be submitted to the editor for consideration as a softcover reprint." Elizabeth, however, did not see Bantam or any other reprint house as an opportunity. Reprinters looked for books that would sell "in the hundreds of thousands," while *Maud Martha* was subtle and appealed to the discriminating few. Reprinters looked either for the mark of the classic or for outstanding sales of the original publication. Gwendolyn's best approach would be to write another book.[11]

By March 1958, Gwendolyn was planning two new works. One book would be entitled "Capsule Course in Poetry Writing" in thirty or forty thousand words, written in familiar style and including illustrative details. She sent a simple outline to Elizabeth, but the editor's reaction was that the book would be too special for Harper to handle.

Gwendolyn's second project was a sequel to *Maud Martha:* "The Rise of Maud Martha," which would take place after the accidental death of Maud's husband. Gwendolyn enclosed two chapters, one of which had already been published in the old *Chicago* magazine. Despite the drift of the opening chapters of "The Rise of Maud Martha," she planned "to 'strain' the story through the light of humor."[12]

In the surviving first chapter, Gwendolyn presents Maud Martha at the funeral of her husband, Paul, who has died in a fire, in circumstances the same as a fire that actually occurred in Chicago during the 1950s. Maud sorts out her feelings after having seen Paul and having more recently confronted his sealed casket. Paul was burned "black with a more 'dreadful' blackness than that which he had ever known and despised—hairless, eroded chin outthrust, and with never one more dream of sophistication remaining, all she could feel was a big surprise that this was happening to her. In the course of the chapter her surprise dissipates into the realization that she had stopped loving her husband before the accident took place. She did not feel sorry for herself as the loser by his death, as a lover should, but merely sorry for him as a destroyed person who "had so loved physical beauty, in the end a fire-used, repulsive thing." Instead of grief, she feels herself freed and rising into a new citizenship—apparently of the cosmos. "A road was again clean before her . . . . all was up to her."[13]

It will be recalled that one of Elizabeth Lawrence's reservations about

Maud Martha had been the question of what Maud had found in Paul and wherein lay the basic conflict of the novel. Her immediate reaction to the new proposal was that the title was bad and the idea of a sequel not good. The story did not have to be that of Maud Martha. There could be a new character who would not require the reader's acquaintance with the earlier novel. Maud was not a "dramatic personality." She was like others yearning for more than life had granted. The new character could resemble Maud in terms of the general pattern of her life and temperament.

Elizabeth then mentioned her concern that Gwendolyn extend her range and explore in her work personalities outside her usual province. The editor wondered if, along with the achievement of self-knowledge, Maud might come to a more profound knowledge and understanding of her husband. Would she be moved to sympathy and compassion by understanding the stresses of an imperfect partner? Elizabeth wished that Maud would attain the wisdom to reevaluate the marriage. She had felt within Maud a touch of self-pity, a sense "of being wronged." Perhaps that was the case, or perhaps neither one was suitable for the other. In any case, a husband's death could reveal some startling matters and enlarge the field to be explored. She urged the writer to see whether the new novel could be separated from the earlier one and given greater scope and magnitude.[14]

Gwendolyn recognized that the issue of extending herself beyond the autobiographical and the question of Maud's relationship to Paul had been raised five years earlier by Elizabeth. Her own desire to extend herself was working itself forward at its own rhythm in some of the poems that she was now writing under the tentative title "Bronzeville." She was also once again struggling with another version of *In the Mecca,* a work that would certainly present people distant from her own personality and intimate involvements.

Her private and public lives were going pleasantly. Nora seemed to be having a very happy childhood. Unlike her brother, she absorbed an unlimited number of public occasions and did not reach a saturation point with crowds. With two hundred partying people sitting around the house and on her bed, she seemed not only at home but in her element. During her early school years, Gwendolyn dressed her in pretty clothes and was delightfully surprised to have her return home with her dresses still immaculately clean. From her brother Nora learned to play chess and astonished his friends by beating them at the game. She was worshipful in her attitude toward her brother and added drama to his graduation from Paul Cornell Elementary School by repeating loudly before the silent audience of parents and other kinspeople the principal's words summoning Henry forth: " 'Henry Lowington Blakely!' Here—come—Henry!" However, her early effort to be a chorus for her mother's achievements met with failure. When she announced grandly, "My mother is Gwendolyn Brooks," small children responded with a blank stare and the question, Who? For Gwendolyn, Nora increased the joy of the household just as Henry Jr., in his adolescent years, was being drawn more into the outer world.

In public life, Gwendolyn was a reviewer of books, one of the acknowl-edged high-ranking citizens of cultural affairs to be called on for ceremonial occasions, as well as a reader of her own poetry. On December 2, 1957, she was among one hundred outstanding Chicagoans selected by a committee for the Jesuit Centennial Celebration and photographed at a dinner given for them at the Palmer House hotel. Her mother and husband attended. On February 12, 1958, she and Henry Rago, editor of *Poetry*, traveled through what the *Chicago Daily Tribune* called "zero bound Chicago," to read their poetry at Lewis Towers, Loyola University, at 8:00 P.M. The newspaper anticipated that "undeterred by icy blasts, hundreds of admirers of Gwen-dolyn Brooks and Henry Rago will be thronging to Lewis Towers." Presented by Loyola as its "second season of Visiting Poet Readings," the occasion was underwritten by David B. Steinman, "noted architect–engineer and patron of the arts."

On February 26, 1958, as a Lenten Feature, the *Chicago American* carried her essay "What Prayer Did for Me," in which she described moving from her belief that people are completely able to sustain themselves to one in which, thinking of her own five-month-old Nora, she prayed for the life of a dying child who miraculously recovered. Out of the experience, she received a "strength superior to any that I have known." Her self-reliance remained, but God also remained available, as a friend with whom to discuss tragedy, aspiration, "or the loveliness of flowers and blue air."

On June 11, the *Chicago Daily News* announced that, along with James McBurney, dean of Northwestern's School of Speech, and John Reich, director of the Goodman Theater, Gwendolyn would serve as a judge of language arts in the *Daily News* Silver Knight awards program. The ten youths chosen from more than a hundred candidates as outstanding students were to receive $500 savings bonds and silver trophies. Others would be given certificates and silver medallions. In a photograph, the newspaper showed the judges going over the entries.

More important, the writer drove ahead with the new version of *In the Mecca*, now presented as a work for adults, and with the poems for "Bronzeville Men and Women"—a title that would eventually be changed to *The Bean Eaters*. On December 21, 1958, she mailed to Harper fifty-two pages of *In the Mecca* with an outline of ten additional chapters and several poems. Then she fully involved herself in enjoying the Christmas season with the family.

Again, the poetry would win the better response from the publisher. The novel manuscript and outline, however, slammed immediately into a wall of rejection. One reader's plot summary tells the story. The novel involved down-at-the-heels life in the Mecca, a tenement occupied by blacks and by whites married to them. Once more we have Giovanna as the talented heroine. She is torn between the ambitions of her white mother and the simpler goals of her black father, who merely wants her to marry a stable black, ideally a mailman, and settle down before she gets into problems. Great Gram, who lives with the family in its small space, would like Giovanna to give up her dreamy ways and accept the fact that hard work has always been the black heritage. Her mother, India, feels that Giovanna's making a white marriage would erase her own disgrace. But Giovanna becomes attracted to Virgil, a boy without the qualities either parent wants.

According to the proposed outline, subsequent chapters will tell of a movement to catastrophe. India is angered when Giovanna becomes pregnant, and Giovanna soon takes a dark son to new living quarters with Virgil and his parents. Finding Giovanna away from home, India borrows the baby and drowns him in his bath. The murder is avenged when India and Great Gram perish in a fire in the Mecca, with India burned blacker than the darkest black in the building. A final chapter takes place in the Mecca as Giovanna, with her two other children by Virgil, revisits the building as it is about to be torn down. The conclusion will also give glimpses of the lives of others residing there.

A reader's comments point both to "deficiencies" and to the fact that Gwendolyn was extending her reach: "This is a poet's novel, evoking occasionally moving insights into the lives and the hearts of these characters. But in this effort the author is grappling with more 'plot' than she attempted in 'Maud Martha.' And to my mind the structure tends to be mannered, more precious than convincing. India, especially, seems to me an artificial characterization. I'm something less than enthusiastic about it. But it should have a second reading."

Elizabeth Lawrence echoed some of the reader's comments and added others on behalf of herself and the staff: melodrama, improbable characterization of India, ineffective organization for a novel, and an ending that stands to "serve the author's purpose" instead of arising inevitably out of the situation. Gwendolyn's problem seemed to be that she compulsively approached dramatic prose with the disciplines of poetry that she had learned so well. Instead of scene, character, and events, Gwendolyn focused upon "precious microscopic details." Elizabeth was, therefore, returning the novel for Gwendolyn to rescue if she could.

The editor was enthusiastic about the poetry, however, and spoke immediately of the joy of looking forward to publishing another of Gwendolyn's books. She found "superb stuff in this collection," and viewed "A Bronzeville Mother Loiters in Mississippi . . . ," "The Last Quatrain of Emmett Till," and "The Chicago *Defender* Sends a Man to Little Rock, Fall, 1957" as "major achievements." But she thought the title unsuitable ("flat and unevocative") and that it "too emphatically draws the color line around the poems." A few poems were not very successful but could be dealt with later. The ballads showed that Gwendolyn still had the power of "spontaneous" song, despite the pressures of the world. However, even the twenty-eight poems that she thought Gwendolyn was planning would not be enough and she would hopefully await the arrival of others. There was plenty of time, in any case, since publication before the next year would not be possible.[15]

Gwendolyn found the news regarding the poetry wonderful enough to soften the blow of what amounted to a rejection of the proposed novel. She was already planning to include more than the twenty-eight poems she had sent. In fact, she was working on several. She wanted to make the new book of poems "as good and as solid and as interesting as I can possibly make it." She asked Elizabeth whether *Harper's* magazine could use any of the poems. She had read, twice, the editor's evaluation of the novel "In the Mecca" and found herself agreeing that the manuscript's problems were, indeed, very serious. "As usual," she wrote to Elizabeth, "you have put a clarifying finger on the trouble—or, in this case, troubles. There isn't a thing you said concerning it that isn't true. Some day I do hope to write a decent novel. The next thing I'd like to tackle is a meaty verse novel, with historical background, illuminating the life and times of a dramatic figure."[16]

She felt very much renewed and plunged into the writing. On March 28, 1959, she sent to Harper fourteen more poems;[17] twelve of them would appear in the published volume in the spring of 1960. *Harper's* magazine accepted for publication "The Explorer" and a second poem with the satiric title "For Clarice It Is Terrible Because with This He Takes Away All the Popular Songs and the Moonlights and Still Night Hushes and the Movies with Star-eyed Girls and Simpering Males." Other poems went to *Poetry*, and "The Bean Eaters," "Old Mary," "We Real Cool," and "Strong Men Riding Horses" would appear in its September issue. By March 30, Gwendolyn had changed the title of her forthcoming book to *The Bean Eaters*.

Other happenings were both relaxing and exciting. Writer, teacher, and labor organizer Frank London Brown, who had worked, although in vain, to secure a teaching position for her at Roosevelt University, invited Gwendolyn to see Lorraine Hansberry's play *A Raisin in the Sun* on its opening night in Chicago in company with him and his publishers. The excitement started even before this because Brown's novel *Trumbull Park* was scheduled to be released on April 13, 1959, reviewed by Alan Paton for the *Chicago Daily Tribune*, and given a full-page ad in the *New York Times*.

Gwendolyn thought that *A Raisin in the Sun* was the best play ever written by a Negro. Unless the New York drama year had been "SUPER-grand," it merited the Pulitzer Prize. In the theater, she had felt tears come to her eyes. "There were so many telling touches—as, the mother, gathering up her poor little plant, against her 'up-to-date' daughter's wishes: 'IT expresses ME.' Wasn't the African student wonderful? And that scene where Sidney Poitier and the daughter are doing the 'African' dance, and *he* springs to the table. Oh my gosh—I could rave about that play forever." It was full of "the universally interesting details" for which she had always "furiously . . . waved the banner."[18]

Besides its other solid merits, *A Raisin in the Sun* did an extraordinary job of portraying a black family's struggle to find housing, and it would probably not be too far afield to assume that Gwendolyn would see in it something of her parents' struggle and her own. An additional excitement came to her that afternoon in a conversation with Era Bell Thompson. *A Raisin in the Sun* was not only a good play; it was a moneymaker. The report was that the play was scooping up money from theater tills and had brought $300,000 from Universal Studios. Gwendolyn had had her own dreams of ending all economic problems with a sudden strike that would produce a somewhat more than *moderate* flowing of gold into the pot, a role she would have been delighted to have *Maud Martha* experience. For it, there would be over many years movie prospects—but no movie. Yet it was good to savor such an experience even when it was a vicarious one only. For now, she sent to Harper another poem to join those being examined. Soon she was to become absorbed in Brown's *Trumbull Park*, which Elizabeth felt was "more limited than *A Raisin in the Sun* as a work of literary art" but nevertheless a work of strength, which clothed "its somewhat reportorial theme with believable characters." The work had special meaning for Gwendolyn, since it was the story of blacks embattled over the right to housing and a direct reflection of the Trumbull Park disturbances.

The overall feeling at Harper about the poems of *The Bean Eaters* was that they made an extraordinary collection, although there was dissension about particular poems. One evaluation sheet carried such marks of praise as: "Even more excellent upon rereading"; "more outstandingly human than the other two"; "a definite advance"; "will re-establish author's reputation as poet of importance." Another states, "This collection deals with big things as well as with the little and very personal. The others [earlier books] were concerned with the small personal details of life almost exclusively." Thus Gwendolyn had communicated to at least one reader her further reaching out into her complicated world. The feeling was to be shared by a large number of the book's readers.

Elizabeth's mettle as editor reveals itself in her dealing with the dissension. Her comments show a readiness to stand her ground quite firmly where a reader's own failure of sensitivity was involved. One reader suggested leaving out a number of poems: "The Last Quatrain of the Ballad of Emmett Till," "We Real Cool," "Old Mary," "Pete at the Zoo," "The Ballad of Rudolph Reed," "Callie Ford," "The Crazy Woman," "A Penitent Considers Another Coming of Mary," "A Man of the Middle Class," and two others. The editor's responses to requests for either omission or revision are frequently pointed and illuminating. Her concept of the collection was that it was about "people beleaguered by confusions and terror, going about their daily trifling businesses, finding in the clichés of existence the nourishment necessary to endurance." In that light, "Old Mary" gave voice to "a moment of recognition in everyone's experience." "We Real Cool" would serve as an "accent piece, the only one in modern vernacular." On "The Ballad of Rudolph Reed": Yes, "this jars. I wonder whether the ballad form was chosen for that very reason." The "Pocketbook. Pot" refrain, though she conceded that it jarred rhythmically in the poem "Mrs. Small," was to be retained because it emphasized Mrs. Small's confusion. In response to a suggestion to omit "The Crazy Woman," the simplest back-up: "I like this."[19] Having worked with Gwendolyn over the years, Elizabeth could more readily perceive what the poet was achieving through various technical moves.

The bookmaking process now began to speed up. By mid-May Elizabeth had set the machinery in motion for the publication of *The Bean Eaters* in a first printing of 2,500 copies. Gwendolyn would receive an advance of $100. As she always enjoyed the entire process of producing a book, she conscientiously read the Harper promotional material for her latest work, which she found "exciting and effective," with one exception: the references to cockroaches. Although the insects were no strangers to the South Side tenement buildings, they did not deserve such emphasis as a marked feature of the territory. Elizabeth had all references to them deleted from the book promotions. As several of her poems began to appear in *Poetry* and *Harper's* magazine, Gwendolyn found pleasure in the way they stood out on the printed page. She was caught up in the rising tide of prepublication excitement.

In May 1959, at the banquet given by the Society of Midland Authors, Gwendolyn met Mark Van Doren, who would become a friend, and the writers Bob and Alice Cromie, with whom she became friends almost immediately. She was serving as a judge for the society's awards and had voted for both Mark and Bob, who did win prizes. The Cromies moved among a large circle of people and were known for generously forwarding the fortunes of others in any way they could. At their home Gwendolyn and Henry would meet such outstanding people as Claudia McNeil, Cleveland Amory, John Dreiske, Albert Memmi, Howard Greenfield, John Fischetti, and Fran Loving. Bob was able to introduce Gwendolyn to new opportunities in lecturing and reviewing and eventually to help Henry secure for his new insurance company a sizable contract. The two families found each other compatible and companionable.

Gwendolyn had been occupied with not only revising poems for her forthcoming book but also going over in her mind a verse biography of the slave Phillis Wheatley, a matter she had begun considering when her last prose version of In the Mecca was returned. After being engaged so very much with contemporary life, she wanted to write a "meaty" work on the past. It would, she felt, require a good deal of research, time, peace, and release from immediate pressures. Elizabeth encouraged the idea, since she felt that in exercising her poetic talents Gwendolyn would be working from strength.

The poet was also steadily involved in reviewing books. For the June 21, 1959, issue of the Chicago Sun-Times, she reviewed William Carlos Williams's biography of his mother, in which "we meet Raquel Helene Rose Hoheb Williams and settle down with her, and very properly stare, for here is a woman of spirit, a little woman of lively energy, physical and mental. A woman proud and challenging, even to her own detriment, self-willed, self-important, dependent upon others chiefly for the sake of the frame for her own picture that they were able to provide."

The Sun-Times of June 28 carried her review of Noel Clad's Love and Money, a novel that she said pulsated with life and presented people fully without singling out any character for the role of hero or heroine. In the Sun-Times of August 16, Gwendolyn opened her review of Hugh Kenner's The Invisible Poet dramatically: "You may ask, Why another of these studies? Why another venture into the careful candors of Eliot-land? But Hugh

Kenner's book does direct, respectfully and with concerned vigilance, further light on the excellences of Nobel Prize winner Thomas Stearns Eliot, who has become almost a legend in his lifetime." She stressed the book's comprehensiveness, its revelation of important influences upon Eliot, and Kenner's methodology.

In such work, Gwendolyn found at least temporary relief from worries about her father's health. David Brooks had been ailing and was not responding well to treatment. She had always looked to him for warmth, kindness, stability, and a protection against the feelings of isolation and loneliness that invade all lives. Her own children saw him as another father, and her mother, of course, had built her life around him. He had been treated at Provident Hospital for stomach and heart problems and had undergone an operation. It became apparent that he would not make a total recovery and that what could be done for him by the medical profession had been done. His family took him home that he might be in his own house and that they might be with him. Though he seemed to be resting quietly, Keziah, apparently sensing the onset of a crisis, called for Gwendolyn to come to the family residence. Her brother Raymond came also and tried to encourage his father to rally.

Although Keziah seemed to have composed herself to face her husband's imminent death, she wanted Gwendolyn to be satisfied that all efforts had been made to save him. Gwendolyn could not accept the inevitability, and insisted after one doctor had given up that still another be called. David seemed relaxed or resigned, smiling gently. The additional medical treatment, however, caused him much pain and he lapsed again into semiconsciousness. Rousing briefly on November 21, he spoke of the coolness in the room and asked to have the window closed. Keziah attended to it, then sat holding his hand and talking to him tenderly. Suddenly, he jerked a foot from under the covers and was dead. Gwendolyn saw her father, a man who had unflaggingly confronted existence, peacefully move out of it. At later moments, when the balance tilted toward consolation instead of grief, she would remember the profound serenity of his departure and would say that from the moment she witnessed how peaceful death could be, she no longer feared it.

Gwendolyn was able to express something of her feelings in the obituary that it fell her lot to write. David Anderson Brooks, she wrote,

left . . . a large number of friends to mourn his demise.
    His soul was beautiful, his heart was gentle, warm and reaching, his mind was inquiring and clear.

He was a good man. He was an honest man. He was a kind and hence beloved man. He was a Gentleman.

At the funeral ceremonies, the Reverend Theodore Richardson brought out the exemplary qualities for which David was known, although his religion as an adult had not included regular church attendance. Margaret Burroughs, old friend, painter, and founder of the DuSable Museum, eulogized him. Waiting with the rest of the family outside the chapel at 4445 South Parkway to be taken to Lincoln Cemetery, Gwendolyn remembers the day as gray—the threatening color for her. Her eyes fell upon Nora and her heart went out to the child. Earlier Nora had stood with a world-weary look on her eight-year-old face on the steps of the Metropolitan Funeral Home on King Drive. Now, waiting again, she looked bleakly away.

Gwendolyn expressed her feelings further in the poem that would become the dedication for The Bean Eaters, "In Honor of David Anderson Brooks, My Father." In it she pushed herself beyond simple grief or the feelings from which a dirge is created; instead, the poem registers the goodness of his earthly existence and the triumph and purity of his new, unconfined being. The meeting of life with death is expressed in the first stanza:

A dryness is upon the house
My father loved and tended.
Beyond his firm and sculptured door
His light and lease have ended.

Sending the dedication statement to Elizabeth on December 2, Gwendolyn confided some of her grief. Elizabeth remembered David well, remembered the "gentle kindly warmth he gave out. Your poem is a lovely memorial until time can give him back to you as he was, without the presence of pain. I do know that the first loss of a parent is an overwhelming experience. But we are among the fortunate to have had ours so long."[20]

The forces at work in the poet's life at this time had largely to do with her new book. Elizabeth had sought prepublication evaluations by those whose prominence and recognized qualifications would be helpful to the book. Gwendolyn knew that she had been fortunate to receive, on the whole, so much praise from critics and reviewers over the past fifteen years, and that she would be foolish not to anticipate "dissenting notes. (Maybe there'll be bricks!)"[21] Among the most positive responses to The Bean Eaters were those of Peter Viereck: "The air is being cleared at last of the need to write poetry—(arid, sapless)—only for explicators. Here is poetry that laughs and cries and dances, poetry—in such refreshing lyrics as 'Bessie of

Bronzeville Visits' and 'The Artists' and Models' Ball'—that throws back its head and sings aloud. This dedicated artist has already won one Pulitzer Prize, and I hope she wins another."[22]

In *The Bean Eaters*, Gwendolyn's movement beyond the autobiographical territory seems, at first examination, to create a universe in which significant gestures are rarely possible. Earlier works, of course, had presented numerous instances in which the triumph of human gesture was sustained primarily by illusion, but they carried more than images of futility. On closer examination, there are similar small victories in *The Bean Eaters*. Mrs. Small seems somehow to triumph in the poem of that name, though her role is confined to homemaking and dealing with the pandemonium of children, by her insistence upon carrying out her part of the world's business in defiance of its power to confuse. In "A Lovely Love," the couple seems to defy the lack of social and cosmic symbols for expressing their emotion. Other characters exhaust the moment or make something out of what little is at hand. In the desperate and heroic defense of home and family made by Rudolph Reed, however, it must be admitted that the universe itself seems to have no promise, and the human spirit is sustained only by its will not to fall.

In "The Explorer," the opening poem, the speaker, his hopes disintegrating, seeks not some far-away Eldorado but "A satin peace somewhere. / A room of wily hush somewhere within."

> So tipping down the scrambled halls he set
> Vague hands on throbbing knobs. There were behind
> Only spiraling, high human voices,
> The scream of nervous affairs,
> Wee griefs,
> Grand griefs. And choices.

Of these, the explorer fears most "the choices, that cried to be taken." The "choices," if taken, might lead to the grandly significant, but our overwhelming tendency to seek "satin" peace will prevent that or any other discovery. The powerful expressionistic imagery marks the inner human condition; the rhymes are scattered, sometimes conventional and sometimes the kind of near-rhymes that signal disharmony. The lines are irregular, well-paced to comport with the nervous uncertainty of the poem's speaker. It is difficult not to feel the poem's tremendous weight within the book, which presents several scenarios that bear out the explorer's discoveries. It is also difficult not to read "The Explorer" as a symbol of the discoveries of the poet.

"The Contemplation of Suicide: The Temptation of Timothy," had been submitted earlier, for inclusion in *Annie Allen*. Although it was thus written much earlier than most of the other poems in *The Bean Eaters*, it underlines the philosophy of "The Explorer," and since it comes late in the book it helps to complete an explicit philosophical framework. In it, one contemplates suicide after having come through confusions ("mazes"), touches of beauty ("robins"), and unfulfilled strivings and attempts to tear away that in existence which blinds (fog), only to observe one's foolish end. Those "downtown" not contemplating suicide are the "sluggish" who are shrugging their shoulders, slinking, talking. But even this awake and questioning observer clings ignominiously to life:

Then, though one can think of no fact, no path, no ground,
Some little thing, remarkless and daily, relates
Its common cliché. One lunges or lags on, prates.—
Too selfish to be nothing while beams break, surf's epileptic chicken reeks or
    squalls.

The clinging would seem to be not quite ignominious but based on Maud Martha's suggestion that somehow the fact of life itself is good, though one surrounded with considerable disappointment. One thus keeps going in a universe that readily surrounds one with terror.

Yet if we go back to the explicit findings of Maud Martha, a work admittedly heavily infused with autobiography, we find a universe that rarely provides "tragedy." "The truth was," Maud Martha says in the chapter "on Thirty-fourth Street," "if you got a good Tragedy out of a lifetime, one good, ripping tragedy, thorough, unridiculous, bottom-scraping, *not* the issue of human stupidity, you were doing, she thought, very well, you were doing well." One was more likely to be caught up in a comedy and to find oneself either laughable or ridiculous. Yet the universe seemed also basically strange, its strangeness compounded by human stupidity and other unlovely human qualities, a fact which made the act of laughter necessary as a bulwark against insanity. One also needed something to lean upon which was constantly available, but human things were inconstant, and the behavior of the Creator seemed not to be useful to one in this life. In "Tim" we read: "Maud Martha saw people, after having all but knocked themselves out below, climbing up the golden, golden stairs, to a throne where sat Jesus, or the Almighty God; who promptly opened a Book, similar to the arithmetic book she had had in grammar school, turned to the back, and pointed out—the Answers! And the people, poor little things, nodding and cackling among themselves—So that was it all the time! that is what I should have done!' 'But—so simple! so *easy*! I should just have turned here! instead of there!' How wonderful! Was it true? Were people to get the Answers in the sky? Were people really going to understand It better by and by? When it was too late?"

Maud Martha and Annie Allen also counted upon extracting from moments what was at hand. Paradoxically, it is all the more necessary, in the face of the social and metaphysical discouragements afforded by this universe, to confront existence with a resilience of spirit—to retain, as Annie Allen's parents did not, the light that "bites and terrifies." The poem "the parents—" seems to suggest that there is an outside chance of retaining in one's life the qualities of swans and swallows, or that the struggle to retain such qualities is itself worthwhile.

The Bean Eaters seems to endorse the adventurous life as the rewarding one, regardless. "Naomi," without assuming that tangible rewards are inevitable, emphasizes this theme. Naomi herself is too vigorously searching out the density of existence to make a blueprint for her brother or to warn her "dull mother" that life is richer than her domesticity evidences, or to urge her "small father" not to become static among his small commercial treasures. She could not etch out what she hoped to get from her "hunt" or state what it was not. Hope existed only if one diligently cared to find out what life was for. "For certainly what it was not for was forbearing."

A recognition of the possibilities of the human spirit in this somewhat ambiguous universe, as seen in the foregoing poems, enables us to see both human errors in approaching it and the complexity with which Gwendolyn imaged the situation. In "My Little 'Bout-town Gal," a rather slight poem, the human spirit defeats itself by cultivating its own corruptness. "Strong Men, Riding Horses" is more challenging. In it Lester uses the illusion cast by a "Western" movie to measure his own smallness. Ironically, the example of courage afforded by the movie is so simply drawn that it offers nothing to the complexity of Lester's situation in the city, where he must deal with "illegible landlords" and robbers and must pay rent for the small space he is allowed to claim for his intimate needs. The images of the movie run an allegory before him: Strong men in vast spaces, always ready to confront Rough Man, as the Challenger, an image giving full scope to physical manliness and the natural entitlement to space. Lester cannot make the Walter Mitty escapist identification with a fictitious model and cringes in self-recognition.

> I am not like that. I pay rent, am addled
> By illegible landlords, run, if robbers call.

What mannerisms I present, employ,
Are camouflage, and what my mouths remark
To word-wall off that broadness of the dark
Is pitiful.
I am not brave at all.

"The Bean Eaters," "Old Mary," and "A Sunset of the City," are representative of those whom time has reduced by its erosions. The title poem, "The Bean Eaters," has its source in Gwendolyn's familiarity with the life and environment of a poor, elderly aunt and uncle who "could make a pound of beans go further than a pound of potatoes."[23] The title itself was inspired by Van Gogh's "The Potato Eaters." The old couple of "The Bean Eaters," though merely good people who have had their day and exist now as time-markers, have still their memories of both pleasures and defeats ("Remembering, with twinklings and twinges"). Presumably, Old Mary, who now can think of experiences she will not have without being pained, has nonetheless had enjoyable ones. In "A Sunset of the City," Kathleen Eileen seems to be a complete loser whose former lovers, husband, and children afford no rich memories. She is pictured thinking of suicide. The poem is one of those somewhat marred by lines and postures too reminiscent of T.S. Eliot:

I am cold in this cold house this house
Whose washed echoes are tremulous down lost halls.
I am a woman, and dusty, standing among new affairs.
I am a woman who hurries through her prayers.

The Eliot echoes occur also in poems dealing with sterility, such as "A Man of the Middle Class," "The Chicago *Defender* Sends a Man to Little Rock," and, less importantly, "The Lovers of the Poor." But such poems also represent the terror of the universe compounded by human deficiencies. The lighter poems, "The Crazy Woman" and "Pete at the Zoo," represent what seems to be a terror simply endemic to the universe. The crazy woman will sing terribly in November, a month foreshadowing death, instead of in May. Pete wonders simply whether the deserted elephant at the zoo experiences loneliness in the same way he does.

Other poems, as earlier suggested, represent the dangers of the universe compounded with individual error and social stupidity. In "We Real Cool," the naïve confrontations of youth with the ills of life will lead to their doom, and the situation is presented with pathos by the suggestions of self-doubt and baffled pride in the youths' halting and emphatic boasts. The reader will

also see a social basis for the youths' situation, although Gwendolyn con-
fines herself to their statements of their intentions.

Among poems reflecting the stupidity of man's social arrangements, the
least effective are "A Bronzeville Mother Loiters in Mississippi. Meanwhile,
a Mississippi Mother Burns Bacon" and "The Chicago *Defender* Sends a
Man to Little Rock." Elizabeth had felt that Gwendolyn stopped being an
artist when a white character showed up in her literary creations and that
when Gwendolyn could laugh at and pity whites in the way she could laugh
at and pity blacks, she "would command the show." It is clear, of course, that
in actual life Gwendolyn did and does sympathize with all humanity, but in
"Bronzeville Mother . . . Mississippi Mother" she seems determined to
present the reader with unmistakable evidence of this. The poem is obviously inspired by the lynching of Emmett "Bobo" Till, a fourteen-year-old
Chicago black boy who was brutally killed and dumped into a Mississippi
river because he allegedly made "advances" to a young white woman in a
Mississippi crossroads store during the summer of 1955. The local Mississippi courts tried and, with some dispatch, acquitted the husband and his
massive friend of the deed.

Gwendolyn thought of the situation in terms of the common denominator Mother. How, on both sides, would a mother feel in such a
situation? The young white woman of the poem is seen through the concept
of motherhood and the chilvaric tradition of the ballad—the framework
through which she herself looks at the crime. She is the "maid mild / Of the
ballad" who must be worth the killing performed in her behalf by the Fine
Prince. After a feeling of temporary exaltation at seeing herself in this
storybook role, it occurs to her that the Dark Villain really lacked the
matured evil to validate the ritual: the fun was all but destroyed when the
villain was not the murderer of many "eaten knights and princesses" but "a
blackish child / Of fourteen, with eyes still too young to be dirty, / And a
mouth too young to have lost every reminder / Of its infant softness."

There are interesting but very obvious dramatic devices. At breakfast,
the husband is concerned with his hands as the instrument of the boy's
murder, though he spews contempt for northern newspapers, the northern
black mother, and outsiders in general. His proneness to violence overtakes
him when the younger baby throws molasses in his brother's face and the
Fine Prince leans across the table and slaps him. The hand now becomes the
Hand and is seen by the young white wife in association with blood as the
husband deals with the children and approaches her for the night's inti-
macies. "She heard no hoof-beat of the horse and saw no flash of the shining
steel." When he kisses her his red mouth also becomes associated with

blood. The movement of the poem is thus one in which hard realities break through the universe of romance in which the sensitive woman had heretofore found her worth. Thus a deep hatred for her husband forms within her.

Gwendolyn had certainly operated as creative artist and had boldly entered the consciousness of a white character, a risk rarely taken by William Faulkner in his portrayal of blacks and one taken, with disastrous consequences, by William Styron in his portrayal of Nat Turner. Unfortunately, Gwendolyn's portrait also seems psychologically false. The pressure of public and historical knowledge of such lynching situations made them rituals through which white southern women of almost any "moral" condition were instantly transformed into Miss Southern White Woman, and the rhythms of southern culture and tradition arose to absorb their "conscience" in the "conscience of the community." Where cultural and historical circumstances press a counter image upon the mind, the artist has more to do to show great strain and struggle before the simple universal woman's heart emerges. It is a matter of charging artistic illusion with sufficient power.

Basically, the same judgment is called for regarding "The Chicago *Defender* Sends a Man to Little Rock," a poem inspired by the very bitter outbreak of violence against young black boys and girls when mobs in Little Rock attempted to prevent desegregation of schools. As in the preceding poem, there are brilliant lines and mastery of the homely detail. The poem contains a kind of truth—but one not sufficiently dramatized against the city's cultural context. Little Rock arrives at the universal by a quick striptease of its cultural clothing and by immediate emphasis upon what it shares in common with others. Thus we light upon the universal: "They are like people everywhere."

"The Lovers of the Poor" and "Bronzeville Woman in a Red Hat" hold as tightly to the historical as the two preceding poems do to the universal. They form sharp contrasts and make no bones about offering offenders against decency the powerful satirical purge. The women of "The Lovers of the Poor" represent those who would give without charity and prescribe all the conditions of giving. Gwendolyn represents them as too repelled by the conditions of people in a slum building to be able to offer the gifts they have brought. At the climax of their encounter with humanity, the women recoil.

> Tin can, blocked fire escape and chitterling
> And swaggering seeking youth and the puzzled wreckage
> Of the middle passage, and urine and stale shames

> And, again, the porridges of the underslung
> And children children children. Heavens! That
> Was a rat, surely, off there, in the shadows? Long
> And long-tailed? Gray?

The ladies from the Ladies' Betterment League make a comical exit:

> Keeping their scented bodies in the center
> Of the hall as they walk down the hysterical hall,
> They allow their lovely skirts to graze no wall,
> Are off at what they manage of a canter,
> And, resuming all the clues of what they were,
> Try to avoid inhaling the laden air.

The ladies conceive themselves as having no kinship with the rest of mankind—a pharisaic disease.

In "Bronzeville Woman in a Red Hat," Gwendolyn administers the purge for pretentiousness with still greater forthrightness. Mrs. Miles, a haughty woman, treats domestics as her slaves. Since she offends against both an Irishwoman servant (Patsy Houlihan) and the black woman in the red hat, Gwendolyn sees her as basically an offender against the poor, although she makes it clear that whereas Mrs. Miles considers the Irishwoman in slave terms, she goes a step further with the black woman and considers her no better than an animal. Mrs. Miles is emotionally sterile. Her responses to her child are based upon the studied guides for rearing children, on which she is entirely dependent.

> —This was the way to put it, this the relief.
> This sprayed a honey upon marvelous grime.
> This told it possible to postpone the reef.
> Fashioned a huggable darling out of crime.
> Made monster personable in personal sight
> By cracking mirrors down the personal night.

Thus, like the ladies from the Ladies' Betterment Society, she can love the child only by re-creating for herself its image so that its features are pleasant and undisturbing. Therefore, she loses the affections of her child to the maid, who responds to it spontaneously and offends by caressing the child: "Her creamy child kissed by the black maid! square on the mouth!"

Whereas the lovers of the poor were shown to be ridiculous by being placed in undignified postures, Mrs. Miles is undermined by being described in stylized and set verse, which implies that she is common and easily defined.

> She, quite supposing purity despoiled,
> Committed to sourness, disordered, soiled,
> Went in to pry the ordure from the cream.
> Cooing, "Come." (Come out of the cannibal wilderness,
> Dirt, dark, into the sun and bloomful air.)

Stylized verse is used also to give emphasis to the simple and natural responses of the child: "Conscious of kindness, easy creature bond. / Love had been handy and rapid to respond."

Obviously, such poems reveal the extent to which man compounds the difficulties endemic to his cramped universe. In contrast to the poems that indict the white middle class, in particular, for narrowness, sterility, and racism, "Bessie of Bronzeville Visits Mary and Norman at a Beach-house in New Buffalo" tells of a black woman who enjoys herself with the white couple she visits.

> And I was hurt by cider in the air.
> And what the lake-wash did was dizzying.
> I thought of England, as I watched you bring
> The speckled pebbles,
> The smooth quartz; I thought of Italy.
>
> Italy and England come.
> A sea sits up and starts to sing to me.

Gwendolyn had in mind Mary and Norman Springer, a couple involved in liberal politics and academia. They had come to a party she had given for Langston Hughes, and she and Henry had accepted an invitation to visit them and had had a lovely time. Once when Norman had taken Gwendolyn on public transportation to visit his writing group on the North Side of Chicago, other passengers had stared at the apparently interracial couple, making Gwendolyn self-conscious and embarrassed. It was difficult in America to escape the impact of racism, even in the company of a liberal white.

The vagaries of intraracial relations played their role in compounding the difficulties of man's inherent situation. Gwendolyn expected the social oppression to be apparent even in "My Little 'Bout-town Gal," in which, on the surface, the conflict seems restricted to the man and woman of the poem. The theme is that of a woman wandering about the city seeking to find the self which she is unable to discover and support through the meager humanity afforded by her husband. Apparently the man is "cheating" the woman of all he would like to give but can't because he himself has been cheated by society. His own victimization, however, is not given imposing evidence in the poem. In reading it today, there may be some danger that the reader will think of "Roger of Rhodes" as a pimp and the "gal" as a prostitute, whereas Roger is her husband. Rhodes refers to Rhodes Avenue, on which Gwendolyn once resided.

If the subtleties, symbols, and silences can be seen as allowing for errant interpretations, certainly "Jessie Mitchell's Mother" seems quite explicit. It is an attack upon the destructiveness of intraracial prejudice, exemplified here in the conflicts usually existing between the young and older generation. Jessie has contempt for her aging and disintegrating mother whom she considers foolish and spineless. The mother, envying her daughter's youth and conscious of having been reduced by marriage to a poor man, has her yellow color as her trump card: Jessie is black-skinned and will suffer more— without the compensating moments of "loveliness" gained by the mother's possession of a yellow skin.

> She, almost hating her daughter,
> Crept into an old sly refuge: "Jessie's black
> And her way will be black, and jerkier even than mine.
> Mine, in fact, because I was lovely, had flowers
> Tucked in the jerks, flowers were here and there. . . . "
> She revived for the moment settled and dried-up triumphs,
> Forced perfume into old petals, pulled up the droop,
> Refueled
> Triumphant long-exhaled breaths.
> Her exquisite yellow youth. . . .

The mother thus reveals her spiritual impoverishment, a condition given more emphasis than the distant arrogance of her youthful daughter.

The consequences of man's compounding his already limited condition are a variety of responses from those who would see him better situated. "Leftist Orator in Washington Park Pleasantly Punishes the Gropers" reveals a concept of man as frightened, beseeching, blind, and unheroic. The orator may in part hope to arouse some spark within him. The second stanza:

> I foretell the heat and yawn of eye and the drop of the mouth and the screech,
> The foolish, unhappy screech hanging high on the air.
> Because you had no dream or belief or reach.
> Because you could only beseech.

In the eyes of the orator, such people are capable of only a meaningless existence: "there will be No Thing for which you fall." The narrator of "The Artists' and Models' Ball," however, sees mankind as unconfused by "wonders" but confused by small things that seem easily settled but change behind us once we think we have settled them. In "A Penitent Considers Another Coming of Mary," dedicated to the Reverend Theodore Richardson, who had preached her father's funeral, a returning Mary would pity, not punish, mankind. She would thus again offer her son for man's salvation.

> She would not shake her head and leave
> This military air,
> But ratify a modern hay,
> And put her baby there.

The final word, however, is given in "In Emanuel's Nightmare: Another Coming of Christ." In briefer compass the poem has something of the agility and at times the light touch of Robert Frost's masques. Christ came again to eliminate from the earth the "dirtiness of war." But He discovered that mankind desired war very much, that "it was their creed, and their good joy. / And what they lived for." Thus Christ failed in his mission, not because he lacked the power to accomplish it, but because He "had not the heart / To take away their chief sweet delectation." So far we have a relatively light touch. But the poem ends with Christ grieved and crying the tears of men because we have "no need of peace." Man cannot really live without the nourishment war provides.

Thus the universe of *The Bean Eaters* is a very complicated one. It has, when closely observed, numerous balances in the consideration of its issues: the racial and the intraracial; the social and the metaphysical; the individual and the group. The tumultuous outer universe is comprised of the tearing flesh and blood in Chicago and in the nation as a whole. The poet recalls hostile responses to *The Bean Eaters* from white critics who accused her of forsaking lyricism for polemics and felt that the book was too "social." Both "The Lovers of the Poor" and "The Chicago *Defender* Sends a Man to Little Rock" (later to be over-anthologized) met with dislike. In her autobiography she credits Robert H. Glauber of the *Beloit Poetry Journal* with being "courageous enough to break the dead silence which for months met my 'too social' 1960 volume, *The Bean Eaters*, with a long and glowing review."[24] In this case, she seems to be referring to the local Chicago press rather than to the national publications, which, while finding deficiencies, tended on the whole to praise the book.

On the level of simple personal potential, one still feels tensions in this complicated universe, tensions deriving from Gwendolyn's holding—not so much in balance as in perspective—opposing ideas regarding man's capacity to deal with his root situation. Here it might be useful to quote again from her February 26, 1958, statement in the *Chicago American* ("What Prayer Did for Me"). "People," she had believed, " are stronger than they think. I considered. They bring about events themselves. They can save themselves. They need not wail in the night or day, wanting and hunting some Love that will hold them like babies, and protect them from the stresses of nature, and from the Strains imposed on themselves by themselves." The statement is a report on her modification of that view, since the experience of prayer made God for her "seem a near reality." But, read closely, the statement retains much of the earlier view, and God becomes a reserve resource, with the individual still working from the belief that he or she can help self, can make things happen and be mainly self-sustaining. "I rarely ask him for anything—a little lingering independence of spirit still whispers to me somewhat, telling me that it is wrong (if not bad) to ask God for help where it appears that you can help yourself." This personal philosophy seemed to enter the poetic considerations of this universe in behalf of the adventurous quester of "The Egg Boiler," the searching "Naomi," the arrogant "Leftist Orator," and the lovers of "A Lovely Love."

The meaning of the book in technical terms resides in her continued mastery of certain outstanding devices and in the confident way in which she creates a highly flexible form at will. The diversity in the manipulation of syntax, the striking range between realism and expressionism in the employment of imagery, the diction that creates sudden delighting verbal surprises are all well-preserved jewels from the past. The loosening up felt in her approach to form registers a further development over the older approaches. In *Annie Allen* she had loosened up the form of the sonnet in "the rites for Cousin Vit" with the use of elliptical syntax, the pressures of colloquial speech, and forcing of all operating devices to create the impact of hyperbole. Cousin Vit, it will be recalled, was simply too big and vital to have died and thus continued to do "the snake-hips with a hiss." In *The Bean Eaters* she loosened up the sonnet form in "A Lovely Love," with the adaptation of the rhyme scheme of the Petrarchan sonnet, the intermingling of brief and long complete statements with a sudden elliptical one, and the management of a nervous rhythm that imposes the illusion of being a one-to-one imitation of the behavior of the narrators. Although the elliptical structures are more numerous and informal in "Cousin Vit," the rhythm of "A Lovely Love" seems to be the greater achievement. Another technical development is her movement at will into a free verse appropriate to the situation and sometimes dotted with rhyme. The range can be seen in such poems as "The Explorer," "Mrs. Small," and "A Bronzeville Mother. . . . " This advance will be more noticeable in her next major poem.

Coming so closely after her father's death, the publication of *The Bean Eaters* put the lift of new achievement into Gwendolyn's life, but she was unable to push back entirely a generalized feeling of tightness and somberness. There had been, before his death, a sense of being overtaken by her own spontaneity, a side of herself that she tended to hide from all except those very close to her—something of Maud Martha's excited whispers: "What, *what*, am I to do with all of this life?" Her daughter, Nora, remembers times when Gwendolyn would suddenly put a record of Errol Garner on the record player and, soapy with dishwater, go "diddy-bopping" through the house, stamping out the rhythm of the beat. It was difficult for Gwendolyn to get going that way now.

Suddenly the household was due for a shake-up, as Henry Jr. decided it was time for him to be out on his own, bringing to an end what he still looks back upon as a sheltered life. The argument that preceded his decision he now sees as simply the creator of the occasion. His parents, rearing their children with confidence, had given both Nora and Henry Jr. what they needed to be independent. Nora remembers being encouraged, prior to school age, to be able to back up her opinions. On one occasion, she had announced grandly that she was for John F. Kennedy for president, thinking it enough of a reason that the rest of the family also supported Kennedy; instead, she found her parents pressing her to explain her preference, to give good sound reasons.

Ironically, self-reliance seems to have made Henry Jr. restive under the household rules. From his parents' point of view, he was beginning to run with a fast crowd. They objected to one of his girlfriends, who seemed to express in her behavior an unusual degree of hipness. One evening when his father objected both to the girl and to the party Henry Jr. was about to attend with her, the young man responded furiously and defiantly. To his father's statement that "as long as you are living in this house you'll abide by my rules," Henry Jr. retorted, "All right, I'll be out by next Saturday." He was firm in this decision in the face of his mother's admonition: "Now, you understand, Henry, that if you leave, that's fine, but you're not to return to live here. I'll expect you to support yourself." Gwendolyn later regretted the statement, but Henry Jr. felt that it strengthened him by helping him face up to what he was doing and making him realize the energy needed to back up his decision.

His father was caught feeling that, yes, at almost nineteen, it was natural for his son to want to move out, but on the other hand, well, no, he was a boy who would benefit from remaining a bit longer at home. Gwendolyn was caught between the natural disturbance of the mother over the departure of the firstborn and her desire to be "sensible." Looking back, Nora feels that Gwendolyn was overly cool and composed, failing to consider how Henry Jr.'s leaving might affect his sister. For Nora, Henry Jr. represented not only a companion devoid of the conventional brotherly irritability with a "kid" sister, but also a god to be idolized. He was part of the older group with whom she preferred to associate instead of with youngsters of her own age. Though Nora got along very well with her own age group, she did not find them essential until she was well into her high school years. Meanwhile, she had shared with her brother not only fun but also growth.

He had changed from an unsteady student into a strong one through developing an interest in science. In one scientific experiment, Nora remembers, fluid shaken up in a bottle blew the cap off and left brown spots on the kitchen ceiling that remained there for years. Another experiment their father ate from the ice-box, as it had appeared to be jello. Later, at Hirsch High School, Henry Jr. won second place in a science competition with his creation of a robot complete with motors and lights and made it to the finals sponsored by the city, in competition with very advanced students.

When Henry Jr. left home, the family watched him walk down the alley toward the '51 Chevrolet his father had given him. Nora tried for her own version of toughness by telling herself that now she would get his room. But after they exchanged waves and he had disappeared she burst into tears and was periodically hysterical for the next two days. Gwendolyn's ability to appear calm and self-contained came in handy. Fortunately, it turned out that Henry Jr. was moving to the Y.M.C.A. and then to quarters on the North Side of Chicago, so visits lessened the impact of the move.

Given the family's economic circumstances, Gwendolyn stressed need in requesting, on August 15, 1960, that Elizabeth recommend her for a Ford Foundation grant. She intended to use the reward to write a biographical novel in verse about Phillis Wheatley, the eighteenth-century black poet, a project she had discussed with Elizabeth during a relatively recent Chicago visit. She enclosed a biographical sketch of Phillis from Arna Bontemps and Langston Hughes's *The Poetry of the Negro*, a piece stressing Phillis's sensitivity, her swift acquisition of the language and literature of her "captors," her rise to fame, and her painful life when her patrons died and she suffered an apparently unhappy marriage in poverty. She died "as a servant in a cheap lodging house at the age of thirty-one." Gwendolyn would emphasize the dramatic conflicts. "The *Drama* WILL BE FEATURED, NOT THE POETRY," she wrote under the plot summary. "I SEE THE MOST EXCITING POS-SIBILITIES HERE, AND HAVE SKETCHED OUT MY BASIC PLAN. MUCH RE-SEARCH IS INVOLVED, HOWEVER, AND MUCH CAREFUL WRITING. I NEED TIME, PEACE, AND MONEY."

No time, peace, or money would be forthcoming in the capital-letter terms she had called for. Elizabeth soon discovered that the Ford Foundation was not at that time making grants for poetry or literature and that it was too late in the year for the board of chancellors of the Academy of American Poets even to consider nominating Gwendolyn for a fellowship. Elizabeth recommended Gwendolyn for the Shelley Memorial Award offered by the Poetry Society of America, but the award did not go to Gwendolyn.[25]

Henry Sr. was meeting his own discouragements at the same time. Some of the poems he had written were liked at Harper, but he had too few of those—or of any kind—to make a request for book publication viable. His massive novel "The Dry Well Papers" had not met with favor at Harper or elsewhere, although it had led to exciting discussions of writing with his friend Frank London Brown. Financial setbacks added to their trials: Gwendolyn meditated sardonically upon a story then making it through the literary circles that the wife of an extremely well-known author, without the pressures of need, had spent grant money to buy a Cadillac.

But if there was not to be "TIME, PEACE, AND MONEY," still available were struggle, tension, and good moments—none of which was despised in Gwendolyn's philosophy. Since Elizabeth had encouraged the Phillis Wheatley project, she reviewed her plan sheet and went to work. Surviving portions of the plan suggest a Phillis Wheatley who awakens to great pain and then experiences tragedy. An incomplete fragment reads:

1. Description of cabin
2. And incumbent reminiscence
3. The way the morning passes. Food, work
4. The surreptitious trip to the place in the bushes from which she can see the Big House children's afternoon tea (whenever she can get away). Their activities (as opposed to the cabin children's.)
5. The fluffy dress
6. Her determination . . .

A more inclusive plan reveals the kind of plot with which Gwendolyn was working.

1. Description of little P.'s life in Africa. The little girl running about in the land of Africa. . . .
2. Capture and crossing. Reactions
3. The slave mart. Reactions
4. Purchase by "kindly" people and description of life in their home.
5. The quality and quantity of P.'s adjustment. Her poetry writing.
6. Other slaves. Her reaction to them, theirs to her.
7. Clash with——, a rebellious slave who wants at the very least to escape himself, and/or better, to start a revolt among all slaves accessible to him. She, abhoring violence, tries to smooth his hate away. He tries to get her to understand his claims, telling her that she has been lulled by ~~the fruits of the~~ favors she has found in the "family." He describes the grim life of most of the other slaves. (Brief description.) He then takes her to see some of the slaves and their lives. Takes her by night & secretly.
8. She *is* horrified, by what she sees for the first time. What can she do? She answers she can at least share the starkness of her countrymen's condition. (Resurrection of her past glories, the European trip, the attentions, the admiration, etc.) She marries a "lowly" Negro.
9. Description of marriage. The bleakness. The death.

Infiltrate throughout the poem subtle appreciations of hers—of beauty of the sky, of books, of the little finenesses in people & in her surroundings. Also many sharp pictures of the contemporary scene. Politics. G. Washington. Current customs, social, moral, intellectual.

Unfortunately, the Phillis Wheatley story was not to be completed. Later Gwendolyn would think of the meaning of the title "To Disembark"—how it felt to be brought to America—and apply it to another work.

Book reviews, meanwhile, were rapidly moving through her typewriter: Pedro Antonio de Alarcón's *The Infant with the Globe*, Frederic Prokosch's *A Ballad of Love*, Randall Jarrell's *The Woman at the Washington Zoo*, John Frederick Nims's *Knowledge of the Evening*, Witter Bynner's *New Poems— 1960*, John Ciardi's *39 Poems*, Vern Sneider's *The King from Ashtabula*, John Betjeman's *Summoned by Bells*, and others.

She was fascinated by the gumption of her friend Frank London Brown, who in the *Daily Defender* of July 21, 1960, criticized blacks for neglecting their writers, of whom he saw Gwendolyn as an outstanding example. In an analogy with black musicians, Brown contended that black writers wanted to sing for black people, but were able to keep going, in the face of black neglect, only by white recognition. Brown warned that "People who don't read their writers lose their writers." Frank Yerby, now famous for historical novels featuring whites, had "started out writing books for YOU." Richard Wright was in exile in France and Willard Motley in Mexico. Margaret Danner had left Chicago to acquire much recognition at Wayne State in Detroit.

There was also much evidence that Gwendolyn had not been neglected by readers. She was "wildly excited" by Ruby Dee's dramatic rendering of several of her poems on the CBS television station in New York: "kitchenette building," "the old-marrieds," "We Real Cool," "Pete at the Zoo," and "A Bronzeville Mother." "How could she know so well my own feelings, how could she draw them out with such sensitiveness! Wonderful, wonderful."[26] The program drew close to a thousand letters.[27]

Early in 1961, at the invitation of Richard Eberhart, Poetry Consultant to the Library of Congress, Gwendolyn recorded her own poems for an hour at the Library. Eberhart showed her where the records were put away for posterity and for occasional loan. He also showed her a view of Washington from the gallery—"a vision never to be forgotten."[28]

The Bean Eaters forms a coda to one long period of encounter, for it registers the complete achievement of Gwendolyn's sensibility in embracing both the autobiographical world and the main strands of the larger universe. With its publication she had a body of work that placed her stamp on poetry. One could recognize a Gwendolyn Brooks poem. She had now produced most of the poetry geared primarily to what might be called revelation. Before the end of the coming decade she would move instead to the creation of a poetry of liberation and celebration.

7

Foreshadowings

Despite the variety in Gwendolyn's experiences, there were, surprisingly, no indications in the early 1960s that her life would be fundamentally altered in the coming decade as her racial consciousness achieved a different focus and she broke with the white liberal critical consensus that had guided most of her career. The break would seem so dramatic that she would give it dimensions similar to the Apostle Paul's sudden conversion on the road to Damascus. It would produce basic changes in her personality, her art, her financial situation, and her relations with others. Not unrelated to these developments would be a radical change in her domestic circumstances.

That the change in Gwendolyn's racial consciousness would be not merely one of degree but also one of kind was not foreshadowed in the early 1960s, which created an intensity of expectations regarding the fulfillment of traditional integrationist goals. Thus the consciousness that produced "Negro Hero" (*A Street in Bronzeville*) seemed merely to have extended itself in the production of "The Ballad of Rudolph Reed" (*The Bean Eaters*) or the poems on the integration debacle in Little Rock and the murder of Emmett Till in Mississippi. What seems to emerge in her writing before her dramatic expression of change in 1967 is hope accompanied by close attention to the spiritual meanings of the civil rights struggle.

On the one hand, she could be seen as pictured in the *Chicago Daily News* of July 1, 1961, which in part described her response to the absence of other Negroes in the area of her home on South Evans during 1945, a time when blacks were confined to a boundary seven blocks to the north. " 'If Bronzeville keeps spreading,' said Miss Brooks with a shy smile, 'I may run out of material. It won't be Bronzeville anymore. We will all be just human beings. Then I'll have to find something else to write about.' " The article describes the extent of black residential resources in 1961 as having resulted from the post–World War II "breakout" of "hundreds of thousands of pent-in souls seeking more living space."

On the other hand, Gwendolyn welcomed the stately presence of Africans in the United Nations Assembly and approved the exploding activities of black students, which soon had the South capitulating to many desegregation demands. In an interview with me, the poet confessed that she had always liked people who got things done; part of her childhood training had been to do something about one's problems. She was particularly impressed by the direct actions of youth during the early 1960s, recalling her own Block Club's effective approach to the discriminatory hiring by the neighborhood Hi-Lo grocery store. Under the club's direction, Gwendolyn had first sent a letter to the company demanding equal employment opportunities. When Hi-Lo refused to make any changes, her young neighbor Harold Hill had organized picketing that forced the company to change their employment practices. It was a local instance of the source of her great respect for young blacks.

A few events revealed that she was also interested in maintaining her role as writer at the center of the struggle. In January 1962, John V.B. Sullivan, vice president and general manager of radio station WNEW in New York, refused to allow the broadcasting of her poem "of De Witt Williams on his way to Lincoln Cemetery," which had been set to music by Oscar Brown, Jr., because it used the word "black" ("just a plain black boy"). In a letter of January 29 to the Edward B. Marks Music Company, Mr. Sullivan stated: "The entertainment value of 'Elegy' is questionable, and while it is not our feeling that music must deal only with fantasy and the kind of world that will never be, a man's inhumanity to man is not necessarily ideal subject material for the music a radio station offers its listeners." A similar letter from Mr. Sullivan to Gwendolyn stated: "I hope, however, that you will appreciate that it [the action] was taken without caprice or any superficial reaction to the observation in your song that Negroes are not white."

Gwendolyn wrote a note of appreciation to the music company condemning Sullivan's action and expressing the hope that the company and Oscar Brown and others would not suffer "because of a clean and sincere, three-word, twenty-year-old phrase of mine."[1] She also enclosed the "defense" she had sent to Mr. Sullivan, which stated her understanding that his reason for rejecting the song was "chiefly a fear of possible Negro indignation over the presence in the poem of the phrase 'plain black boy.' " Accusing the radio stations of undue timidity, she pointed out that the poem had been received enthusiastically, North and South, since 1943. "There is no reason why the Oscar Brown music, which, incidentally, is an amazing repetition, enhancement and fulfillment of my own thought and sense of the life and death of a pitiful yet proud and lip-out-thrusting, chest-announcing youth, should alarm. It is a tasteful rendering in exquisite and sensitive italics."

The remainder of the paragraph expresses sharply her state of consciousness and pride in her own role: "There have been racial advances since then, many of them dearly paid for by both Negroes and whites. Don't expect *me* to do anything, or personally to allow anything, treacherous to those advances. In which I judge I've joined. For seventeen years. Without ever detouring from my Business—which is being a writer. Many of the banners so brightly (and originally, they think) waved by today's youngsters I waved twenty years ago, and published sixteen years ago." She also described a new force that was reshaping consciousness: "Why should American Negroes, now developing an ever more intense race pride—due considerably to current emergences of African power and bearing—resent the use of the word 'black'? The Africans they admire are endorsing, promoting, and exulting in the word and the fact." Perhaps part of the problem she was then having in trying to write about dream and misery in the old Chicago Mecca Building was that rendering the situation required a change in consciousness. In any case, work on the poem was about to take a back seat to the effort to publish a volume of selected poems.

Feeling that the time was ripe and that another set of "reading folks" had arrived on the scene since she was first published in 1945, Gwendolyn queried her editor as to whether she might publish a collection of her work. "1960 was such a year for Collections and Selections (nobody seems to wait for death anymore) that I am inspired to ask—Do you think I may have a 'Selected Poems' of my own this year? It would be a pleasure to re-examine the books of verse now, and with your help to exclude certain items that will not contribute to a simple cohesive impression." Elizabeth felt that such a volume should not be published during that year or the next because it would follow too closely upon 1960's *The Bean Eaters*, but the editor suggested that they begin to work toward the collection which would eventually present both new work and the best of the old.[2]

In mid-1962 Gwendolyn again raised the issue. "This is my problem. I'm writing now a book-length poem—2,000 lines at least, thick with story and music and sound-and-fury and I hope idea and sense—based on life 'in the Mecca.' (I can't give up the thing; it has a grip on me.) I don't want to do anything else—of an extended nature—just now. It will, however, take a year or more to finish. Meanwhile, I'd like to have out a 'Selected Poems'— I'm constantly asked to tell where 'A Street in Bronzeville' and 'Annie Allen' can be bought—but I wonder if you feel that fall of 1963 is all right? I would *love* that—but you may know of reasons why it would not be good." If that date was agreeable, the poet would send a "tentative list of contents for your suggestions, or, if you can 'see' the manuscript better (nice and big at last!) all typed out a-fresh, I'll be happy to do that."[3] She also had a few new poems and would write two or three more to provide additional bulk and substance.

Understanding Gwendolyn's obsession with her Mecca experiences, Elizabeth encouraged both projects. She felt that if the poems could be assembled by early 1963 they could be published in the following fall.[4]

Gwendolyn replied "warmly and excitedly" on September 9, reacting also to an article on her work by Harvey Curtis Webster in the September 1 issue of *The Nation*. "I was overwhelmed when I read this article, because it is the sort of thing I had hoped would be said of me (by respectable critics) *after* death." Webster's essay sets up the hurdles he sees Gwendolyn transcending and begins a discussion of *A Street in Bronzeville, Annie Allen,* and *The Bean Eaters*.

In times as troubled as ours what sensitive writer can avoid a certain obsession with contemporary ills that may be temporary? Gwendolyn Brooks, from her very good *A Street in Bronzeville,* through her nearly as good *Annie Allen,* to her better *The Bean Eaters,* has never denied her engagement in the contemporary situation or been over-obsessed by it. In her engagement she resembles Langston Hughes, Countee Cullen and Margaret Walker, to name the other Negro poets I know best. In her ability to see through the temporal she equals Richard Wright, James Baldwin and Ralph Ellison, writers of fiction who accept Negro-ness as prizeable differentiation and a dilemma, include it to transcend it. Of course she writes of Emmett Till, of Little Rock, of Dorie Miller, of a white maid [sic] disgusted to see her child embrace the Negro maid. Of course she uses (less frequently and less successfully than Langston Hughes) blues rhythms, writes of the blessing-curse, the accident of color. Like all good writers she acknowledges Now by vivifying it, accepts herself and the distinguishing background that is part of her distinction. But she refuses to let Negro-ness limit her humanity. She does not "marvel at this curious thing:/ to make a poet black, and bid him sing" [a quotation from Countee Cullen's "Yet Do I Marvel"]. Gwendolyn Brooks accepts to transcend.[5]

Such remarks comprise the standard script inscribed by the white liberal critical consensus on the test sheets of those blacks about to be admitted into the company of true writers. But Webster also improves upon the script. On the one hand, her poems about "the Negro dilemma" seem to him her best poems "because they help me and others to identify as we must." On the other hand, in truly the best of her poems, "Negroness, the contemporary situation, Miss Brooks's individuality, mastered craft and foreverness coalesce. . . . Race is then an accident; the contemporary situation a source of detail; craft the skilled accomplice of matter; Miss Brooks everywoman differentiated. Increasingly in each of her books these poems have appeared." Webster cites the sonnet beginning "Surely you stay my certain own . . . " (*A Street in Bronzeville*), "pygmies are pygmies still . . . " (*Annie Allen*), and "A Lovely Love" (*The Bean Eaters*).

Webster then praises her technical proficiency: "gradual development of freedom, of her own spontaneity disciplined, culminating in the frequent free verse that is used almost as often as regular forms in *The Bean Eaters*, the book which contains her best work . . . . She is a very good poet, the only superlative I dare use in our time of misusage; compared not to other Negro poets or other women poets but to the best of modern poets, she ranks high."

Webster's essay had immediate impact at Harper. Elizabeth wrote the poet on September 17 that the "lovely" article was right on time "to confirm our resolve to bring out a Selected Poems." Van Allen Bradley, literary editor of the *Chicago Daily News*, would reprint the article during the next year for Gwendolyn's Chicago audience.

For Gwendolyn, the prospect of putting together "Selected Poems" was one way to leaven some of the impact of the loss of the Blakelys' close friend Frank London Brown, who died from the abrupt advance of leukemia on March 12, 1962, at the age of thirty-four. Gwendolyn would remember him for his badinage with Henry and their endless discussion of writing. More personally, her memory was of the friend who could detect the slightest tip in her temperament toward depression, and of his insistence upon making his time and his ear available. Both had lost fathers. Brown had been very preoccupied with his father's death when he discovered that he, too, had only a short time to live. Gwendolyn encouraged him to be frank with his family about his illness, and after his death she recalled that he reminded Henry that a person should try to get his work done, since no one knew the duration of his time. She had found him always "loyal and kind; and gently funny, on top of a deep sobriety, almost a Sorrow, always there no matter how much he laughed."[6]

A director of the Union Leadership School at the University of Chicago, Brown had a strong private and public impact on blacks and whites in Chicago because of his humanism and his courage. During the riots at Chicago's Trumbull Park housing, where he lived, he had refused to be conducted to and fro by police, insisting upon walking on his own, as a citizen.

Gwendolyn tried to catch something of the implications of his character in the poem she read at his funeral. As with memorial poems for her friend

Edward Bland and her father, she stepped back from the kind of concrete details that spoke of specific events and focused on the general ritualistic patterns governing his behavior.

The first stanza, which was quoted by Robert Cromie in his memorial article, seems the most successful.

> He observed
> School and garbage and bright shells,
> The molasses stickiness of stupidity,
> The ticking of quick Time,
> The tender profiles of children,
> Unwieldy
> Prophecy, political persons
> Gone past the place
> And point of grace
> To slitheriness and slime.
>
> Always
> Love and the pledge of the curtain to fall
> Erected such reverence of vagabond View after all.

Such memorial poems as "In Honor of David Anderson Brooks, My Father" (*The Bean Eaters*) and "Medgar Evers" and "Malcolm X" (*In the Mecca*) achieve their success by sustaining the illusion of an inevitable movement from stanza to stanza. "In Honor . . .," for example, builds all the way on the idea of a releasing and fulfilling journey, and the Medgar Evers poem on the transformation of self in a moment of crisis that has been long building. The personhood of the subjects is steadily before us. "Of Frank London Brown" instead moves from a portrait of the subject's ritualistic patterns of response to commentary upon the failure of the community, and then to what we must gain from his legacy. Thus the poem does not achieve an organic form, suggesting that the autobiographical emotion, so early after the friend's death, was still too overwhelming. The poem was published in the September issue of *Negro Digest*.

Besides the memory of comradeship, Gwendolyn also treasured the number of times Brown had tried to turn the sentiment of friendship into deeds. His article calling the black audience's attention to her efforts has already been mentioned. Published in the August 27, 1961, issue of the *Chicago Sunday Tribune* (reprinted in the December issue of *Negro Digest*) was Brown's article "Chicago's Great Lady of Poetry." In it he stressed Gwendolyn's modesty, fame, talent, compassion, and involvement in humanity, and the coherence of qualities that made her the Great Lady of

Poetry. It was an excellent appreciation. Two paragraphs emphasize her achievement and importance to the community:

> She is familiar, now, with the "hollow land of fame," but she has never lost sight of the rainbow. Love is the rainbow she chases—love in the broadest sense: love of each man and woman, *by* each man and woman. She wants to show her readers the golden cord of humanity that unites every girl in a tattered dress and every girl in a gown of silk.
>
> She declares it in her precise but passionate poetry, and in the jazzlike experiments of her one short novel, "Maud Martha." She is saying that birth, happiness, sorrow, and toil are much more extraordinary than they usually seem to us. She is saying that life's real magic lies in these things alone, and that we are still strangers to the reality which we have abandoned in our search for some vague higher truth.

Brown also spoke of her as a "voice of soft power dedicated to people—all people."

Gwendolyn appreciated the article as a whole. But the idea of lady as an achieved condition struck a special chord in her being. She confided to a friend that she had wished to be worthy of the term but had found herself falling short here and there. Thus despite the fact that she had rebelled against the strict conventions of her upbringing, she still responded to this traditional concept of woman. The fact is perhaps a testimony to the unrelenting persistence within her of the more traditional type of woman which her mother, to a large degree, represented.

Only six days prior to his death, Brown's efforts had succeeded in gaining for Gwendolyn an entrée to teaching. On March 6, 1962, his secretary, Freddy L. Nollet, confirmed that she would be teaching American literature in Brown's Union Leadership Program at the University of Chicago, in seven sessions from April 16 through May 7. Although some of her students in the Union Leadership Program had read more American literature than she had, Gwendolyn would find when she began teaching regularly that this first experience helped her to define the teacher's end of the classroom exchange.

At this point, Herbert Hill, then labor secretary for the National Association for the Advancement of Colored People, was putting together an anthology of black literature, *Soon, One Morning* (1963), that would use several of Gwendolyn's pieces: two prose works (a section from *Maud Martha* and the "new" short story "The Life of Lincoln West") as well as nine poems, four from *A Street in Bronzeville* and five from *Annie Allen*. Hill's anthology was designed to display works of black writers from the 1940s to 1962 that went beyond the status of "sociology" and met the criteria of art and literature. Hill's sixteen-page introduction made variations on the theme usually adopted by the white liberal critics in approving individual black writers:

The greater part of contemporary American Negro writing is characterized by a determination to break through the limits of racial parochialism into the whole range of the modern writer's preoccupations. Though the Negro world frequently remains their emotional home, Negro writers in a variety of ways have abandoned the literature of simple and unrelieved protest, and have made the creative act their first consideration. They continue to confront American society as Negroes, but increasingly without the conflict between social and literary aspirations that marked the work of Negro authors in the past. Now most often they use the concepts of "Negro" and "race" as universal symbols in a new concern with the problems of individual consciousness, identity, and alienation.

The work for the Hill anthology obviously did not give her great labors since most pieces were from earlier efforts. Even "The Life of Lincoln West" came from work she was doing in 1954. The situation was quite different with the work going into the shaping up of Selected Poems, since the task required careful evaluation and creation of a sense of overall symmetry. Gwendolyn had at first dedicated to Frank London Brown a poem representing the spirit of the Freedom-Riders, the Sit-Inners, and other courageous protestors against discrimination. Then she decided to divide the dedication of the book as a whole between Brown and Bob and Alice Cromie. She wanted very much to head the book with quotations from Brown and Nelson Algren: "Oh, yes, the mob was still screaming; but now I heard singing—" from Brown's Trumbull Park and ". . . not one should be slighted. / . . . not one should be turned away" from Algren's distillation of Whitman's introduction to The Neon Wilderness. But now she eliminated them because they did not harmonize with the total contents of the book.

She also pondered the use of the customary title "Selected Poems." Would another name be better? "Contemporary Fact," perhaps, "from Walt Whitman's 'the writer should vivify the contemporary fact'?" On the other hand, "of course, 'Selected Poems' has a certain cold dignity."[7] Elizabeth pointed out that "Selected Poems" had more of a specific reference, and Gwendolyn agreed that it had more self-possession.

Larger problems were also rather easily resolved in the ritual in which the editor and her staff played the role of an acute reader. Repeating to herself such expressions as "stripped," "definitive," "uncluttered," the poet rigorously culled the poems to be included. As a result, she left out several that had been highly praised by Harvey Curtis Webster in *The Nation*. Elizabeth, as ever refraining from insisting upon changes but rather exposing the author to the reactions of herself and her staff, responded: "At least two of us who have read the manuscript regret the omission of several poems mentioned by Professor Webster, and we think all of them should be included, since length *per se* is not a problem."[8] Gwendolyn gave the editor carte blanche to include whatever she thought was worth preserving.

Elizabeth stood firm, however, that certain poems should be retained, despite their inclusion in the Harper list of poems not up to the standard of the collection as a whole: "Matthew Cole"; "Riders to the Blood-Red Wrath" ("which has force but not clear direction"); several from "Shy Fish" ("which seem either trivial or not too worked out"); and "Theresa and the Oracle."[9]

Gwendolyn agreed immediately on the exclusion of "Theresa and the Oracle," a poem about a young woman questioning the nature of love; and "red and Rosalind," a poem about a woman's choosing the right dress to enhance her appearance for her lover. She liked "Matthew Cole, poor fellow, but please do as you wish about 'him,'" and felt the same way about "to a winter squirrel" (from "Shy Fish") but it was "too new and spare to weep over."

Her protest: "BUT ELIZABETH! The *only* thing I want to scream over is 'Riders to the Blood-red Wrath,' my salute to the Freedom Riders. I'm so old now that I know when I have written a good poem, and this is one of the best I've ever made. To have been maudlin, propagandistic, declamatory, or even vengeful would have been very easy. I avoided, *escaped* all that. I vigorously believe I made a poem that will stand *as* a poem *outside* the prevailing confusion as well as *inside* it (and *after* as well as *during*). Oh I do hope you will re-consider, will give it a chance."[10]

Elizabeth sent almost immediate reassurance: "Of course we will keep 'Riders to the Blood-red Wrath'—and anything else you feel strongly about. Do not hesitate to speak up, or make changes in the proof if you have second thoughts. I'm sorry if I sounded full of fire and conviction. The final contents of the book must be satisfactory to you."[11] The two women temporarily escaped further basic negotiations by enjoying together a visit to the Chicago Symphony on the occasion of Elizabeth's passing through. Gwendolyn felt "all troubles and irritations and frustrations temporarily just falling away from me."[12] Her spirits were also surging because of reprint requests by the *Chicago Sun-Times* and an inquiry from *Country Beautiful* about writing a Christmas poem for $450.

Soon poet and editor were working out a practical adjustment. The poems they had decided to include in the collection would fill 136 text pages, exceeding the 128 pages allotted to the book under the publisher's paging system. The page allotment could be increased only in units of 16 or 32 pages, and the extra pages would add to the retail price. Though quality and not profit would be the first consideration, Elizabeth asked Gwendolyn's frank response as to whether the omission of "the murder," "downtown vaudeville," "the ballad of the light-eyed little girl," "We Real Cool," "Pete at the Zoo," and "Leftist Orator" would be too great a sacrifice.

Gwendolyn was reluctant to withhold "We Real Cool" and "the ballad of the light-eyed little girl," poems that "always get an enthusiastic reaction from audiences and have found favor with many of the readers who have written to me. I hope you will leave these two in, for I have done things in them that I have done in no other poems and can not, because of their little peculiarities, do again." Instead, she authorized the removal of "the funeral," "the soft man," and "obituary for a living lady" (A Street in Bronzeville), and "my own sweet good" (Annie Allen).[13]

From then on, the process went rapidly. By May 12, 1963, the proofs had arrived for Gwendolyn: "After eighteen years, Proof Day is still an exhilarating 'holiday.' What I feel on that day is awe: at the drama of ideas and fancies actually achieving the Birth that 'cold print' allows." When bound copies reached her, she telegraphed her editor that it was "one of the most beautiful books that I have ever seen. I love the design the print the wide pages. I love everything about it. And I am ever so grateful to Harper for the obvious enthusiasm imagination and hard work that went into its production."[14] By October 9, the poet reported, "Booksellers here tell me that they have sold out, and have reordered copies."

Selected Poems was, on the whole, immediately well received. Carl Morse's review in the New York Times of October 6 recognized the volume's invitation to examine it as evidence of the poet's total achievement to date:

Gwendolyn Brooks does not exactly hymn 'at heaven's gates,' but she takes care of things below in a likable and knowing way. She has a warm heart, a cool head and practices the art of poetry with professional naturalness. Her ability to distinguish between what is sad and what is silly is unfailing, and she deals with race, love, war and other matters with uncommon common sense and a mellow humor that is as much a rarity as it is a relief. Sometimes she is overly sentimental or gets too involved with furniture and ephemera, but on the whole this selected volume, which collects three earlier books, otherwise out of print, and a group of new poems, is a pleasure to read.

In Poetry magazine for March 1964, Bruce Cutler admired Gwendolyn's wide-ranging technical resources, her ability to exploit the spoken language to make it work for her, and her existence as "a whole person behind her poems." He concluded, "She is one of the very best poets." Robert D. Spector observed in the *Saturday Review* of February 1, 1964: "Beneath the indignation in her *Selected Poems* . . . there is a special quality of tenderness. Most often that indignation is directed against the outrages of racism. But her power of anger and sympathy runs deeper than the color of her skin, responding to all victims of poverty and loneliness, whoever they may be. In the sweet, sad strains of her ballad and blues rhythms she exhibits technical proficiency; but it is in her ability to feel and make others feel that she truly reveals the essential qualities of a poet."

Ironically, the review that would make its author's name well known among blacks contained the jarring formulaic kind of judgment that often seemed prepackaged by the white liberal critical consensus. Louis Simpson, in the October 27, 1963, issue of the *New York Herald Tribune Book Week*, approached the *Selected Poems* last among several books he was reviewing, and began innocently enough: "Gwendolyn Brooks' 'Selected Poems' contains some lively pictures of Negro life." But his next statement offended many blacks: "I am not sure it is possible for a Negro to write well without making us aware he is a Negro; on the other hand, if being a Negro is the only subject, the writing is not important." Does "being a Negro" preclude being universal? Or is Negro life deprived of universality? At any rate, blacks took Simpson to task for the statement on numerous occasions during the 1960s. Of the many poems of recognized complexity, he selected only two for positive comment: "Jessie Mitchell's Mother," an ironic portrait of conflict between a light-skinned mother and a dark-skinned daughter, and "The Bean Eaters," a compassionate portrait of an older couple rising above the limitations of their lives through their memories of more pleasant times.

But on the whole the responses to *Selected Poems* gave the book credit for being illustrative of Gwendolyn's capacities. A total count of poems not included is somewhat misleading, since many of them were quite short, but it is suggestive. Of the 110 poems in her first three books, thirty-nine, or something over a third, were not included. Such omitted poems as "patent leather," "the soft man," the Hattie Scott group (*A Street in Bronzeville*), "my own sweet good," "beauty shoppe," "intermission" (*Annie Allen*), "Kid Bruin," "Pete at the Zoo," and "For Clarice—" are obviously light, and their type is easily and quickly enough represented by other poems. But a number of more complex poems also bit the dust: "the old-marrieds," "the birth in a narrow room," "downtown vaudeville," and "The Explorer." The overall result, however, is a more focused, more cohesive body of work, without any sacrifice of range and depth.

The essential framework of A *Street in Bronzeville,* for example, was a gallery of portraits by the speaker-observer as he moved through Bronzeville and into the larger world. The surviving poems from A *Street* preserve the journey, retain a distinct flavor of the street, and end on a strong note, with the sonnets and the complex longer poems "The Sundays of Satin-Legs Smith" and "Negro Hero." In terms of form, subject, or theme, the movement of the poems, for the most part, is from apparent simplicity and directness to obvious complexity and some indirection. The new arrangement, however, in leaving out the story of the speechless "old-marrieds," does plunge us more abruptly into the struggle for beauty against overwhelmingly debilitating circumstances by making "kitchenette building" the opening poem.

The first two poems in *Annie Allen,* "the birth in a narrow room" and "Maxie Allen," portraits of early childhood, lead gradually through the life of the imagination into that of disillusion. With the removal of these two from *Selected Poems,* the reader at once confronts "the parents" ("Clogged and soft and sloppy eyes"), who have sacrificed the richness of existence for sterile comfort. The overall design of the original volume is, however, retained, portraying the girlhood, young womanhood, and maturity of one who must extract her gains and losses not from the sensational but from the daily rounds and rhythms of existence. *Annie Allen* loses, all told, only nine poems—the smallest loss of any of the three books. The development of Annie from the status of the light-hearted and somewhat flippant girl and young woman of "After the baths and bowel-work . . . " and "Late Annie in her bower lay" or the first part of "The Anniad" into the pensive and spirited woman of "The Womanhood" poems is also clear in collection.

Selected Poems retains the original pattern of *The Bean Eaters,* including its introduction with "In Honor of David Anderson Brooks, My father," a poem that at once memorializes and celebrates the less sensational virtues that provide modern man with the possibility of the fulfilled life. I personally miss the omitted second poem, "The Explorer," which emphasized the philosophical concerns of the book—the hurdles of despair with which little humanity is threatened and its tendency to win or lose according to its capacity to remain adventurous or simply coherent in doing its part of the world's business. But I can see that to retain it would require eliminating the relatively trivial "My Little 'Bout-town Gal," which followed, and would then present the reader with two successive poems of intense despair, since "Strong Men, Riding Horses" would be its replacement. Perhaps another strategic choice for the *Selected Poems* was to end with "The Ballad of Rudolph Reed" instead of "In Emanuel's Nightmare: Another Coming of

Christ," which concluded the original volume. The choice seems essentially one between a tightly built poem emphasizing desperate courage
("Reed") and the more quietly moving poem emphasizing man's littleness
and Christ's anguished compassion. The tendency in the original and the
collection is toward some sense of possibility and some gleam of the
unfulfilled promise of mankind, and the selection retains the best poems of
the original volume.

Selected Poems has the kind of organization and integrity that afford a fair
examination of Gwendolyn's achievement up to the early 1960s. Although
the new poems in the collection do not measurably increase her stature,
neither do they detract from it. Her high rank among contemporary American poets remains obvious. In the words of the Rocky Mountain Herald,
September 21, 1963, Gwendolyn's poetry evidences the "life-long commitment to the whole welter of experience that distinguishes the true poet from
the intellectualoid."

In a feature story in the Chicago Daily News of September 28, 1963,
Gwendolyn emphasized the writer's concern with a self other than that of
the artist:

I don't like to think of myself as a poet. I think of myself as the commonest kind of
human being there can be—who likes to write poetry. I think it would be terrible
and would kill your efforts if you were aware of yourself as a "poet."
    Maybe I would have done better as a poet if I didn't think that nothing that I do
is more important than being a mother, taking care of my husband, and getting a
meal together. Living is the most important thing to do, and poetry comes after
that. That's how I feel.

    As the article's headnote stated, "Gwendolyn Brooks is at least two
women."

One is the poet whose slim volumes offer lovely poems of a deceptive simplicity.
This is Miss Brooks, the Pulitzer Prize–winner, the champion of causes, the writer.
This is the woman who claims the quiet daylight moments when her husband is at
work and her daughter is in school, to bend over the dining room table to work on
an idea, a right word, a rhythm.
    The other woman is the wife of Henry Blakely, 46, an insurance adjuster, and
the mother of Henry Jr., 22, a Marine stationed in Hawaii, and of Nora, 9. Mrs.
Blakely is a good neighbor, worries over her food budget, nudges Nora to eat
properly, sees that her husband has enough white shirts to last the week.
    The two halves meld in her poetry. The mother and the wife are never apart
from the poet in the modest frame South Side home on Evans Avenue.

In giving a glimpse of the poetic process, Gwendolyn begins by describing an experience available to "the commonest kind of human being there can be . . .

cooking some chitterlings one winter day two years ago when I noticed a squirrel outside my kitchen window. It was natural for me, I suppose, to try to think about how he felt about life. He scurried up the back stairs and down, across the yard, and then up a tree.

I worried about him, out there in the cold, but then dismissed the worry with, "Well, you're as God made you." Just the stray thought not related to anything. No, that's not entirely right. I related it to me. Here was I, in a nice warm kitchen and I didn't have to scurry around and look for food in the winter. I thought how much luckier I was than the squirrel.

Well, that's the kind of material a poor poet has to work with. What we observe or experience—such plain material—and make our own.

That was two years ago. That night I jotted down three lines to save the thought about the squirrel. I find it valuable to keep notebooks for these ideas—as I grow older, my memory gets worse and worse. So the notebooks serve as a larder.

Instead of writing about herself, the poet chose as her subject a young woman in "a poor shabby kitchen" and named her Merdice to give the poem a Negro flavor. "A lot of Negro girls have names ending in d-i-c-e. And Mer seemed to have an unfortunate deprived sound to it for me. It suggested something murdered. So I began: 'Merdice can cook. Merdice / Of murdered heart and docked sarcastic [soul] Merdice . . . . '" Gwendolyn wanted to "get the idea into it that something had happened to her, to her inner life, something outside of her had murdered a part of her soul. 'Merdice . . . Merdice . . . murdered . . . Merdice.' That's the chorus of that line, the sound I wanted." Other explanations of diction follow, with emphasis on their relationship to the character of Merdice. She "of docked sarcastic soul" who "cooked guts; and sits in gas," confronting the world with the "shellac of her look," was also "a bolted nomad"—a person who retains spirit and would like to enjoy "the beautiful wildness of life." But she is "bolted by her stove, by her existence." The squirrel, whatever his other handicaps, has what Merdice does not have—"the enjoyment of his gypsy life."

Gwendolyn also explained her new attraction to mixing "long [lines] with rather short ones that get an idea across with a sudden impact. The longer line of the shawl and the coal—I could have made another stanza of it, but I like the contrast of the blunt opening phrases with the long swinging sound." She returned to the human element. "This is a little poem, nothing crucial about it. I like it because it has lots of reality and is rather delicately done. It has earthiness and meat to it. It makes its point without being an outright protest. I see in it a poor young woman of color who can find no way out of her slum misery. But she still has some imagination, some ability to enjoy life if only she was free."

The *Chicago Daily News* carried the full text of "To a Winter Squirrel":

That is the way God made you.
And what is wrong with it? Why, nothing.
Except that you are cold and cannot cook.
Merdice can cook. Merdice
Of murdered heart and docked sarcastic soul.
Merdice
The bolted nomad, on a winter noon
Cooks guts; and sits in gas. (She has no shawl, her landlord has no coal.)
You out beyond the shellac of her look
And of her sill!
She envies you your fury
Buffoonery
That enfolds your silver skill.
She thinks you are a mountain and a star, unbaffleable;
With sentient twitch and scurry.

Slightly altered in punctuation and capitalization, and printed in three stanzas, "To a Winter Squirrel," having been excluded from the *Selected Poems*, would appear in *In the Mecca* (1968), whose title poem Gwendolyn was now struggling with.

The article "At least two women" helped Chicago sales of *Selected Poems* and placed beside the poetry a well-projected personality. Sales at the *Sun-Times* Book and Author Luncheon went briskly, and in the central district of Chicago, Gwendolyn autographed copies for sale. Robert Cromie of the *Chicago Tribune* was soon reporting that the book was virtually out of stock in Chicago. Like all of Gwendolyn's earlier volumes, *Selected Poems* was justifying itself financially as well as critically.[15] A *Street in Bronzeville* had sold the greatest number of copies, 4,762, with 538 remaindered, but now it was out of print. Still in print, *Bronzeville Boys and Girls* had sold 4,236 copies, and *The Bean Eaters* had achieved sales and disposals of 1,686 copies. *Annie Allen*, out of print, had sold or disposed of 2,841 copies, with 378 remaindered, and the novel *Maud Martha*, which would be reissued through a paperback reprint publisher, had sold 3,221 copies, with 1,932 remaindered.

The talent Gwendolyn revealed in the *Daily News* article for articulating the functioning machinery of a poem would soon stand her in good stead in the classroom. Mirron Alexandroff, president of Columbia College, which specialized in the communication arts, asked her to conduct a poetry workshop at the college. "Do anything you want with it," Gwendolyn reports him saying bravely. "Take it outdoors. Take it to a restaurant—run it in a restaurant, a coffee shop. Do absolutely anything you want with it. Anything!"[16]

The "Literary Notes" column of the *Chicago Daily News* of October 26, 1963, was headed: "Miss Brooks to Teach at Last." It continued: "Gwendolyn Brooks, Pulitzer Prize–winning poet and a truly great Chicagoan, has agreed to teach at Columbia College, 207 S. Wabash Avenue. Asked why she never taught before, she answered: 'Because no one ever asked me before . . . . I guess because I have three strikes on me. I am a woman. I am a Negro. And I have no college degree.' " Commented the writer of the column, "None of these reasons is big enough, except in the minds of small men." As gracious as the column is, it is also typical of the unrealism with which whites approached the impact of racial discrimination, as implied by the question of why she had not taught before. Institutional racism, against which the blacks of the 1960s would soon be reacting, had, of course, done the dirty work, while the individual liberal or bigot might be unaware that employment as a teacher had been denied to a writer who was often called upon to judge writing in the city's literary contests.

The direct contact with students through the creative medium was most rewarding to Gwendolyn, especially as the audience was young and she was free to experiment. On the other hand, the expectations of the classroom were different from those of an audience awaiting the reading of her own poetry, and she was not yet beyond attacks of shyness. Entering the classroom in a new blue suit, she felt a strong impulse to retreat immediately from the twenty-one students who awaited "the knowledge, the magic, the definitions that I was bringing them surely." But she soon found herself enjoying the work and earning a reputation as a good teacher.

Although a teacher cannot create a poet, Gwendolyn set specific goals to be achieved. She could make clear certain matters of technique and form, but more important, "a teacher can oblige the writing student to write." Her chief requirement in this poetry workshop, and in subsequent ones, was the writing of twenty poems, with ten being in prescribed forms. She instructed the students in Shakespearian and Petrarchan sonnets (the Spenserian being optional), ballads, blank verse, free verse, the Japanese haiku and tanka, the verse play, the "Beat" poem, and the heroic couplet. The students read a good deal of new and old poetry, listened to poetry record-ings, and attempted to write musically ("write a poem—let the music use your fingers in ITS behalf"). There were also "panel discussions, debates, round-robin response to controversial 'creativity'-based questions, verse play enactments, book reviews as opposed to book *reports*, one-page very personal critiques on poets and their poetry, and poetry-trade, or 'revision-verse' (students write, then trade their poems with their neighbors in class for signed criticisms)."[17]

In teaching fiction writing, she required the composition of short stories, or a novella, or the beginning of a novel. When she taught twen-tieth-century poetry and short story at Elmhurst College, required reading included a fifteen-chapter book of twentieth-century criticism. She held firmly to the requirement despite the students' indignation and pleas for modification. All students met the challenge and, she felt, evinced enthusi-asm.

A variety of devices were used in the classroom for exacting creative response, provoking thinking, and broadening exposure to literature, in-cluding French, German, Italian, and Eastern literature in translation, and also black and Jewish literature—areas rare until recently in standard texts. In the later 1960s Gwendolyn would bring cultural and racial ferment into the classroom by putting before the students challenging statements from such blacks as Larry Neal, A.B. Spellman, Lerone Bennett, and Hoyt Fuller. Sometimes the issue was art itself: Alain Robbe-Grillet's "Nothing is as fatal to literature as a concern with 'saying something.' The world is neither significant nor absurd. IT IS—quite simply." Gwendolyn also raised the basic issue: " 'What IS art?' (Oh boy!)"

During her years as a teacher, Gwendolyn entered into the spirit of the young, preparing her for the more intense encounters of the later 1960s and helping her to lose her shyness. At the same time, she was struggling to build the 2,000-line poem "In the Mecca" out of her youthful, haunting, and obsessed experiences in the actual Mecca Building slum. The poem would eventually have both male and female versions of Merdice of "To a Winter Squirrel." In her mind, she returned to places where she had lived in which dreams were hard to keep, and she saw the glazed look of people hiding behind their eyes, a look she had at times encountered on Forty-third Street—people masked in their attempts to sustain spirit amidst misery; people who could not bear the intimacy of the direct gaze.[18] In previous works, a single theme had run through several poems—certain poems representing the street in Bronzeville, groups of sonnets, and poems in *The*

Bean Eaters, for example. But she had not yet tried to sustain a theme throughout a 2,000-line poem, and at this point only the title remained firm.

An assignment from *Ebony* magazine to write a poem for its special Emancipation issue allowed Gwendolyn to express the feelings she shared with other blacks toward what was beginning to be called the "Negro Revolution." Lerone Bennett, Jr., in *Confrontation: Black and White*, astutely analyzed its growth and emergence from stages of the Freedom Movement—sit-ins, freedom rides, church bombings, riots, and marches—which forced "a realignment in Negro leadership circles and this realignment intensified the triple confrontation which in turn forced a further realignment in the Negro community."

Bennett felt that the birth of the movement was ultimately connected with blacks' new sense of the possible, brought about by the Supreme Court decision against segregation in education in 1954.[19] His comments in both *Before the Mayflower* (revised edition) and *Confrontation* point up the collision between spiraling expectations and spiraling frustrations. The southern struggle seemed to have climaxed in the march on Washington, D.C., in August 1963, but its fervor was soon cooled. In the first months of 1963, Bennett points out, Negro unemployment was at the 1930s Depression level, and Negro ghettoes were "spreading like hot lava in every metropolitan area." Negro schools, despite the Supreme Court, existed "separate and transparently unequal." The "revolution" was moving toward explosion in the large northern cities, including Chicago, the most Jim-Crow city in the country.

Gwendolyn had never put poetry or art above the battle and had always participated in changes within the community. On June 12, 1963, the Mississippi civil rights leader Medgar Evers was gunned down outside his home; she would later put into a poem some of his spirit and the decisiveness with which he met the terror of his experiences. There would be poems on Malcolm X and Martin Luther King. And there would be one regarding the November 22, 1963, assassination of President John Fitzgerald Kennedy, whom she had met and who had symbolized for blacks the beam of hope.

For now, Gwendolyn looked the frustrations in the face and held to a somewhat restrained feeling of hope. She wrote for *Ebony* the following lines, entitled "The Sight of the Horizon":

> After such mocks—what Motive?
> What certain Spur? (to find

Among all nervous rebels that bewitch
The melancholy capitals of the mind.)

The Sight of the Horizon.
Possession of our breath:
Possession of our vagrant vision: even
The legendary mammoth of our death.

We seek no clue of green.
We seek a Garden: trees,
the light, the cry, the conscience of the grass.
In this most sociable of all centuries.

We seek informal sun.
A harvest of hurrah.
We seek our center and our radius.
Profound redemption. And America.

The September 1963 issue of *Ebony* carrying the poem would share space with a new catastrophe, which seemed a direct defiance of the hopes raised by the 250,000-strong march on Washington, D.C., on August 28: On September 15, persons unknown bombed the Sixteenth Street Baptist Church in Birmingham, Alabama, killing four young Negro girls. On October 22, 225,000 students boycotted Chicago public schools in a Freedom Day protest of de facto segregation. At this point, Gwendolyn could not so easily say, as she had in 1961, that many days went by without her thinking of race. Her consciousness reflected still the kind of guarded hopefulness and alert pride other blacks were evincing. In the spring of 1962 the Burnside Elementary School at 650 East Ninety-first Place had honored Gwendolyn at an assembly that presented a program of her poetry and of the poems of those pupils who had written under her inspiration. The pupils dedicated the entire program to her. Spontaneously she had announced two awards totaling over $200 for poetry contests to be held at the Burnside and Cornell schools. At the end of the contests, during January 1964, she took note of the talk of freedom in the air, which she found exhilarating. She spoke again of the inspiration provided by the surge toward freedom on the African continent. For publication by *Muhammad Speaks* she selected "Negro Hero," written during World War II to tell the story of Dorie Miller, as a poem "which perhaps best typifies the current model and outlook of black America." The Negro became a hero after defying restriction to kitchen duties in the naval service. The last stanza reads:

Naturally, the important thing is, I helped to save them, them
and a part of their democracy.

Even if I had to kick their law into their teeth in order to
        do that for them.
And I am feeling well and settled in myself because I believe
        it was a good job,
Despite this possible horror: that they might prefer the
Preservation of their law in all its sick dignity and their
        knives
To the continuation of their creed
And their lives.

One of the student contestants, Lillian Myrick, gave a youthful version
of the state of matters:

We marched on Washington for our rights.
We walked for hours, days and nights.
Do you know all men are created equal?
Just because our skin is brown or black,
No more freedom must we lack.
Give me liberty or give me death!
To take my freedom is to take my breath. [20]

But Gwendolyn's consciousness also reflected the apprehensiveness that
blacks, under integrationist compulsions, felt about whites' responses to
unattractive black images. In reviewing Richard Wright's novel *Lawd Today,*
she was careful to put raw images of black life into proper perspective:
" 'Lawd Today,' written before 'Native Son,' is an achingly straight represen-
tation of *a* kind of life. It will not be fair to say 'So that is the way Negroes
live. It will not be fair, on the other hand, to insist defensively that Negroes
like the Jake Jackson here—wife-beater, policy-player, prostitute-client,
prejudice-rider, hair-pamperer—can nowhere be found. People like Jake are
not in the black majority but they do exist."

She explained further that "Wright would have been quick to agree that
all Negroes do not react in this way—just as *all* Irish, Hindus, Puerto Ricans,
Jews do not react in this way. But he was not writing about Ralph Bunche.
He was not featuring Jackie Robinson or Martin Luther King or George
Washington Carver or John H. Johnson, all of whom had beginnings other
than kindly but managed to subdue their tigers. He was interested—at the
time—in giving you one day from the life of what is surely one of nature's
rawest creatures." [21] Then she got on with a paragraph of incisive literary
comments.

Her consciousness was still struggling with balancing the tensions of
utter black misery against the dreams of black humanity in the long poem

she was calling "In the Mecca." With the old feeling that nothing beats a try but a failure, she applied for a third Guggenheim Fellowship to buy time for concentrated work. The Guggenheim Foundation requested a commendation from Elizabeth Lawrence and routinely pointed out that a third Guggenheim was rarely given. The case had to be one of unusual merit.

Elizabeth emphasized the genuineness of Gwendolyn's poetic talent, as standing for saneness and clarity in a time of trouble. The inevitable limitations affecting her talents derived, Elizabeth felt, from her being a Negro and writing of a special world. But she had found few artists who were able to overcome personal limitations of one kind or another. Gwendolyn "succeeds rather better than most in celebrating the human condition above the Negro or special condition." The rest of Elizabeth's recommendation expressed the hope that a financial grant would allow Gwendolyn to develop the poem "In the Mecca," which had "absorbed her for a long time."[22]

Gwendolyn did not get the third Guggenheim but did find some financial release through other awards and activities. She reviewed. She taught. She received the $100 Robert F. Ferguson Memorial Prize for *Selected Poems* from the Friends of Literature at their annual awards dinner. On May 22, 1964, at a dinner at the Sheraton Chicago Hotel, she received the Thurmond L. Monsen Award of $500 for the same work. In June, Columbia College conferred upon her an honorary doctoral degree, the first of a stream of such recognitions. While recompense in these forms could not produce the leisure she needed, it gave some relief from immediate financial pressures and it lifted her spirit.

Something of the old economic dispensations and something of the new appeared on her total calendar of events for 1964. Langston Hughes put together a program for the British Broadcasting Corporation entitled "Negro Poetry Today," including Gwendolyn, Margaret Danner, Samuel Allen, and a variety of other poets. The BBC accepted her recordings of "The Chicago *Defender* Sends a Man to Little Rock" and "We Real Cool," and asked permission to use "kitchenette building"—seemingly on some future occasion. For all poems they were paying "a small fee . . . about $30.00." Gwendolyn had speaking engagements at Wisconsin State College, Stevens Point, on July 23, at the University of California on August 6 and 10, and at Elmhurst College on December 7. More immediately, she was to be one of six guest lecturers at Northwestern University on the "Interpretation of Mid-Century American Writers."

The California engagement would have the most all-around significance. But she saw still another local engagement as an extremely rich opportunity: Henry Rago of *Poetry* magazine had asked her to be "one of five poets of honor to read at this year's Poetry Day benefit." The affair was regarded in Chicago as the most glamorous literary event of the year, and each participating poet received an honorarium of $500. In the preceding year, the readers had been Robert Lowell, Stanley Kunitz, Richard Wilbur, J. V. Cunningham, and Karl Shapiro. Each poet would have some routine functions the day before the reading and for the actual occasion would read for twenty minutes at Orchestra Hall before an expected audience of 2,000. Immediately following the program was a black-tie buffet in honor of the poets at the Casino Club.

Before Poetry Day, however, came President Lyndon B. Johnson's Scholars' Reception at the White House, during which unresolved tensions of Gwendolyn's personality asserted themselves, first in the matter of dress: "I went, beautifully gowned in blue chiffon: for surely, I fancied, White House guests should don their 'best.' I arrived to find all the other ladies in knits, tweeds, linen." The poet was seated between Ogden Nash and Alfred Knopf, whose company had had first chance at publishing her first poems. Gwendolyn introduced herself to Thurgood Marshall, who appeared somewhat cool and passed her on to Lady Bird Johnson, whom she was later to describe as a "wonderfully warm and essentially gracious human being." Then she stood "THAT CLOSE!—to the thirty-sixth president of the United States." But she became "tongue-tied when he directed at me his handsome smile; I never said a word."[23]

Something of Gwendolyn's continued reserve had been noticed a bit before her trip, at the party of a literary agent. Lois Bauer reported in the *Chicago American* of June 3 that "she stood in the same spot on which she stood when she arrived. The people came to her. As she spoke, with sometimes a secret smile in her eyes and sometimes a sadness, we were reminded of this bit from her poetry: 'And if sun comes how shall we greet him? Shall we not dread him after so lengthy a session with the shade?' "[24] Gwendolyn's secret smile, earlier observed by Frank London Brown in "Chicago's Great Lady of Poetry," seemed to suggest her awareness of comedy peeping into the most prestigious human relations. But at the White House she was apparently sufficiently nonplussed to require a subsequent self-lecture. "But *pshaw!* as my mother used to say and says, I had long before met John F. Kennedy and had pumped his hand when he was a mere *senator*. He was the speaker for the *Chicago Daily News* Silver Knight Awards. I was one of the judges and hence was permitted to share the stage with him."[25]

Of her untimely withdrawal from the White House reception, she said: "I made another mistake. I left. I was the first to leave! I was told later, by kind friends, that this was unforgivable. Nobody leaves, said my post-advisors, before the presidential party . . . . I left because at a certain moment in social proceedings I am on FIRE to leave; I have a leaving-FIT."[26] Nonetheless, the trip was one of the most pleasant, and adventurous, functions she experienced in her now almost routine role as cultural arbiter.

In hindsight, it is clear that at this time vast psychic changes were taking place within blacks and within the arts and artists representing them. On the positive side were the far-reaching provisions of the Civil Rights Act of 1964. On the negative side was the mood of stark despair "moving Negro America" since, despite the demonstrations of 1963, despite King and Kennedy, despite pain and bloodshed and pious statements, little had changed. During the Civil Rights debates the Ku Klux Klan recovered its leadership from the White Citizens Councils—once known as the uptown Klan.[27] The North was the scene of the "white backlash." And despite the Civil Rights Act, southern senators "used the national arena as a sounding board for anti-Negro propaganda" in their filibustering. "As a result of these events and others of similar tone and texture, a certain hope died in the Negro ghetto. Tangible proof of this was the rise of a new cadre of leaders who repudiated the tactics of the established civil rights organizations and called for radical new departures. These leaders, who were in the forefront of the Northern school boycotts and demonstrations, were more political and less religious, more cynical and less conciliatory. They called for generalized expressions of disgust aimed at the whole white community—they called, in fact, for massive civil disobedience movements."[28] James Baldwin's *The Fire Next Time* (1963) is a kind of impassioned announcement of a crisis in the relations between the white liberal consensus and blacks. Writers and other artists would have to deal with the crisis, since white approval had always been essential for recognition of the black arts.

Foreshadowing events came to Gwendolyn quietly enough. William Targ, senior editor at Putnam's, wrote to express his company's interest in publishing her autobiography. He felt that a very large number of readers would be interested in the story of her childhood and youth, her early days in Chicago, her "views and observations," her presentations of family and friends and responses to the life around her.[29] Gwendolyn had already had in mind doing her autobiography for Harper and sounded out Elizabeth's opinion.

Elizabeth felt that Harper would most certainly be interested in such a book. Incorrectly, she remembered that Gwendolyn had grown up "partly outside of Chicago, in a community where there were few Negroes" and the fact that her life would not, therefore, be a Chicago story exclusively would give a fresh perpsective. The editor had always assumed that *Maud Martha* was partly a "revelation" of the poet, and it would be interesting to learn more about her as a girl and the worlds she grew up in.

Although Gwendolyn had, of course, grown up entirely in Chicago, after being born in her mother's hometown, Topeka, the locale was incidental at this point; Harper's interest in the work meant that life was again asserting itself as possibility. But Elizabeth's next paragraph came as something of a bombshell:

Regretfully I shall not be with Harper when your next book is published. I shall be retiring the end of September to live in Connecticut . . . . But I shall keep watch from a distance, and certainly I expect to keep in touch with author-friends like you who have made my years in publishing pure (well, almost) joy.

Gene Young, a very charming and able young woman, will succeed me as your editor. She doesn't profess to know a lot about poetry but that will not be necessary, as you do. She knows good writing and she knows publishing. And there is Frances Lindley, whom you met in Washington, who is not an editor but is passionately fond of poetry and one of your long-time admirers. You will be in good hands.[30]

Elizabeth would leave at the end of September, and would continue to have a hand in Harper & Row's affairs when needed.

Elizabeth had been Gwendolyn's editor for twenty years, the whole of her book-publishing life. Gwendolyn wrote in response:

When I read your letter, I felt weak and old.

What a wonderful friend and editor you have been to me. You have helped me and/or sympathized with me in "crises." You have hinted me off the diving board when I seemed determined to drown myself. You have been loyal to me and have maintained faith in my potential ability. You have made each of my books a little work of art, with I believe, not a single error in the twenty years of our association. It is not strange, therefore, that I regard your departure with bleakness and a sense of personal loss.

My best wishes to you in the new life. My best wishes to you for always.

With real love and respect, with gratitude—

Gwendolyn[31]

The poet was to have friendly and constructive relations with her two succeeding editors, Genevieve Young and Ann Harris. But Elizabeth, as the creative engineer of her publishing career, was of both immediate and long-range significance. Elizabeth was the older woman and one of a quite worldy sophistication about the practicalities of life and the vast business world. The correspondence between the two women shows the impact of this sophistication upon their relations. Both women were at times strategic in their use of it. Elizabeth could confidently give firm suggestions as the person initiating the always-struggling author into the ins and outs of bookmaking and the publishing world. On the other hand, Gwendolyn, though aware that she was a stranger in such a world, had faced maturely the essential challenges of life and had developed herself as artist and as resident of another complicated world. Gwendolyn could appear occasionally as the sprightly youth appealing to the adult, or rebuking the adult somewhat for seeming inconsistent. ("Oh I do hope you will reconsider, will give it a chance.") On the other hand, she was also the gracious woman asserting freely the adult imperative. Such roles carried the women through relations that were not without friction but always productive.

Inescapably, however, despite the integrationist script from which both read their lines, the two represented black and white worlds, and the structure of their relationship would later arouse in Gwendolyn ambivalence. Thankful for having been prevented from disastrous plunges, she would still wonder whether this young chicken–mother hen relationship had not persisted too long. Such a response would mean also that she had effected a different relationship with the white liberal climate.

The second foreshadowing of change was the University of California–sponsored Conference on the Negro Writer in the United States at the Monterey Peninsula's Asilomar Conference Center, August 5-9, 1964, in which Gwendolyn, accompanied by her daughter Nora, participated.[32] *Newsweek* magazine stated: "Now, in the summer of 1964, the subject of the Negro writer in America has explosive and far-reaching implications; and an occasion which promises to bring together such participants as Saunders Redding, Arna Bontemps, LeRoi Jones, Horace Clayton, Harvey Swados, James Baldwin, Ralph Ellison, Gwendolyn Brooks, and Nat Hentoff is an important event in our cultural life." Hoyt W. Fuller saw the gathering as "the most impressive array of Negro talent ever assembled for a writers' conference," but he also reported skepticism about Ralph Ellison's reasons for being absent and about the apparent failure to invite such writers as John A. Williams, John Oliver Killens, Langston Hughes, and Louis Lomax.

Besides the invited writers, who were to act as faculty, the gathering consisted of approximately 200 writers, teachers, social workers, students, housewives, artists, and intellectuals. The setting was scenic and rustic: ponderosa pines and cypresses beside the Pacific Ocean, and housing of a few dozen redwood lodges. Directing the conference was Herbert Hill, a man of liberal intellectual and cultural leanings, the editor of the anthology of black writing *Soon, One Morning,* and the NAACP's white secretary for labor.

The conference enlarged Gwendolyn's circle of friends. She and Nora met the poet Sarah Webster Fabio, who took the group in her car on a "lovely trip" to Berkeley to have lunch.

The gathering at the conference represented various viewpoints, which made for tension and ferment. Kenneth Rexroth found that off the platform teachers were angered by the way textbooks were being desegregated: "the castration of Negro history; the new friend who . . . entered the circle of Dick, Sally, Jane, Fluff, Toodles . . . a little light-brown Sambo with his middle-class father, his middle-class mother and his middle-class dog. Poor little guy, they didn't even have the decency to give him a liver-spotted hound, just another Scotty." Young radicals with Afro hair styles and allegiance to LeRoi Jones censured the affair as "an Uncle Tom show" concocted by "white devils," and were themselves referred to as the Mau Mau by the more temperate. "The Freedom Now people objected to the lack of program. The more orthodox Marxists objected even more to lack of program, fuzziness of thinking, and racialism. Certainly, there was no better way to get a big hand from the mixed audience than to give whitey a verbal kicking around. Everytime anybody said, 'I hate all white men,' all the white women in the audience applauded vociferously."

Scattered about the audience were more restrained and composed young people looking on thoughtfully. Rexroth felt that they asked the most "trenchant" questions and "deflated demogogy." They were there from the dangerous southern integration activities, whereas, according to Rexroth, none of the highly militant northerners lived either in the recently rioting Harlem or in any other Negro ghetto. They tended to reject gratuitous racial friction. When a teen-age white boy who had somehow come all the way from West Virginia questioned why he, who only wanted to help, must confront Negro hostility, a group of blacks rose to combat him, but "a startlingly beautiful young woman fresh from the Mississippi Wars . . . stood up, and in language as eloquent as any heard at the conference, embraced the boy, chided his detractors, and wished, in behalf of all her beleaguered colleagues on the Southern battlefields, that there were a few hundred Mississippians like that brave boy who only 'wanted to help.' " The racial tensions were further expressed by a deeply troubled white Chicago teacher who had read the fiery James Baldwin and had heard LeRoi Jones. She could not understand the alienation from middle-class values evidenced by Negro families in the huge Chicago public housing buildings: "They write on the walls and urinate in the hallways."

Gwendolyn was also part of an occasion heated up by individual encounters. Robert Bone, the critic, offended Kenneth Rexroth, who among other things shouted back some unprintable expressions. And the audience was uneasy with individual black youths who had expressed concern as to what they should write about, since they were products of neither the South nor the ghetto.

The civil rights movement, integration, and the relations between blacks and the white liberal consensus thus made themselves felt at the conference. LeRoi Jones provided further radical provocation by accusing critics of sterility and contending that "the Negro writer has to make an intentional break from the mainstream." In disagreement with older writers, particularly with Saunders Redding's orientation toward the mainstream, "he spoke with furious feeling and violent volubility, sweeping much of the audience—white and Negro—before him. In the hipster argot that has become his platform manner, he said: 'Just by being black, the Negro is a committed nonconformist. You don't have to be weird. Man, you are black and in America that's weird.' Attacking the 'white power structure,' he said: 'They say one day there will be a Negro President of the United States. Well, I say who would want to be President of the United States? Like who wants to be a mass murderer?' " *Newsweek* regretted the absence of "our two most important Negro writers—Ellison and Baldwin," who would probably have pushed the discussion in a more strictly literary direction. As it was, Jones "carried the day," and only James Baldwin's substitute, Ossie Davis, was able to argue the necessity of protest and, at the same time, provide a powerful healing experience for the audience. But *Newsweek* also allowed that: "literature had come to seem—amidst the emotional storm of the American dilemma—a matter of secondary and contingent importance."

Still, there were intense literary moments, and the conference sessions themselves, despite the ferment, flowed smoothly. The reminiscences of Horace Cayton, Arna Bontemps, and Saunders Redding regarding the late Richard Wright brought quiet reflection. Bontemps's "spell-binding" discussion of Jean Toomer and the Harlem Renaissance brought strong response from all wings of the audience but particularly from the very militant and the hostile. When he finished, he was confronted with an overwhelming number of hands. The audience wanted to know more about the legendary personalities of the Harlem Renaissance and to discuss the "spiritual and literary problems" of Jean Toomer who, after a period of religious and mystical search, had renounced allegiance to conventional concepts of race. Probably correctly, Rexroth stated that most of the audience had never heard of Toomer but now wanted to hear more.

Gwendolyn and LeRoi Jones provided the third intensely literary moment. There was something of a foreshadowing of the 1967 Fisk Conference in their sharing a platform, though it was one still carrying many of the assumptions of the white liberal American mythology of art. The first part of their program was pleasant. "Gwendolyn Brooks's encores were a revelation to the whites in the audience. People obviously knew her work by heart, and called again and again for one favorite poem after another." The audience was equally attentive to Jones. But the audience also sensed the possibility of a confrontation, since Gwendolyn's "The Sundays of Satin-Legs Smith" had been held up by critic J. Saunders Redding as the way to write poetry, in contrast to Jones's method. In *Home* (1936), Jones had spoken bluntly but somewhat respectfully of Gwendolyn's poem "The Chicago *Defender* Sends a Man to Little Rock" in an essay review entitled "A Dark Bag": "Gwendolyn Brooks, the Pulitzer Prize-winner, who is capable of lyrical preciseness like, 'The blowing of clear wind in your gay hair; / Love changeful in you (like a music, or / Like a sweet mournfulness, or like a dance, / Or like the tender struggle of a fan),' is also capable, under Mr. Bontemps' permissive editorial hand of dumbness like, 'the loveliest lynchee was our Lord.' " (Gwendolyn herself would later disavow the image.)

On the platform, the two poets were respectfully deferent to each other until Gwendolyn, suddenly responding to unfair attacks upon Jones, found herself rising to his defense and proclaiming, "He is a master of language." She found Jones looking at her strangely.[33]

Despite this spontaneous sense of oneness with the young man who had turned away from the mainstream, Gwendolyn's own turning would not take on tangibility until a few more years had passed. Not yet would she say, as Jay Robert Nash put it:

Goodbye social teas. Goodbye aesthetic podiums. Goodbye tokenism awards. Goodbye fair-skinned writers.
Goodbye, goodbye.[34]

8

Changes

During the 1960s the "Negro Civil Rights Revolution" interacted painfully with a stubborn and unyielding racism that seemed to require blacks to develop resources from within if they were to stand upon the earth as men and women. This interaction wrought far-reaching psychic changes in most American blacks—Gwendolyn and other artists, of course, included. One "moderate" black stated that the radical black movement of the 1960s did more to create wholeness within blacks than all efforts made during the preceding sixty years, although she herself felt that her life was so fundamentally intertwined with those of whites that she would have to leave the country if blacks decreed an absolute separatism.

Lerone Bennett, Jr., historian, observer, and participant in the social scene, has rendered a complex, blow-by-blow analysis of developments in such books as *Before the Mayflower* (the latter part of the revised edition, 1964), *The Negro Mood* (1964), and *Confrontation: Black and White* (1965). In them he points out that the developments of the 1960s were culminations of earlier ones, and he intricately analyzes crucial turning points. By 1964 the Freedom Movement was losing much of its polite, middle-class character, as impatient black masses forced even conservative leaders to take more extreme stands, dramatizing the separateness of the interests of American blacks and whites—in Bennett's phrase, "the broken community." In light of the revolutionary structural changes required for America to deal with racism and with blacks' misery and despair, many blacks began to feel that whites either wanted more inclusion of blacks in defective existing structures or would make merely ritualistic concessions. Hence the white liberals, whose indulgent nod had been crucial for the welfare of blacks and the progress of black artists since the days of slavery, became irrelevant.

Brilliantly, James Baldwin—in such works as *Notes of a Native Son* (1955), *Nobody Knows My Name* (1961), *Another Country* (1962), *The Fire Next Time* (1963), and *Blues for Mr. Charlie* (1964)—dramatized the sterility of white liberalism and of an America unable to achieve identity because of its inability to confront the past. Certain of his phrases voiced so well the inarticulate responses of others that they seemed made to order for slogans. *The Fire Next Time* ends with a ringing challenge to white liberals to join with blacks to save America or to face, in the words of a slave, "the fire next time." His expression "Who wants to be integrated into a burning house?" found echoes in the hearts of many.

Malcolm X, with his street background and an identity achieved through the Muslim leader Elijah Muhammed, also spoke for the masses, breaking through with a new language and a way of thinking that cut shams to ribbons. He exposed the moral bewilderment imposed by such popular expressions as "second-class citizenship" by pointing out that one either was or was not a citizen. He created an electrifying shock of recognition by declaring that he (and, by implication, other blacks) was not a part of the American Dream but of the American nightmare.

Malcolm thus provided steps for a liberation of thinking. In 1903 W.E.B. DuBois had used the term double-consciousness to describe blacks' awareness of the unintegrated existence of the self as Negro and the self as American, the result being two warring dark selves in one dark body locked into a world that yielded no true self-consciousness, no identity. The new direction of the 1960s aspired to a single black consciousness. Chaotic at first, then crystallizing as the decade wore on and as assassinations and other horrors grew apace on the American scene, nationalistic developments posed for the artist new choices of allegiance and new sources of health.

Inspiration from the Freedom movement is already firmly evident in the statements of some of the writers participating in the April 1965 symposium of the *Negro Digest*, who addressed the following question: "What is the task of the Negro writer concerned with creating a work of art in a segregated society and how does his task differ from that of the white writer—if it differs at all?" Gwendolyn (and others) responded with old formulations: "The task of the Negro writer in any sort of society is the task of every writer: to clarify his interior and to deliver, thoroughly and only, the 'messages' urged by that clarity." Her language would retain pretty much intact the older formulations until very late in the 1960s. In her summer 1967 interview with Paul Angle, for example, she posed for herself the following question: "Has much of your poetry a racial element?" Answer: "Yes. It is organic, not imposed. It is my privilege to state 'Negroes' not as curios but as people."[1] The 1968 publication of *In the Mecca* would reveal the impact of the new climate and also that she had been responding to it for some time, but no coherent reformulation can be drawn from her 1965 response to the symposium.

The newer responses of the symposium ranged from strong black consciousness statements to revolutionary ones. Lerone Bennett spoke of the necessity to hack through myths to get to one's authenticity as a man, to achieve one's identity, to come to terms with his own history. The writer must "accept the color of his skin and the ambiguity and tension of *his* experience; . . . see with his own eyes and . . . hear with his own ears and . . . find a new language and new forms." He should relate the black experience to the great struggles for liberation and free himself from the tyranny of a white audience. He is, if authentic, the engaged artist participating directly and as writer in the liberation struggle. William Melvin Kelley called for the writer to address a black audience rather than a white regarding his pain: "The Negro writer believes that he must tell the white man where it's at, as if the white man has oppressed the Negro for the last 346 years without really being aware of it." Instead, "the Negro writer must use his art (and art it must be, not propaganda) to help the Negro to find those things that were robbed from him on the shores of Africa, to help repair the damage done to the soul of the Negro in the past three centuries." Such writers as Ossie Davis, William Branch, and John O. Killens made various black consciousness statements.

LeRoi Jones (later Amiri Baraka) represents the most revolutionary position. He had paid dues in Bohemia and at one time had associated himself with Beat and other poets and had theorized about poetic technique. By 1965 he was ready to make a statement of revolutionary social implications, which in turn would dictate the literary: "The Black Artist's role in America is to aid in the destruction of America as he knows it. His role is to report and reflect so precisely the nature of the society, and of himself, in that society, that other men will be moved by the exactness of his rendering, and if they are black men, grow strong through this moving, having seen their own strength and weakness, and if they are white men, tremble, curse, and go mad, because they will be drenched with the filth of their evil." The artist would band his people in a common understanding of the world, nature, the human soul, and America; rescue them from American sterility; and teach them how to achieve the death of the "white eyes." In 1966, Jones's *Home* would describe the full journey to revolutionary writing and theaters; workshops, conferences, publishing companies, and other literary efforts would be flowering in the new way, although not all black writers would attune themselves to the racial and revolutionary preoccupations.

For quite some time, Gwendolyn's life pattern maintained much of the mold into which it had settled. The domestic situation provided its intensities. Although Nora continued to be a source of joy and companionship, she occasionally startled Gwendolyn into minor protests or corrections. At fourteen, she would return from vigorous recreational activities with her clothes bearing the evidence of confrontations with wind, weather, and soil. Nora remembers Gwendolyn recalling the more ordered behavior of her childhood and exclaiming: "You were such a good child!" Given her own phone, Nora made somewhat more than the typical adolescent use of it. While holding long telephone conversations, she would sometimes pause to read silently but would also read the livelier passages to her friend. When the friend responded in kind, the conversation would continue until it seemed that whole books were being consumed.

Gwendolyn felt herself moved into another stage of family life by her son Henry's marriage on April 17, 1965, an event that came after he had moved about a good deal. After attending the University of Illinois and Roosevelt University, where he was mainly interested in physics, he had spent eighteen months in the Marine Corps and, while in service, attended the University of Hawaii. His marriage to Kathleen Hardiman at the Park Manor Christian Church seemed to emphasize his return from the military. Gwendolyn allowed herself to picture grandmotherhood.

She also continued her complex role as citizen of Chicago. On March 13, 1965, she participated at the Chatham YMCA in a program sponsored by the Frank London Brown Negro History Club, highlighted by Val Gray Ward's dramatic reading of "Walk in Freedom" from Brown's *Trumbull Park* and by the presentation of the Frank London Brown Memorial Award to Lerone Bennett, Jr., for his historical writings. Gwendolyn served as an honorary vice chairman of the club, and the last stanza of her eulogy was printed on the back of the program.

On Sunday, October 24, she and another memorial poem were part of a program saluting the late Adlai Stevenson before an audience of over 4,000 in the Chicago Auditorium theater. Gwendolyn placed him in the context of other "Fallen Great"—Medgar Evers and John F. Kennedy—and concluded with a brief tribute to Hubert Humphrey, "a believer in AMERICANS ALL." In her speech-poem she seemed anxious to correct any neglected emphasis upon broader significance and the role of blacks. Malcolm X had been assassinated in February 1965, and the Watts rebellion had occurred in August. In late July an estimated 30,000 blacks and whites, led by Martin Luther King, Jr., had marched for civil rights and equal education from Buckingham Fountain to the Chicago City Hall, from which the mayor was absent. Reportedly, a Catholic priest spoke of finding more tension in Chicago than in Selma, Alabama.[2]

Panorama Magazine of the *Chicago Daily News*, on July 31, 1965, carried a photo of the poet among the "62 Best People in Chicago." The citation read: "Gwendolyn Brooks, gentle woman, loving wife and mother, Pulitzer Prize poet, an unpretentious and gracious writer whose works do credit to herself and to Chicago." (Ironically, balancing off the list of the conventionally distinguished is Slim Brundage, "alumnus of the Hobo College and the Dill Pickle Club and janitor of both the old and the new College of Complexes, an audacious and fully discredited institution of learning, where next week's discussion topics include 'Move the Capital of the United States from Wall Street to Wells Street' and 'All Poets are Putrid.' " His name found alphabetical listing just below Brooks, the editors feeling that he "qualifies, as a contankerous [sic] character in a city that doesn't have too many interesting cantankerous characters.")

In the *Chicago Tribune* of December 2, Gwendolyn is pictured between Lieutenant Governor Samuel J. Shapiro and Dr. Rudolph Ganza—the three being first recipients of Chicago Hadassah's Myrtle Wreath, awarded at a luncheon at the Pick-Congress Hotel. Honorary degrees came from Lake Forest College and Northwestern University. Such recognitions underlined her position as a Chicago institution.

Among the more touching recognitions were those from the young she was struggling to influence and aid. A National Merit Scholar just graduated from Wendell Phillips High School, Judith Brown, included Gwendolyn among various distinguished and historical figures inspiring her determination to achieve: "Gwendolyn Brooks, Pulitzer Prize winner from our own Chicago, looked about her at the struggles of the individual against demands of urban life, wrote her penetrating poetry, revealing the electrifying pains of the human soul as it strives for identity and happiness." Earlier, Gwendolyn had broadened her Fine Arts Award to include prose and plays, in addition to poems and short stories.[3] And on December 9, she was guest of honor at Hirsch High School's Students' Honors Day Program.

Teaching and writing remained the dependable sources of satisfaction. In teaching, the poet made a major effort to assist the student in breaking through to a language that truly expressed personal feelings, since she found that the young sometimes had difficulty bridging the gap between what famous poets thought and what they themselves were thinking. Yet the writer is partly made by reading other writers. Remembering her own experiences in school, she avoided having students memorize poems, which had delayed her appreciating Emily Dickinson's "I Never Saw a Moor," Carl Sandburg's "Fog," and Edwin Arlington Robinson's "Miniver Cheevy" until she encountered them again after school.

One evening she played a recording of Edgar Lee Masters's *Spoon River Anthology* for her students. Finding them impressed and interested, she told them to go home and write a "series of poems about their own community— a Marina Towers anthology or an Oak Park album." She delighted at seeing them really "letting their hair down. They criticized their neighbors. They summed up their neighbors. They said what they thought and felt and experienced at home. Some of the poems were very good." She watched them fight language that falsified feeling. She noticed similar fine effects from playing records of Beat poets, who seemed to her to have revived in the young an interest in poetry. "Those who are afraid to say what *they* mean seem to loosen up when they hear the Beats."[4]

Yet, though the teaching was mainly about writing, it operated in tension with her own efforts to write. She dreamed of new directions as she struggled with what was in front of her, including the long poem "In the Mecca." She wanted to do more free verse—long lines that nearly become paragraphs but remain poetry; not the elaborate prose that she felt was mixed with dots of poetry here and there in "A Bronzeville Mother . . . " but more on the order of Walt Whitman's work. More narrative interest might exploit people's liking for stories without losing the poetic style: she wanted to reach people more effectively. Another challenge: "I want to write short verse plays," she told Robert Glauber. "If I am successful with what I plan, it will be impossible to produce these works as plays. I want them to be pieces of literature—true poems cast in the form of drama."[5]

A critic of her own poetry, she was uneasy about some recent pieces. Although she rarely wrote poems to order, she had done so in an Illinois Bell assignment to write a poem on the city of Chicago. Despite its conflicting qualities, she loved Chicago, but her subject was people and she would not have thought of writing about a city had she not been asked. The subject had an intimidating vastness. She was still dissatisfied with the ending of her 1964 poem "I See Chicago."

> Up-chinned, redemptive, obdurate and fond!
> I see Chicago leaning toward a light
> Indelible, substantial—to unite
> Fever and ice in dialogue and bond.
>
> Iron is the will below the flying smile.
> Hale is the heart of this rich rebel whose

> Scars alter, furies falter and diffuse,
> Vagueness reverses, in a little while.
> I see Chicago, city of yeast and yield.
> City of clangor.
> City of lunge and langor.
> City of maul and mercy, city of the
> out-stuck neck, city of perils repealed.
> Already grand, already harvested.
> With grander range and grander reach ahead.

She had tried to bring Chicago into what she called a "singlicity." She had been told only to keep the poem short—an agreeable directive. But she did not think that the last two lines were the "bell-ringers" she had hoped for. "They are . . . perhaps a little too sentimental." She believed that most poets felt better satisfied with individual lines and stanzas in their works than with complete poems. She herself liked a couple of sonnets in *Annie Allen's* section "the children of the poor." She thought especially well of the ending of the fifth sonnet, about deprived children who see something right in death:

> I say they may, so granitely discreet,
> The little crooked questionings inbound,
> Concede themselves on most familiar ground,
> Cold an old predicament of the breath:
> Adroit, the shapely prefaces complete,
> Acecpt the university of death.

Ironically, in a few years she would be trying to change the style that she admired here. A series of writers' conferences and some institution-building had already drawn certain enterprising blacks. Increasingly, the conferences would give direction to writers and allow them to see each other as sharing common problems and needing to share more of a common consciousness. Gwendolyn would be among those affected.

Near the end of March 1965, the American Society of African Culture sponsored a three-day conference for student news editors that provided a frank exchange between a few African students and American black students. Accused by an American black student of complaining about American institutions though lacking better ones in their own countries, Africans responded that they were disillusioned by America's lack of the democracy they had been told to emulate and by American mistreatment of their black brothers. *Negro Digest* editor Hoyt W. Fuller, reporting the conference in June 1965, stated that spontaneous applause ensued from the audience,

although it was not clear that mutual bridges of understanding had de-
veloped. As resource people, the conference had a mix of writers and civil
rights advocates: J. Saunders Redding, then writer-in-residence at Duke
University; Mal Goode, newsman of ABC-TV; John McCormally of the
Hutchinson (Kansas) *News*; and James Farmer of CORE, fresh from the
"Southern wars."

Other writers' conferences were more mature, less weighted toward the
white critical consensus. The Harlem Writers Guild and the New School for
Social Research in New York City combined to sponsor a conference on
April 23-25, 1965. According to Hoyt Fuller, Richard Gilman, drama critic
for *Newsweek*, in effect (though not in exact words) told black playwrights
that they could not create good plays at present because they were still trying
to establish their being, whereas the creation of fine plays requires that the
playwright be free to consider and explore the *nature* of being. To Fuller's
astonishment, no one bothered to reply except LeRoi Jones who, having "all
but ceased *trying* to communicate with white people, mostly shrugged Mr.
Gilman away."[6]

James Baldwin delivered the keynote address, "The Negro Writer's
Vision of America," and stated that " 'the liberation of this country' . . .
depends on whether or not we are able to make a real confrontation with our
history." The novelist John O. Killens felt that "Black writers must save
America" if it is to be saved. Novelist Paule Marshall, according to Fuller,
most stirred the audience with her paper "The Negro Woman in American
Literature." Generally, the women provided the most "moving panel discussion." The conference presented a very large array of writers and some
fireworks, mainly from clashes of consciousness among blacks. The "inevitable young man" who could discover no relations between himself and
Africans other than skin color was accused of being brainwashed and was
fiercely directed by another writer to recover himself by consulting works by
and about blacks in the Schomburg Collection at the Harlem Branch of the
New York Public Library.[7] It was a historic occasion, and one that might set
the precedent for something "better—if not bigger—next time around."

The New York conference was followed on April 29-30 by what was
apparently the first black writers' conference on a black campus, at Alabama
A.&M. College, Normal, Alabama. The sparkplug for it was the Dutch
woman Rosey Poole, who had maintained the admiration of the slightly
radical because of her presentation of black poetry in anthologies and her
no-nonsense response to American whites who would patronize it. The
conference theme was "The Negro Writer in Our Time," and it included
contributions by poet Robert Hayden and novelist John O. Killens, both

from Fisk; poet Mari Evans from Indianapolis, who composed an original poem for the conference ("Fling Me Your Challenge"); and poet-playwright Owen Dodson from Howard University. The conference, as reported by Fuller in *Negro Digest,* stuck to its point and allowed no "wandering into political waters . . . no hassling with black nationalists intent on disruption." The audience was attentive and very responsive.

Conferences, of course, were not all of one mind. Several simply celebrated black heritage, with varying amounts of white participation. In March 1965, Gwendolyn was part of a wide-ranging conference sponsored by Rockford College, Rockford, Illinois, a conservative setting about ninety miles west of Chicago. The *Negro Digest* of April 1965 reported that the conference was "stupendous" and gave exposure to all the arts. (In announcing the conference the month before, however, the magazine had implied another kind of politics operating: "Programmers are trying for Ellison as headliner, feeling that Baldwin—if available—would be too 'controversial.' ")[8] There were exhibitions of African and Melanesian art "worthy of a major museum," collections of painting and sculpture by distinguished black American artists, lectures on American and African history by distinguished black historians, folk-singing and various other performances, as well as poetry readings. Gwendolyn and Robert Hayden read from their works.

But John Killens in 1966 was creating at Fisk University the type of conference that would give the artist the most intense self-confrontation, the kind at which Gwendolyn in 1967 would feel a rebirth. David Llorens expressed the hopes riding on such a conference: "One attends a writers' conference anticipating new ideas, pertinent criticisms, enhanced perspective—a touch of the inexplicable as well as the profound—but one also secretly hopes for that person who will rise to the occasion and provide the emotional stimulus that transforms writers' conferences into good old 'down home' Baptist conventions—for at least a little while."

At the Asilomar conference, the role of transformer had fallen upon LeRoi Jones and Ossie Davis. David Llorens's report in *Negro Digest* suggests that at Fisk the role was ably performed by Killens himself, Melvin Tolson, and Davis, who gave the closing speech of the session. Bluntly, Killens challenged the audience to make their own definitions: "For too long we have looked into the eyes of the white master for an image of ourselves." Later in the conference, he stated that "The Negro revolt is part and parcel of a worldwide revolution. Our literature should have social relevance to the world struggle, and especially to the struggle of black Americans." The writer has responsibility for "de-brainwashing."

Melvin Tolson, speaking sometimes softly and with seeming reverence and then in a booming voice that roared through the Fisk Jubilee Hall, worked through the biological, sociological, and psychological circumstances that gave man identity to demonstrate that he was not accidentally or incidentally a Negro. "I'm a black poet, an African America poet, a Negro poet. I'm no accident—and I don't give a damn what you think."9 Ossie Davis, while eulogizing Malcolm X and LeRoi Jones, gave a rousing call for the development of a new language and a new image through which blacks must overcome being made the expendables of America. In the process, the artist would eschew the images of the dead Uncle Tom and the Honorary White Man and create those having relationship to the man in the gutter and capable of appealing to him.

As it confronted issues, the Fisk conference had its direct and sometimes agonizing clashes and challenges. Saunders Redding, after first receiving applause, attacked several black writers for making in their fiction "heroes out of heels": John A. Williams in *Nightsong*, Chester Himes in *If He Hollers Let Him Go*, Rosa Guy in *Bird in My Window*, and James Baldwin in *Another Country*. Counterattacked, he was viewed as overcoming his opponents with the tense statement, "Oh Lord, I don't want to argue." The argument resurfaced, nevertheless. There were conflicts with such white writers as Bert Gilden and Margaret Halsey. Their belief that whites sinned against blacks from ignorance was countered by blacks' doubts that whites exploited unconsciously, were unknowing of what they were doing. Gilden's statement that blacks were without self-hatred was met by advice that he not try creating Negro characters "until you find out something about Negroes." Commented observer-reporter David Llorens: "By this time, the enormous gap between the way white and black Americans view the world was revealing itself both in and out of the 'official' conference sessions."10

Conflicts among blacks also continued, sometimes representing differences in the consciousness of a younger and an older generation. At one point, Robert Hayden, who had taken the unpopular stand that a poet of Negro classification was "a poet who happens to be a Negro," stated that he was tired of being attacked at every writers' conference. James Forman pressed for black writers to be in touch with the Freedom movement, an idea that had already been introduced by John Killens and by the novelist William Melvin Kelley's call for a revolutionary black literature addressed to blacks. Lasting issues arose at the conference: Negro writer versus the concept of writer who happens to be Negro; addressing a white audience versus a black one; protest versus literature; pleading one's individual status and merits versus forthright assertion of one's right to be; achieving true black identity and an appropriate stance toward Western culture; and old images and language versus the need to create new ones.

At this and other writers' conferences, much thinking went into the expressions of roles of the writers, the building of appropriate institutions, and the struggle simply to create freshly or in a revolutionary way. In the process, there was an increase in the authority of blacks to influence black writings and a corresponding reduction of the authority of the white liberal consensus with which Gwendolyn had so long negotiated. Gwendolyn would find the air still more charged by the next Fisk Conference, in 1967.

In 1966 she was already having encounters that would influence her future direction. In February 1966 she met the poet-publisher Dudley Randall, whose reviews she had been reading in *Negro Digest*. On the basis of the reviews she had felt he must be something of a terror, but she was immediately impressed by his gentleness, despite his firm features and powerful physique. Randall recalls her saying, "Oh you're Dudley Randall. I thought you were terrible but you're all right." They were both reading their poetry in a program at Oakland University, Rochester, Michigan, an occasion that Randall had helped to plan. Afterward, Gwendolyn, in company with such poets as Oliver LaGrone, Joyce Whitsit, and Harold Lawrence, dined at Randall's home. He had read *A Street in Bronzeville* shortly after it came out and had been impressed especially by the compression and economy of the poetry. Not a free verse man, he admired the sonnets and liked the other forms in which the flow of language seemed natural and easy. In the company Gwendolyn seemed to him very modest, not striving for attention but allowing others to express themselves—not the most common behavior in a gathering of artists. Mostly she listened to others give their theories. Thus began a friendship and literary association which would grow in warmth, affection, and admiration, and would partake strongly of her new spiritual directions.

Randall's background was somewhat similar to Gwendolyn's, although he had grown up in a rougher neighborhood, on Detroit's Lower East Side, from which had come also poet Robert Hayden and Detroit's mayor, Coleman Young. In their neighborhood there had been "blind pigs" (houses illegally selling alcohol), houses of prostitution, and some violence, but no organized gang activity. The neighborhood provided colorful memories without essentially challenging Randall's childhood innocence. Before marriage his mother had taught school and had secretly written poetry, an activity not particularly fostered in the neighborhood. His father had been trained as a minister but worked in a Ford factory most of the time. He too had aspired to other work, hoped to get a job in personnel, and became a salesman for the Gray Motor Company until it failed. His parents kept an ordered home and encouraged education. He remembered his mother's exclaiming on one occasion, "I don't give a darn," and his father responding, "Mother, watch your language." Dudley completed his education at Wayne State and became a librarian because of his liking for books; he had been a poet from the age of thirteen.

What immediately continued the association between Gwendolyn and Dudley was his publishing activities. He had started the Broadside Press in an effort to secure a copywright for his poem "Ballad of Birmingham," which folk singer Jerry Lewis wished to set to music. Continuing the press as an outlet for other black writers, he first published broadsides. Gwendolyn came aboard with such broadsides as "We Real Cool" and "Martin Luther King," which sold for fifty cents each. Impressed as usual with people who get things done, Gwendolyn continued to contribute to Dudley's independent publishing company. She gave her poem "For Malcolm" to Broadside, without fee, for inclusion in the anthology devoted to Malcolm X. Later she would recommend other poets for publication in the Broadside Press series and pay the printing costs for some of them. Through her would come several books, and Broadside would finally become her publisher. This collaboration brought her further out into the stream of new black literary movements.

A less pleasant experience more directly dramatized tensions in her inner weather during 1966. While at a reading in California, she was interviewed by a reporter for the *San Jose Mercury*. She related to him a comment that had been made to her by "a progressive elderly gentleman" in 1945: "Oh, Miss Brooks, if only you would write marching songs for the people! *Then* you would be really writing poetry." The newspaper gave the story a front-page spot and headed it: "Negro Poet Just Couldn't Write Songs for Marches." The story read in part: "Gwendolyn Brooks, the only Negro poet to win the Pulitzer Prize, admits she had to turn down requests from civil rights groups to save her literary integrity. 'They wanted me to write marching songs,' Miss Brooks said. 'I just couldn't do that.' "

Gwendolyn felt compelled to demand a correction of the reporter's story and to make a statement in *Negro Digest* regarding what had actually been said. In her letter to the paper, she stated: "Mr. Miller [the reporter] has presented to the public a picture of an addled and simpering Negro woman who is a traitor to her race, and I cannot allow such libel to proceed unimpeded." The reporter's aim, she said, was to present her as "a 'serene,' stupid, smug, uninvolved, bloodless, cold-eyed housewife of 48. He *did* get the age right!—not suspecting, perhaps, that I am proud, not sorry, to have achieved such a rich heritage, and the fruits thereof." She explained her serenity as the avoidance of bustle, under "medical necessity. But surely everyone today is churning under-mask; and properly so."[11]

Refuting the statement that she had said, "I just couldn't . . . " she referred to her 1950 statement about the necessity for the Negro poet to transform raw materials into art. "Lilting libel. I am, first of all, not the kind of prissy touch-me-not who chirps 'I Just Couldn't.' NEITHER-EITHER would I ever think of referring to 'my literary integrity.' That kind of twaddle is for fools, and I do not belong in the listing. Most important, however: NO CIVIL RIGHTS GROUPS HAVE EVER REQUESTED THAT I WRITE MARCHING OR ANY OTHER SONGS. Perhaps because 'We Shall Overcome'—the authorship of which would have been a special pride—is still *mighty* strong." Instead of believing, as reported, that "she is a poet and not a propagandist," she believed that "the poet is a most certain kind of propagandist." Her quoting of her 1950 statement suggested that the Negro poet is one who transforms propaganda ("raw materials") into art.

Her last paragraph in *Negro Digest* revealed her concept of her role in the struggle and the relevance of her own work: "It is true that I have not marched in the streets. Not only am I still regularly writing, but I have judged important the very difficult creation of poems and fictions and essays which even a quarter of a century ago were—and are now (Mr. Miller 'admits' he has not read my work)—bearers of a hot burden. BUT I MAKE NO PROMISES! As Gemini, I'm adjustable: I do what the particular instance and its toil inspire me to do."[12]

Gwendolyn's response registers the tensions in her consciousness. Her statement seems to go beyond refutation of the reporter. It reveals her sensitivity to the Freedom struggle, her need to sustain a close connection with the directions it was taking, and her revulsion at the idea of noninvolvement or the "traitorous." For the daily round of existence, there was the self proclaimed by *Panorama Magazine:* "gentle woman, loving wife and mother, Pulitzer Prize poet, an unpretentious and gracious writer whose works do credit to herself and to Chicago." The unfortunate San Jose incident made clear the equally real existence of a formidable, passionate, and fighting self, not lightly to be crossed on a matter of principle.

Other, less tense, selves were evoked by other situations. On April 18-22, 1966, she was writer-in-residence at Aurora College, Aurora, Illinois, where she fulfilled a busy schedule with the young and attracted, in addition to Aurora students, about 150 high school English and creative writing students from "as far away as DeKalb as well as East, West and parochial high schools of Aurora." On July 25 at the Indiana University

Writers' Conference she held her audience "spellbound" while reading the final lines from her abortion poem "The Mother": "Believe me, I loved, I loved you / All." She defined poetry as "life pushed through a strainer." In November, she and fellow judges David Etter, author of *Go Read the River*, and Robert Glauber, founder and editor of the *Beloit Poetry Journal* and a senior writer in Illinois Bell's Public Relations Department, chose the prize-winning poems of high school youngsters in a contest sponsored by Illinois Bell.[13]

Gwendolyn also published in *Negro Digest* an incisive review of Robert Hayden's *Selected Poems*, which had resounding overtones of her own persisting convictions. In a variation of her 1950 *Phylon* magazine statement regarding the obligations of black poets, she spoke of them as participating in the rawness of existence but divided into two categories by their approach to poetic art:

We need the poet who 'lives in life,' mixes with mud, rolls in rot, claws the scoundrels, bleeds and bloodies, and, grasping in the field, writes right there, his wounds like faucets above his page, at once besmutching and ennobling it. We need, also, the poet who finds life always interesting, sometimes appalling, sometimes appealing, but consistently amenable to a clarifying enchantment via the powers of art. His reverence for the word Art is what chiefly distinguishes him from Poet I. Poet II, moreover, may postpone composition until he is off the field, rid of the fray's insignia, and has had a bath.[14]

Hayden was one of the Poet IIs of the world—"one of a growing number of Negro poets believing that matter is not enough, believing that there should be marriage between matter and manner." Approvingly, she noted that Hayden's *Selected Poems* developed from a rich artistic process that refines life without destroying it. She illustrated his power by quotations from several poems which by now are well known and admired: "The Ballad of Nat Turner," portraying the feelings of the leader of the Virginia slave revolt of 1830; "Runagate, Runagate," exhibiting the courage of the runaway slave and the terrors of his situation; "The Whipping," presenting a mother's cruelty to her child and her feelings about the deed; "Middle Passage," showing the suffering of slaves experiencing the famous passage across the ocean into slavery; and "Those Winter Sundays," portraying a man's discovering, in retrospect, the love expressed by his father in a powerful form that, as a child, he had been unequipped to perceive. Stressing both life and art, she declared that "Robert Hayden is brother to many things—dolor, premise, apprehension, sublimity, homage, terror, origin; other relatives are love and a dedication to the highest of which he himself is capable." At the end, her emphasis upon Hayden's involvement and art is also reflected in her scorn for the book jacket statement: "The Jacket of *Selected Poems* is disfigured with this legend: 'Writing, of course, out of his experience as an American Negro, his lines are NEVERTHELESS carefully controlled and disciplined.' The furious capitalization and italics are mine."[15]

Gwendolyn's 1950 *Phylon* statement on the Negro poet had recoiled from the artist who fails to transform the raw dough of experience into art: "It is like throwing dough to the not-so-hungry mob. The mob will look, may handle, but cannot be expected to eat. Although your produce be made of ever so sincere a wheat. You have got to cook that dough, alter it, until it is unrecognizable. Then the mob will not know it is accepting something that will be good for it. Then it will eat, enjoy, and prosper." She stated that just by being Negro, every Negro has important things to say, that his "mere body" is an "eloquence." His silent walk on the street is itself an address to the people, "a rebuke . . . a plea . . . a school." She concluded, "But no real artist is going to be content with offering raw materials. The Negro poet's most urgent duty, at present, is to polish his technique, his way of presenting his truths and his beauties, that these may be more insinuating, and, therefore, more overwhelming."[16]

Her praise for Robert Hayden thus relates very closely to her 1950 position. What is added in the Hayden review is the emphasis upon the poet's *engaged* condition and the acknowledgment of our need for the poet who is not concerned about art. True, having acknowledged this Poet I, she has no more to say about him, no further explanations at this time. But the area of tolerance seems extended to meet recently felt needs. It would appear that the Freedom movement had stimulated her to bring into the foreground slightly broader considerations than those that appeared in 1950. It will be instructive to weigh future comments on writing and thus see shiftings in consciousness.

The consciousness expressed in the Hayden review seems to be the one that Gwendolyn took to the Second Annual Writers' Conference at Fisk University on April 21-23, 1967. She came from South Dakota State College, where she had been warmly received and enthusiastically embraced by an audience that was very white indeed. She would recall seeing only one black at the school, and she, in terms of the turbulent times, did not seem very black. The audience reception was that of whites to whom blacks were rather new, as they were in various places in the United States.

The Fisk Conference, by contrast, would be passionately racial. It would initiate a fundamental change in the poet's consciousness, her commitment to art and audience, and her perception of the black situation in America.

She was coming to Fisk at a time when the highly tense confrontation between literature and civil rights had transformed itself into a pronounced nationalistic concern with literature and the black writer's role. In contrast to the Asilomar Conference, this assembly had gone beyond the restraints of white liberal control. With the novelist John O. Killens directing and participating, the speakers were Ronald Fair and Killens, novelists; Lerone Bennett and John Henrik Clarke, nonfiction writers; Gwendolyn and Margaret Danner, poets; and LeRoi Jones and Ronald Milner, playwrights. The aggressive and bold stance of the conference is immediately suggested by the fact that a petition supporting the then-controversial stand of Dr. Martin Luther King, Jr., against the war in Vietnam emerged from the final session and was signed by several panelists and others.[17]

The simple fact was that the Black Power thrust, which Stokely Carmichael had raised in his conflict with King in June 1966 during the completion of the James Meredith Freedom March, was triumphing. Students and others were moving away from the black and white unity of the song "We Shall Overcome" and closer to Malcolm X and black consciousness. Gwendolyn was "first aware of a general energy, an electricity, in look, walk, speech, *gesture* of the young blackness I saw all about me." She was aware of reborn young people and would feel that through them she herself was also reborn. But whereas she had been loved at South Dakota State College, she was at Fisk "coldly Respected." The coldness may have been in contrast to the degree of warmth accorded other panelists, but the audience also gave her applause at times.[18]

The conference theme was "The Black Writer and Human Rights," and the setting was Jubilee Hall, a building owing its existence to funds raised by an early Fisk choir by presenting spirituals in its national and international tours. A bit wide-eyed in this new atmosphere, Gwendolyn joined a large and enthusiastic crowd in the hall. The morning panel opened with speeches by Bennett and Clarke, two engaged historians outstanding for their ability to move audiences. Clarke, whose manner owed a good deal to the southern folk preacher, would represent the pressures of both southern and urban life. Like the folk preacher, he presented history as a total world view. He first presented evidence from the pre-colonial period of African history to show that blacks brought to America during the slave trade did not come empty of history and culture and that the African identity had been firm and well-buttressed. In responding to a destructive assault on identity, blacks in America created instruments for their survival—the slave narratives, a literature of petition asking that their human status be acknowledged. Periods following the abolition of slavery created a literature of Restoration, led by W. E. B. DuBois (and outside America in the nineteenth century by Wilmot Blyden), which was designed to give back to blacks their heroes. The struggle persisted through the Harlem Renaissance. A dynamic literature of protest had emerged with Richard Wright and persisted through World War II. More recent was the appearance of the new slave narratives of James Baldwin, John Oliver Killens, William Melvin Kelley, and others. Many new writers had also returned ideologically to Africa and achieved "a reconsideration of the African culture and a reconsideration of our relationship to it," from which might come a whole new literature. "It is singularly the mission of the black writer," he concluded, "to tell his people what they have been, in order for them to understand what they are. And from this the people will clearly understand what they still must be."

Clarke's speech drew laughter and applause when he pointed out that the writer of the new slave narratives is angrier than the original creators of the genre, having "beheld, with his attaché case and his horn-rimmed glasses and his house, sometimes split-leveled, that he is still on the auction block and that very often the auction block is air-conditioned."

One concept seems to have made an especially strong impression upon Gwendolyn, since she referred to it later, at the beginning of her own presentation. Clarke had said, "There is no such thing as a Negro in the true ethnic sense. They gave us a name that referred to a condition, and took away the name that referred to land, history, and culture. When you say *English*, a history comes to your mind of a land—a history and a culture. When you say *Negro*, a condition comes to mind." Clarke pointed out that some blacks were now replacing the word Negro with Afro-American.

Since Clarke had talked about the literature of the past and the present, Lerone Bennett stated that he would talk of the future and thus of a literature of transformation. Bennett felt that, in an oppressive and sterile world where art and literature are made into entertainment for the privileged few, the writer's business is revolution and whatever leads to it. Embodying the will and consciousness of a people engaged in a "total struggle for human rights," black writers should respond to the revolution within and the revolution without. But, since it is clear that the revolution without cannot succeed without the prior achievement of the revolution within, black writers of nonfiction had, he thought, "a peculiar, if not exclusive responsibility, in projecting the need for and the content of such an internal revolution." There must be a complete redefining of all tools and concepts, since they contained white supremacist assumptions and were devised to keep blacks from seeing; and removal of the last elements of white supremacy from the "minds and hearts of black writers, themselves." The result would be a new vision of human rights, humanity, and the "relationships of art, literature, and human struggle." In the process, the writers, if successful, would replace the false excluding humanism of Western Europe by one of benefit to all mankind. Again the audience also responded to several sharp shafts. Perhaps the most relevant to the general tone of the audience was the call for the writer to come home to the black community. Bennett found it extraordinary "that a man or an oppressed person would choose to address his oppressors, primarily," and pointed out that behind the myth of the ill-equipped black audience were a people "hungry for knowledge."

Gwendolyn was to describe the impact of the conference in *Report from Part One:* "I was in some inscrutable and uncomfortable wonderland." She was like the woman in the Helen Hokinson cartoon who in "a wild world" has a sign saying, "Will someone please tell me what is going on?" The poet did not know "what to make of what surrounded me, of what with hot sureness began almost immediately to invade me. *I* had never been, before, in the general presence of such insouciance, such live firmness, such confident vigor, such determination to mold or carve something DEFI-NITE."[19]

The session in which Gwendolyn was to follow Margaret Danner at first lost momentum as an overly zealous male student introduced the panel by describing the glories of poetry in the black man's struggle during the Harlem Renaissance in literature, its decline from glory, and the need for it now to align with the black man's struggle. He clearly had in mind a revolutionary black poetry, produced by numerous LeRoi Joneses. The student's remarks revealed an ignorance of the black poetry developed since the Black Renaissance of the 1920s; since he praised the Renaissance poetry, which was not revolutionary nor even very knowledgeable about the real Africa, it was apparent that he was unaware of the poetry of deep social reference, whose tough fiber was clearly related to the "black man's struggle" and invested with an economic realism not a part of the Renaissance poetic achievement.

Margaret Danner began with an attack upon this ignorance, accusing the young man, and those like him, of "not reading the poems that we have struggled so many years to bring to our public." Stating that the poem speaks more particularly to the audience than other literary forms because it is involved in emotion, she urged: "All that you have to *do* is *read* the poetry."

The audience seemed to appreciate the saltiness of her counterattack, which ranged in tone between bitterness and motherly concern, as she stressed the rigor of the poet's struggle and the lack of awareness of his black audience.

Gwendolyn's presentation followed Danner's. She prepared it with the statement that she would not "try to wring the neck of our introducer because Mrs. Danner has said everything I could have wanted to say to him, and much better." She spoke of what she had learned from the morning session, her appreciation of the astuteness of the students and their questions, and then read her "tiny" speech.

Whatever a creature is, has managed and sustained, that will be the statement of the work thereby. Perhaps it is not always easy to sustain Negrohood, for what is it? I am interested in the pleasing sneer of the young African poet Rurwar Chiri. (Wonder how many of you have ever heard of him?) 'Ah,' he asks, 'Where is Negroland?' But it does seem to me that every poet of African extraction must understand that his product will be either italicized or seasoned by the fact and significance of his heritage. How fine! How delightful! (All of this and much more Mr. Clarke has already said. But here I am.)

One of the more anxious wants of fundamental man is variety. The man from Africa is able to provide some because of the influence of an old music, an old and colorful land, because of the amazing crimes visited upon him, because of the rich quantity and quality of his response to those crimes. As I have said in Langston Hughes' *New Negro Poets USA*, in the works of Negro poets the reader will discover evidence of double dedication, hints that the artists have accepted a two-headed responsibility.

Few have favored a track without flags or emblems of any racial kind, and even those few in their deliberate "renunciation" have offered race fed testimony of several sorts. I continue and violently to believe that, whatever the stimulating persuasion, poetry, not journalism, must be the result of involvement with emotions and idea and ink and paper.

"And that's all the vital prose that I have for you, Mr. Killens," she concluded. (Audience laughter and applause.) She then turned to give most of the time to reading her poetry: "Malcolm X," "Boy Breaking Glass," "kitchenette building," "the mother," "Negro Hero." Each poem she introduced with an easygoing informality and understated humor that apparently reflected the achievement of a rapport with her audience that was increasingly characteristic of her readings. The audience responded with applause and frequent appreciative laughter.

The audience remained quiet after her reading of the second sonnet of "the children of the poor" and "Beverly Hills, Chicago." "We Real Cool" brought sighs of appreciation and sustained applause, and the response to

"The Ballad of Rudolph Reed" was notable. Apologetically, she stated, "The poems that I have that deal at length with the struggle for human rights are too long to read here. Some are four pages long. Some are seven pages long." But she ended her poetry selection with the last stanza of "Riders to the Blood-red Wrath," to sustained applause.

The climax of her reading was the then-prose piece "The Life of Lincoln West." She explained that her fiction was usually referred to as "an attempt at poetry. And perhaps it is because when I try to write fiction I find myself giving each phrase and word just as much concentration as I do when I'm writing 'an orthodox poem.' " She began with a vigorous reading of the first line, "Ugliest little boy that everyone ever saw." Interrupted by audience laughter, she stated: "Well, it would be nicer if I'd say quickly that I, too, am a Lincoln West," and joined in the laughter. When she finished reading, the audience responded with resounding applause.

Gwendolyn then introduced Oscar Brown, Jr.'s musical adaptation of her poem "of DeWitt Williams on his way to Lincoln Cemetery" and told briefly how the New York radio station had rejected the musical version, feeling that blacks would find part of the poem offensive. "They failed to understand that a phrase I have in there, 'Nothing but a plain black boy,' was supposed to be a poem in itself and a high cry of excruciating sarcasm."

Near the end of Brown's music and singing, LeRoi Jones walked in. Gwendolyn announced his presence, and "there was jubilee in Jubilee Hall." From that moment, the conference was in the hands of the more radical social critics and the visionary young.

Both Margaret Danner and Gwendolyn had clearly shown themselves to be artists whose works had been important in the struggle for human rights. But the young in the audience were heady from direct experiences in the civil rights struggles, which now involved colleges across the country and provided them with a pantheon of heroes and heroines and wars fought, won, and lost over a period of seven years. Although they reacted strongly to Margaret Danner, the more radical would be unlikely to respond with reverence to her citations of such establishment institutions as Poetry magazine and the Pulitzer Prize. Although they would have to admit that Gwendolyn's poetry was a powerful element in the human rights struggle, their ultimate demand came closer to being satisfied by a literature that asserted a hearty rejection of middle-class values, a violent response to oppression, and an exclusive identification with the black community.

Gwendolyn continued to feel the impact of the electricity, the determination to mold and create, with which the atmosphere itself seemed charged. The young woman introducing the evening panel stressed the necessity to act in line with one's deepest feelings, to reject nonviolence, and to create a true drama of the actual feelings involved in black life. An activist who confessed to having been involved in "disturbance," she ended with a challenge: "That is the drama of Negro life: its violence, its blues, its coolness, a drama that unfolds itself twenty-four hours a day, a drama that explodes with sudden violence and not only takes the country by surprise but the people caught up in their need for physical expression. Too long have honest emotions been distorted and used for an excuse for further exploitation. Too long have we been looking in the rear view mirror to steer in the head-on-coming traffic. Too long, and it's time we started looking forward, and honestly reacting to what we see. The black playwright can help to draw our attention to the front and to focus on what lies ahead." She then introduced LeRoi Jones and Ronald Milner.

Gwendolyn listened as Milner called for black theater to return to the black community. "If a new black theater is to be born, sustain itself, and justify its own being, it must go home. Go home psychically, mentally, aesthetically, and I think physically." He visualized the community as being in a confusing, grinding state of being that once was called blues but now simply Blackness, a state in which all the universals were distorted by white racism. The theater would show the community its victimization and its stubbornly retained beauty and would inspire it to "more essential levels in their new black theater of living, new visions of life."

LeRoi Jones, using a low-key approach, gradually built the intensity which his audience obviously expected and brought the scene to a high stage of excitement with his attacks upon American sterility and the corrupting whiteness within blacks. Drama, he pointed out, re-presented the self and life experience, a necessary act since the individual cannot fully understand his own experience in his capacity as the actor of it. He contrasted the great creative energy of James Brown with the sterility of American society, as demonstrated by its monstrousness in Vietnam.

Instead of going into immediate questioning of the participants, the audience demanded that Jones read some of his poems. With his reading of "A Poem for Half-White College Students," he lifted the audience higher. Near the end of his poem celebrating James Brown, the audience suddenly joined him in chanting in high exultation: "Yeah! Yeah! Yeah!" During the reading of "Magic Words," Gwendolyn observed that "a pensive (until that moment) white man of thirty or thirty-three abruptly shot himself into the heavy air, screaming, 'Yeah! Yeah! Up against the wall, Brother! KILL 'EM ALL! KILL 'EM ALL.' "[20]

The Milner-Jones panel fully dramatized the marriage of the Black

Power and Black Arts movements and the hard tones and desperation of life in the Northern ghettoes. Milner said at one point, "When you stand on those hot streets feeling this whimpering going on under the beast's muzzle, when the myriad poisons are part of your natural everyday element, the needs will either come bursting out of your pen onto your stages or they'll drive you sick with your own faggot cowardice."[21]

At the Fisk Conference, Gwendolyn absorbed positive images of the young and was unconcerned with specific concepts such as "cultural nationalism." In a later interview with Charles Lynch she would respond to that term: "Is that what you call it? You may use any label that you wish. All I know is when young people started talking about blacks loving, respecting, and helping one another, that was enough for me."[22] Her response to the images the young were casting has sources in her more conservative yearnings, as seen in several early poems. Certain poems written during her seventeenth year, it will be recalled, recoiled from persons either uneasy about their own blackness or all too efficient in adopting the white standards that made them ugly purveyors of intraracial prejudice. The narrator of the 1935 poem "Negroid" scorned the black woman who wrote on a job application, "I've Negroid features, but they're finely spaced." There is little question that she was testifying from the authority of her own experience in her poem "Thoughts of Prejudice" (May 28, 1935):

> But little men of Afric's swarthy shores,
> There is more prejudice within your race
> Than out beyond its shadowed bar; far more
> Within your tract than any other space.
> Why search for foreign dung, why seethe and foam
> When so much mucky filth lies loose at home?

And, since she herself identified with Lincoln West, there was that deep bonding on a level important to the young radicals.

There were, of course, differences that would show up as therapeutic quarrels within the group. In their self-intoxication and the very vigor of their forward stride, the young frequently lose strength by confining their vision too strictly to the present. Even the bearer of such imposing credentials as John O. Killens would occasionally find hungry elements of the younger generation trying to tread him down into a "happened" rather than a "happening." Gwendolyn, for her part, now looked to the larger spirit promising the rebirth of a people and of the individual self.

9

Recognized in Her Country

Gwendolyn brought back to Chicago the excitement aroused in her by the Fisk University Writers' Conference. Nora found her mother a bundle of energy, walking "three feet in the air" and looking for ways to express her new consciousness. She found such an opportunity among the accumulated mail awaiting her on her return, a telegram from the producer-singer Oscar Brown, Jr., which invited her to a preview of his latest work, "Opportunity Please Knock," a show created from the talents of the Blackstone Rangers street gang. What Brown had done with the youths, who were usually considered problems, seemed to her another inspiring example of what could be achieved by those who cared about human beings. She had been hearing about the gang for a couple of years and had yearned, she embarrassedly confessed later, "to do something for them." Finding that there were writers among them, Gwendolyn offered to conduct a writing workshop. Since certain gang members had already asked Brown whether they could show Gwendolyn their manuscripts, the proposal was quickly accepted and arranged.

By telephone, Brown introduced Gwendolyn to Walter Bradford, a Wilson Junior College student who worked with teenagers. Interested in writing and at a turning point in his own life where he was seeking an outlet other than social work, Walter would be her link with the Rangers. He would also become one of Gwendolyn's lifelong friends and would eventually take over the teaching of the workshop. Walter was awed by Gwendolyn's stature as a poet and by her directness and plainness. He remembers their first meeting at the First Presbyterian Church—the site of the Rangers' headquarters, the rehearsals for "Opportunity Please Knock," and the forthcoming workshop. "The cab pulls up, and this little lady gets out. Two little dudes ran across the street right away: 'Hey, you want us to carry your bags for you?' Little cats we called 'shorties,' you know. I greeted her at the door and introduced myself. They gave her back her bag and we went upstairs and started the first workshop."[1]

Gwendolyn walked through groups of Rangers, the room next to the one appointed for the workshop being the site for the gang's council meeting. She moved, Walter recalled, as if she knew what she was doing "and went right on and did it." She began at once to talk about poetry and writing. "The Stones were kind of sitting around looking like—well man, you know, what is this? They were absolutely quiet. Absolutely quiet. Nobody said anything out of place, and when they wanted to talk they would raise their hand. She started out talking about John Donne and Shakespeare and people like that, you know. I think, after awhile, she got a couple of yawns out of some of them. So she changed the format."

According to Gwendolyn, she consumed some early meetings in going over the complexities of the sonnet form. The Rangers laughed at her for her interest in the sonnet and her efforts to teach them iambic pentameter. But they brought manuscripts. Lively discussions developed; Gwendolyn ceased speaking of the sonnet and became a counselor and friend.

Actually, the Rangers were not as stern a challenge as the group of black college students to whom Walter was introducing her. Responding to the media announcements of the workshop's existence, they began to drop by and, as Gwendolyn relinquished her Rangers work to Walter, began to meet as a writers' workshop at her home. Walter knew them from his own college or from work in the liberation struggle, which by now blended the civil rights thrust with that of Black Power. Though they were not a monolithic group, several were responding strongly to the pressures of the streets and the crisis atmosphere and were likely to feel out carefully anyone over thirty bringing gifts.

Perhaps Walter and Don L. Lee (now Haki R. Madhubuti), in their contrasting responses to street and environmental pressures while growing up, would mark out boundaries within which some other visitors also fell. Walter, though fully responding to current racial tensions, had at the foreground of consciousness an afterglow in his memories—warm and spontaneous triumphs of the environmental and street situations over adversity. Born in Chicago at Thirty-seventh and Wabash of a Chicago mother and an Arkansas emigrant father, he recalled his neighborhood as a warm black community that was almost like a small southern town. Tragedy entered the family with the murder of his father when Walter was nine, but he formed a strong relationship with his stepfather, who brought into the home humor and stories of the South. He was surrounded by a large clan that included a grandfather, several aunts and their children, and his own immediate siblings, a setting that left memories of spontaneity and great fun. Everyone in the neighborhood knew everyone else, and the taverns and clubs provided mischievous encounters with outstanding entertainers who would make history. Some hangers-on made money dancing in front of the nightclubs for contributions from the crowd, and "big time" gangsters were also part of the tavern and entertainment scene.

Thus, although Gwendolyn's poem "In the Mecca" later delivered its load of frustration and misery to Walter, it also caused him to re-create from his old neighborhood what had been pleasant during his youth. "When I did discover the key, I remember sitting in my back room one morning and simply soaring right out of my seat. It was like when I was a little dude on Forty-seventh Street. They used to have a tavern on the corner called the Dixie Liquors, and Muddy Waters and Howling Wolf and them used to play in there—all those guys. We would peep in the back door, those cats would be getting down in there, and they would chase us away. All of a sudden I was right there again—running up and down Forty-seventh Street looking in the taverns, listening to people talk. The fights were going on. There were the pretty women and their perfume, the men in double-breasted suits, the guitar players."

Walter would become, after minor negative workshop responses, part of a small intimate group with whom Gwendolyn discussed serious concerns over the telephone. Their relationship was marked by easy enjoyments. There were pleasant conversations and counsel regarding Walter's flamboyant tendencies, but also the easily sustained comradeship characterized by such simple outings as going for an ice cream cone or finding a restaurant that served "fantastic" cornbread. Gwendolyn seems to have supplied tolerance and understanding to what Walter called the "wayward son" in him which he had drawn upon from earlier maternal figures.

Don L. Lee, on the other hand, had searing memories of the devastating powers of street and environmental pressures, although he was now outwitting those that were not backed by disastrous acts of God and nature. Born in Detroit, he had seen much of his family disintegrate, amid vicious responses from whites and certain blacks. His mother gave way under the burden of raising a family and became an alcoholic and a prostitute, bringing chaos into the home. Turned away by the nearby white hospital, she died from hemorrhaging of the brain before the family was able to get her to the Detroit city hospital. But the home and environmental difficulties caused Don to see school as a haven and to profit by his mother's reading habits. He committed himself absolutely to his schooling and escaped the havoc being wreaked by youth gangs by using his intelligence to help certain gang members get through school.

But his hard-won entry to one of Detroit's best high schools for that day, Cass Tech, was of short tenure, since he could not afford the books and supplies. After his mother died, he struggled through Chicago's Dunbar High School, where he met Walter. At first he was unable to get a job because, at six-feet-one in height, he weighed only 131 pounds. After enlisting in the army he found regular meals—but also white racism. Back in Chicago, he became part of the labor force on the docks, where blacks were hired by the day only, with the regular jobs being given to white "ethnics," many of whom could not speak English, while the blacks hired as their "helpers" did most of the work of loading trains.

Black life seemed, at times, to intensify oppressive situations. When Don lived almost next door to one of Detroit's major Congregational churches during his childhood, he tried to become part of its youth program. But the church was doing no missionary work in the community, serving instead well-dressed blacks who arrived from outside the neighborhood in big cars. Don was gradually laughed out of the children's sessions because he came in ill-fitting second-hand clothes from the Salvation Army. It seemed to him that the church people were trying hard not to appear like other black people—or, as he would later be able to conceptualize it, were trying to be white.

When Gwendolyn met him, Don had been educating himself through a rigorous program of reading and the more formal resources of Wilson Junior College and the DuSable Museum, where he worked and received encouragement from the director, Margaret Burroughs, and her staff. Like Walter, Don represented a set of experiences that were finding a more coherent outlet through the various black movements, although Don's were more on the bitter side. By the time of his and Gwendolyn's meeting, he had published his first book, *Think Black* (1967), and had evolved into a tough and obsessed seeker. His vision of how things really were derived its authority, force, and energy from hard environmental realities, the movements, and a demanding moral consciousness.

When Gwendolyn's more ordered background encountered Don's sense of urgencies, there were at first strong conflicts. But he would become an adopted son and comrade. Gwendolyn spoke of him as "One whom I have recognized as a star for black people, young and old, uncompromising, serious, consistent—warmth inside a mail of necessary cold, *History* but not impressed by the fact." She described their "working easily and earnestly and enjoyably together when there are jobs to be done."[2]

Others, including several young women, shared the struggle for identity, as indicated by the anthology of their work, *Jump Bad* (1971), edited by Gwendolyn. Attempting to clarify their direction both as persons and as artists, they discussed the values from American culture that should be rejected and the values, often directly from black life, that they themselves supported. Integration, black solidarity, American systems of validation (such as money, prizes, and degrees), class divisions, competition, individualism, economic alternatives—all shared discussion space with ideas of the role of the artist in regard to himself and an oppressed society, the nature of an appropriate literature, ways of writing, and criteria for judging black writing. Since the overall unity was grounded primarily in the reaction to oppression and the need for identity, the discussions often produced considerable heat. A few of the younger women held out for the independence of the individual writer and the artist's freedom to follow his or her impulse in choosing subject matter. Flowers, the natural scene, and personal emotions, in this view, were as important as poems directly devoted to liberation of the group. Val Gray Ward, the actress, not a writer, brought into the discussion the pressure of having grown up in an all-black town, Mound Bayou, Mississippi. She felt conflicts in the departures from folk values existing prior to the ascendance of street lore, and the popularity of such words as "motherfucker."

Thus the group's heat was often turned upon itself. But, especially in the early meetings at Gwendolyn's house, there were conflicts between this young group and the distinguished writer of an older generation. Don L. Lee had mildly confronted her at the Rangers Workshop over her reliance on the work of white writers and what he felt was a European perspective "at a certain level of structure." But he could see that the workshop, whatever the limitations, was moving forward and helping individual Rangers. When he gave her his first book, *Think Black*, she commented on a few of the poems but later confessed that she had had difficulty in seeing some of the work as poetry.

Today, outside the supporting atmosphere of the liberation movement, *Think Black's* writing reveals serious shortcomings but is still raw and vital material for the time. Gwendolyn would write an introduction for Don's third book, *Don't Cry, Scream* (1969), a work revealing dramatic improvement in writing and control of form. The stage for conflict would be set at Gwendolyn's, however, because of various differences across which she and the group would eventually build a bridge. Though committed to black solidarity, Gwendolyn retained reflexes based upon broad ideals of art—integration, bourgeois democracy, and Christianity—which would only gradually relax their force. Despite differences in the group, most of the young were closer to sources of the radical definitions characterizing the time: Malcolm X's viewpoints, Marxist or Maoist speculations, and various theories emphasizing blacks' going it alone. Several also strongly valued street definitions of existence.

Walter recalls the group's filing into Gwendolyn's home with the still relatively new symbols of black revolt conspicuously showing. "Here we were with naturals and sandals on and dashikis and shirts that were open or tied around our waists. Beards hanging all down, ladies wearing their hair in all kinds of different ways." One of the more serious conflicts arose over Gwendolyn's reading a paper questioning the idea sometimes expressed in the group that whites were of a different breed. Over the years of her career, she had sometimes used the example that we are all "bathroom goers" to point out people's common share of mortality and imperfection. In the paper, she spoke of lions and elephants and their shared animalhood in producing wastes. Although her poetry firmly registers her recognition of kinship with a black group, it is based primarily on the idea that "people are people." Her way with blacks was to portray complexity and distinctiveness, to show that they were human beings and not "curios." In the group, on the other hand, there was strong feeling that it was not so simple to account for the murderous responses of whites toward the civil rights movement, the urban horrors and despair deriving from systematic exploitation, America's general racial intransigence, and European wholesale destruction of indigenous human life in so many geographical areas.

Other than a couple of aborted walkouts, group members dealt with their disagreement on these issues by defending their conclusions as a logical extension of the awareness that she herself had shown in such poems as "kitchenette building" and "The Ballad of Rudolph Reed." Amidst tensions, Gwendolyn brought the issue up at other meetings, asking whether they didn't think there could be one or two whites who were all right. The response was "Yes, but they don't count because they don't make up enough difference to keep the rest of them chumps off our case." Those who came over to the side of blacks to suffer with them, it was felt, ironically showed that they were as powerless as the blacks they thought they were espousing. A basic difference was thus Gwendolyn's anchorage in simple moral views and the principle, shared by some of the younger group, of power relations espoused by the Black Power movement; they felt free to characterize the enemy from evidence on the historical record.

Eventually, the group bridged the question by stating that they were not concerned with "them," but with "us." Whites were not part of their conversation, and they were trying to write poetry not for "them" but for "us." A walkout issue for Don L. Lee was Gwendolyn's questioning the value of so much profanity in a work of art, an objection shared by Val Gray Ward, who had dramatized the works of earlier black writers who seemed to achieve much without it. It was Gwendolyn's view that profanity at some point became trite, detracting from the quality of the work. Don at first felt that this judgment derived from her parochialism, although he had deep respect for her work, which he had known during the period of his troubled youth. After almost getting into a shouting match with Gwendolyn, he left the meeting, and they did not talk, as he recalls, for quite a while. "But after thinking about it for some time, my conclusion was that it [her judgment] was a combination of both [artistic principle and parochialism]. I think that what she said had definite validity. On the other hand, it was still another phase for her, and it would take some time for her to get used to it."

The confrontation caused Don to look more critically at his own work, seeking to create a quickly communicating poetry that would not require elaborate knowledge of literary conventions; humor, street rapping, and a complex method of insinuation known in black folk literature as the "signifying tradition" permeated much of his early work. A considerable freedom in the use of language was important to the method. In subsequent talk over brunch at Gwendolyn's, Don and Gwendolyn discussed their frustrations and reached "a level of communication that was much tighter and closer."

Gwendolyn and the group were aware of each other in ways that would create a harmony among the differences. She admired their energy, definiteness, determination, and talent. They were becoming a family, as reflected in some of her poems. In *Family Pictures* (1970), Don is "Beautiful. Impudent. / Ready for life. / A tied storm." Walter Bradford is "a whipstopper . . . Tree-planting man." For their part, the kinship group was aware of her as a distinguished poet who had entered the big literary battles and had won with integrity. Life as they had known it was genuinely represented in her poetry, and they had experienced her sincerity and openness and her process of undergoing change. Many were also aware that they were still in the process of forming themselves or facing a significant turning point in their lives. The group's ideological certainty was thus sometimes a projection that masked uncertainties about their lives and their own writing. Don confessed ambivalence about challenging an elder and a person whose writing had meant much to him over the years.

As Gwendolyn and the group moved beyond the "therapy" sessions and into writing as their main concern, Val Gray Ward saw in her a greater vitality, like that she had experienced at Gwendolyn's earlier "nice" interracial parties. "She was high, she was spiritual, she was like a little girl jumping around." The earlier parties had been good, but the current gatherings were "exhilarating." "It was a different kind of spiritual feeling. . . . She would let loose. . . . If I hadn't got my screaming session on by then, she would say, 'Is Val OK?' She would say, 'What do you think of so' n' so? You going to let that go by?' " Larry Neal, the New York–based critic, was reminded by Gwendolyn's relationship to the young of John Coltrane and Ornette Coleman: like them, she needed to put herself into the context of the energy that the young represented.

The relationship between Gwendolyn and younger writers reached its first climax at the dedication of the Wall of Respect at Forty-third and Langley on August 27, 1967, to recognize the achievement of the Artists Workshop of the Organization of Black American Culture (OBACC). One of the organizations destined to have considerable influence on artistic creativity of several sorts in Chicago, OBACC (*oh-bah-see*) had, as one of its goals, to achieve a free context within which the artist could explore black experience, providing the black community with positive images of itself. Jeff Donaldson, later head of the Arts Department at Howard University, and other painters had painted on the wall of a slum building images of outstanding blacks whom the community, without prompting by the media, would naturally honor, such as W.E.B. DuBois, Lerone Bennett, Gwendolyn Brooks, H. Rap Brown, James Baldwin, Stokely Carmichael, Wilt Chamberlain, Ornette Coleman, John Coltrane, LeRoi Jones, John Oliver Killens, Martin Luther King, Malcolm X, Thelonius Monk, Max Roach, Nina Simone, and Sara Vaughn. The Wall also carried LeRoi Jones's "S.O.S." poem, which called to all blacks to come in and help to form a black solidarity. Thus the Wall was part of a political thrust, asserting the community's power of self-determination.[3]

On dedication day, the crowd itself, by its sheer size, closed off the street to traffic. Gwendolyn participated in the ceremonies with the writers' group, who read their poems. In the high tide of the excitement, the writers' group took Gwendolyn to the bar at the Playboy Lounge, which was located right off Langley. All the OBACC writers and their leader, Hoyt Fuller, were there. One of the poets went to the front of the bar where a microphone was set up and said, "Say, folks, we're going to lay some poetry on you."

Gwendolyn, who was wondering how the people would receive such offerings, read with the group. People "turned around on their bar stools, with
their drinks behind them, and were listening. Then they applauded."[4] The
audience "sat there for more than an hour listening to us do our thing. And
when we finished, we took the microphone down and turned on the music
and danced. Yes, they really accepted that."[5]

For Gwendolyn the communal quality of the experience was deeply
penetrating, and would, over the years, continue to tease her sensibility and
require different approaches to art. It was only in recent years that she had
been afforded black audiences of such magnitude and consciousness. She
spoke repeatedly of her desire to reach people like those in the bars and
taverns. "I want to write poetry—and it won't be Ezra Pound poetry, as you
can imagine—that will be exciting to such people. And I don't see why it
can't be 'good' poetry." She would not try to do the same thing as the
younger artists; she was not, in 1969, interested in her poems becoming
"social forces." In her interview with George Stavros, she stated that she felt
her future poems would be more like those in A Street in Bronzeville and
would give pictures of black life as she saw it at that time.[6] She would not
preach, nor aim to teach (though she would not object to her poems
teaching something), and she was also thinking of writing small verse plays.

In a 1971 interview with Ida Lewis, she would again speak of the
necessity of reaching the people in bars.[7] As late as 1972, the impact of the
1967 reading in a bar was still evident, though her statements referred to a
broader cross section for her audience: "My aim, in my next future, is to
write poems that will somehow successfully 'call' (see Imamu Baraka's
'SOS') all black people: black people in taverns, black people in alleys, black
people in gutters, schools, offices, factories, prisons, the consulate; I wish to
reach black people in pulpits, black people in mines, on farms, on thrones;
not always to 'teach'—I shall wish often to entertain, to illumine. My newish
voice will not be an imitation of the contemporary young black voice, which
I do so admire, but an extending adaptation of today's G.B. voice."[8]

Listening to the younger poets at readings, she marveled at how well
they could speak out of themselves, as the poetry became merely the script
for a total attempt at communication through various inflections of speech,
song, and sometimes dance. It was the communal quality of the experience
and the very deep level of acceptance that persisted in her memory.

In the Mecca, in both form and content, registers the impact. Gwendolyn spends little time evoking the Mecca Building, the former showplace
that had become a slum and served as the setting for her framework and
related stories. She focuses instead upon what is happening to the holiness

of people's souls in a corrupting universe. Mrs. Sallie Smith, a domestic worker and the sole support of nine children, is the source of the framework story. Returning from oppressive domestic labors, she finds that Pepita, her youngest child, is missing. Eventually, the small girl is found under her murderer's cot amidst the dust and roaches. Thus the framework story provides the ultimate pathos. The search by Mrs. Sallie, her children, and "the Law" provides a tour of the Mecca Building and an exposure to the life stories of Mrs. Sallie's children and several other occupants of the building. We meet a representative group and experience the lostness, isolation, frustration, and debasement that characterize the Mecca as well as more far-flung areas in man's historical experiences.

Apparently expecting a more traditionally developed story, Harper & Row was startled by the *Mecca* manuscript they received early in September 1967. One reader felt it was a complete failure. For this reader, Gwendolyn had not achieved a continuous interweaving of sound and substance in the poetry, and though the four short poems she had originally submitted had defects, they contained more genuine poetry. The piece lacked power to deliver a story and arouse feeling, and the Mecca Building and all it was supposed to represent were inadequately invoked. The mother's voice seemed out of tune with the voices of others; the stories did not relate to the Mecca Building or to the tragedy befalling the child—a lack that dispersed interest, watered down the suspense, and made for a weak ending.

Harper decided to publish the work after securing what changes it could. The editors called for more poems, a request that Gwendolyn was at first hesitant to grant since she did not want them to detract from the longer poem. With the hope of securing changes in style and structure, Harper got the poet's permission to have the work reviewed by Elizabeth Lawrence, who wrote to Gwendolyn regarding the failure of the poem to move her as she thought it should. Its artifice seemed to overwhelm the content. She therefore felt that the book should be larger and more diversified. [9]

Apparently, Gwendolyn saw creative possibilities in adding ten poems. To editor Genevieve Young, she stated that they would be "an advantage for the book. The Ten should be products of *this* time, should speak for, or out of, today's temper and tones—should be derivatives of the Mecca situation. And they should join the four closing poems under the title 'After Mecca' (instead of 'Appendix'). Then the entire book can be called IN THE MECCA (instead of In the Mecca and Other Poems, which does not have a cohesive sound)." The poet enclosed a *Life* magazine article, from November 19, 1951, on the Mecca Building and encircled the picture containing the

staircases up which she herself had "trudged . . . delivering Holy Thunderbolts and Liquid Love Charms" for the spiritual advisor. She felt that the
photo was evocative and that it could be featured on the book jacket. In the
middle of one set of courtyards stood a little lost-looking girl. "That could be
my Pepita," Gwendolyn added.[10]

Harper was delighted with the additional poems. However, since *Life*
refused permission to use the photograph, the poem is introduced only by an
inscription from John Bartlow Martin's "The Strangest Place in Chicago,"[11]
which described the Mecca, and by comments from Chicagoans. On the
adjacent page the book announced itself "In Tribute—Jim Cunningham,
Jim Taylor, Mike Cook, Walter Bradford, Don Lee, Curtis Ellis, Roy Lewis,
Peggy Susberry, Ronda Davis, Carolyn Rodgers, Sharon Scott, Alicia
Johnson, and Jewel Latimore."

In the Mecca contains both the universe of the earlier poems and an
emerging universe of struggle. The outstanding achievement in *The Bean
Eaters* and *Selected Poems* was the evocation of an individual holding onto
some measure of integrity, some capacity to act from the best of the self.
Mrs. Sallie, the heroine of the title poem "In the Mecca," certainly
represents the strong individual of the older universe. Very early Gwendolyn reveals the depths and the heroism in the character of this "ordinary"
domestic servant through an imagery and diction that also convey something of her psychological responses, attitudes, and discipline.

> S. Smith is Mrs. Sallie. Mrs. Sallie
> hies home to Mecca, hies to marvelous rest;
> ascends the sick and influential stair.
> The eye unrinsed, the mouth absurd
> with the last sourings of the master's Feast.
> She plans
> to set severity apart,
> to unclench the heavy folly of the fist.
> Infirm booms
> and suns that have not spoken die behind this
> low-brown butterball. Our prudent partridge.
> A fragmentary attar and armed coma.
> A fugitive attar and a district hymn.

"The sick and influential stair" locution is expressive both of a quality of
the staircase and of how it makes the climber feel. It is thus a character in
itself, one not unknown to climbers in any deteriorating building where the
stairway seems to have absorbed into itself the varying rhythms of its

climbers and to reflect the depression all around. The stairs had a personal meaning for Gwendolyn because she retained so vivid a memory of her own upward trudges with her load of Love Charms and Holy Thunderbolts during the time she worked for the prophet. Up such stairs Mrs. Sallie is going home to "marvelous rest."

A key image revealing the psychological pressures on Mrs. Sallie is "the last sourings of the master's Feast," from which she proceeds with "eye unrinsed" and "mouth absurd." The "sourings" are everything Mrs. Sallie, as a domestic, has had to react to under the tightest discipline. Other images suggest repressed violence, inner explosions: "the heavy folly of the fist," "infirm booms," and unspoken "suns." In "fragmentary attar," "armed coma," "fugitive attar" and "district hymn," Mrs. Sallie is a fine sweetness and fragrance not fully developed or freely asserted, a warrior unable to assault frontally the ills of the domestic scene, and a song from an area unknown to her oppressors. The rest of the poem reveals her passionate commitments and unsettled but stoic confrontation with realities.

Gwendolyn is also interested in revealing Mrs. Sallie's damaged and brainwashed side. Though intensely commited to her family, she sees as the ideal the images of beauty provided by the white family she labors for:

> Mrs. Sallie
> evokes and loves and loathes a pink-lit image
> of the toy-child. Her Lady's.
> Her Lady's pink convulsion, toy-child dances
> in stiff wide pink through Mrs. Sallie. Stiff pink is
> on toy-child's poverty of cream
> under a shiny tended warp of gold.
> What shiny tended gold is an aubade
> for toy-child's head! Has ribbons, too!
> Ribbons. Not Woolworth cotton comedy,
> not rubber band, not string. . . .
> "And that would be my baby be my baby. . . .
> and I would be my lady I my lady. . . .

Comments the poets: "What else is there to say but everything?" Mrs. Sallie's heroism is coexistent with victimization.

Mrs. Sallie's children are usually expending positive energy, though often at odds with society's conventions, and preoccupied with retaining for themselves the autonomous worlds of adolescence and childhood. Yvonne, the oldest, receives generous attention from the poet. Yvonne is at once a person of "bald innocence and gentle fright" and the "undaunted" who once "pushed her thumbs into the eyes of a Thief." An uneasy and uncertain dreamer, she would appear tough to impress her lover but also daydreams of ways and settings by which he can best be brought to marriage. Eventually, the excitement over the missing youngest child, Pepita, stifles within her her primary concerns: "Cannot now conjure spice and soft explosion / Mixing with miffed mosquitoes where the dark / defines and redefines." Gwendolyn deals tenderly with Yvonne's romantic strivings and rationalizations:

> It is not necessary, says Yvonne,
> to have every day him whom
> to the end thereof you will love.
> Because it is tasty to remember
> he is alive, and laughs
> in somebody else's room,
> or is slicing a cold cucumber,
> or is buttoning his cuffs,
> or is signing with his pen
> and will plan
> to touch you again.

When Gwendolyn reads this passage aloud, she looks away, laughs secretly, as if she herself were carried back to the experiences that produced the portraits of love dreamers in such poems as "Annie Allen," "To Be in Love," and "A Lovely Love."

Like Yvonne, most of the other Smith children are caught in isolation. The poem's description of the boy Briggs and his inability to escape gang involvement would seem to apply to many of the other children: "Please pity Briggs. But there is a central height in pity / past which man's hand and sympathy cannot go; / past which the little hurt dog / descends to mass—no longer Joe, / not Bucky, not Cap'n, not Rex, / not Briggs—and is all self-employed, / concerned with Other, / not with Us."

Forced to face harsh realities, the younger group feels its alienation and hates "sewn suburbs." Tennessee identifies with a cat that permits stroking, though he is given milk while crying for meat. Mixing with the affairs of others, he knows already, brings on bruises and regrets. Thomas Earl imaginatively transcends his universe by his love for Johnny Appleseed and his identification with the myth, but in his own universe he feels powerless. Melody Mary is only lightly troubled by headline tragedies and feels that sufficient to the day are the pains immediately in front of her. "Trapped in his privacy of pain / the worried rat expires / and smashed in the grind of a rapid heel / last night's roaches lie." Rats and roaches seem representative of both Mary's broad respect for life and the unpredictable terrors confronting her.

The adult characters who shape and partake of this universe are pathetic, corrupt, or merely contemplative. They are presented in terms of startling imagery, incisive phrases, dramatic encounters, soliloquies, ritualized passages sometimes emphasized by rhymes, special forms, language formalized or made artificial by various devices—sudden shifts into realism, symbolic or abstract language or dialogue, and varied speech tones. Numerous personalities become memorable: insane Sophie, who is to be caged with her "doll, whom none will stun"; Great Gram remembering a slave childhood playing with her sister Pernie Mae where things "squishied" and "creebled" in the cabin's dirt floor; Aunt Dill, sensation monger; and Marian, frustrated by the fact that nothing of her inner self is ever seen, even by her husband.

Memorable younger men, including the historical Don L. Lee, act as choruses. Alfred's is the philosophical voice or perspective in most of the poem—a charming but dissolute teacher, would-be writer, and dreamer of a better world. He is trapped and neutralized within his reveries while articulating the ills of the Mecca. The immediately violent is seen in two men: Way-Out Morgan, collecting guns to avenge the violations that he, his family, and friends have undergone, and Amos, picturing a healthy America arising from violent destruction and rebirth. Loam Norton broadens the picture of misery, historically and geographically, and clearly connects the Mecca scene with that of all the disinherited. His voice gains power through a parody of the Twenty-third Psalm—a reflection upon a god who has not taken care of business.

> Norton considers Belsen and Dachau,
> regrets all old unkindnesses and harms,
> . . . The Lord was their shepherd.
> Yet did they want.
> Joyfully would they have lain in jungles or pastures,
> walked beside waters. Their gaunt
> souls were not restored, their souls were banished.
> In the shadow valley
> they feared the evil, whether with or without God.
> They were comforted by no Rod,
> no Staff, but flayed by, O besieged by, shot a-plenty
> The prepared table was the rot or curd of the day.
> Anointings were of lice. Blood was the spillage of cups.

Don L. Lee's vision, his desire for a completely reborn world, is the black nationalist perspective. Alfred, however, has led the old feelings up to this nationhood stance by calling for "hot estrangement" and the demolition of the old dispensation.

Although Mrs. Sallie and a few others confront life directly and are in touch with the depths of themselves, the universe of "In the Mecca" is both like and unlike that of *The Bean Eaters*. Certainly, much of the poem recalls "The Explorer" of the *Bean Eaters*, his confusions and findings:

> So tipping down the scrambled halls he set
> Vague hands on throbbing knobs. There were behind
> Only spiraling, high human voices,
> The scream of nervous affairs,
> Wee griefs,
> Grand griefs. And choices.

Up to the word "choices," there is a good deal of similarity between the two universes. But circumstances in "In the Mecca" give a different meaning to the significant individual gesture that *The Bean Eaters* celebrated. Persons who salvage something despite being weighed down by external forces can, of course, be cited in "In the Mecca." Alfred, though overtaken by meaninglessness, stands up to make accurate recordings of how things are and, in the end, becomes a prophet. The poem ends on a note of compassion and without a significant change of consciousness in the heroine, Mrs. Sallie, thus recording a simply humanistic pressure amidst the revolutionary. Yet the individual gesture that seemed to take the measure of life and humanity in the earlier books seems to become, in "In the Mecca," the mere pocketing of small change in a gesture of survival. As to choices that "cried to be taken," the poem really implies that one big choice must first be taken—a communal one against the sea of misery. There must be found, as Alfred implies, a "joining thing." Besides the appearance and sentiments of persons of revolutionary vision, it is the implications of this altered universe that would seem to reflect Gwendolyn's encounter with the younger black writers.

Despite numerous criticisms, most reviewers had to admit that the poem had areas of power, and James N. Johnson in *Ramparts* magazine hailed the complete book as Gwendolyn's best work since *A Street in Bronzeville*.[12] The truth is that "In the Mecca," like the novel *Maud Martha*, makes its way on its own terms. That is, what Gwendolyn has to say finds its own form—a major tendency in American poetry of the twentieth century. The poem is concerned with a universe of misery that extends beyond Chicago, geographically and historically. Its form is essentially that of a series of interrelated vignettes that reveal the pervasiveness of the ills expressed by the central catastrophe. The poetry exemplifies every technique that Gwendolyn had learned, and is a culmination of her power to wield a flexible free verse.

The poem, of course, is not without flaws, one of them being inconsistency. Perhaps the poet intended that the exploiting Prophet Williams, despite the opening characterization, should have no greater evil impact than that of a sizable but banal fraud. Yet the tendency is to expect more because of Gwendolyn's shuddering autobiographical references to him, even though such references are outside the poem itself. Alfred is spoken of as "he who might have been a poet-king," although he is said earlier to be aware that he is untalented. Some sections of the poem seem abruptly shoved in, although they tend to justify themselves by their contribution to the poem's thematic development. Expressionistic passages don't always communicate effectively ("In the blasé park, / that winks and mocks but is at all times / tolerant of the virtuous defect, of audit, / and of mangle and of wile . . ."). Besides the overall form, it is the intensity with which Gwendolyn enters the life of several people that makes the poem outstanding.

The remainder of the poems in *In the Mecca* make excellent use of the transition to the present day effected by the title poem. We are carried through stages of disaffection and rebellion in "To a Winter Squirrel" and "Boy Breaking Glass." As "Boy Breaking Glass" puts it, "Each to his grief, each to / his loneliness and fidgety revenge." "Medgar Evers" celebrates the assassinated civil rights leader's inner revolution and his commitment to the creation of a new world, while the assassinated Malcolm X is celebrated as the man of uprightness and honest vision, of power and persuasiveness. Of the two poems devoted to art, "The Chicago Picasso" raises issues relevant to man's appreciation of contemporary Western art, and "The Wall" portrays group celebration involved in the paintings on a slum building. Two poems touch upon gang life, with emphasis upon strength and vitality in reacting to oppression.

The two sermons on the Warpland (America) draw the book to an effective conclusion by moving beyond victimization, rebellion, and celebration, by urging a rich solidarity and living and having "your blooming in the noise and whip of the whirlwind."

In the poem "In the Mecca," the author, as she said in her initial plan, is "interested in a certain detachment, but only as a means of reaching substance with some incisiveness." From time to time, she is part of the choral commentary, and usually she hovers very close to the characters, who are portrayed through an omniscient point of view. This "certain detach-ment" is completely abandoned in "The Wall," where the author dramat-ically appears as part of the group in what is almost a formalized initiation ceremony.

> I mount the rattling wood. Walter [Bradford]
> says, "She is good." Says, "She
> our Sister is." In front of me
> hundreds of faces, red-brown, brown, black, ivory,
> yield me hot trust, their yea and their Announcement
> that they are ready to rile the high-flung ground.

More than any other, this passage registers the author's intensity of personal hunger for the group's validation, and again reminds us of the importance of both the Wall and the tavern experience in Gwendolyn's personal and poetic development. But the sermons on the Warpland make clear that the validation is also an initiation into a role at the center of the group's struggle. George Stavros felt that these two poems were almost "apocalyptic or prophetic," but Gwendolyn declined the role: "They're little addresses to black people, that's all."[13] She stressed that she wanted simply, as part of the changes in her poetry, to create uncompromising poems that would also be meaningful to blacks in general. Whatever Gwendolyn's conscious inten-tion, D.H. Melhem's judgment seems quite accurate: "Thus *In the Mecca* (1968) marks a creative prime meridian for the poet. There the oracular voice, prescriptive and prophetic, is clearly heard. Fact, faction, strangers, friends, history and personal narrative, past, present, future are caught in a dynamo of refining energy."[14]

Gwendolyn spoke of *In the Mecca* quite rightly as her blackest book up to that time. Later she would be apprehensive about the use that might be made of the first part of "The Blackstone Rangers," where the Rangers are presented "As Seen by Disciplines," that is, by those concerned primarily with order: "There they are. / Thirty at the corner. / Black, raw, ready. / Sores in the city / that do not want to heal." Later she would ask Genevieve Young not to "let anyone reprint any part of 'The Blackstone Rangers' without reprinting the entire three-part poem. The people who select the first tiny part *only* are interested, I believe, in suggesting to an eager, waiting public that the Rangers are sores and nothing else—a fallacy I went to some pains to discredit."[15]

In the Mecca got off to a good start with the buying public, selling 2,986 copies in the first week.[16] Local reviewers gave the book a strong push.

Under the heading "Giant of a Poem That Says It All," Robert H. Glauber, in the *Chicago Sun-Times*, stated that "In the Mecca" was the best work of the book and that the book was Gwendolyn's finest. It dealt with what "Jung calls the 'crucial experiences,' powerful emotions, suffering, passion, the stuff of human fate in general." Under the heading "The Rage and the Fire," Van Allen Bradley, in the *Chicago Daily News*, spoke of Gwendolyn as the most celebrated black woman poet since Phillis Wheatley: "In spinning out in spare, blazingly brilliant lines the tragic tale of the death of Pepita Smith, Miss Brooks creates with deft strokes a mini-portrait gallery of Chicago characters unequaled in imaginative power since the creations of Nelson Algren in 'The Man With the Golden Arm.' " He recognized her new militancy, "the signs of a smoldering rage born of centuries of oppression. Yes, it is all unmistakably here—the rage and the fire and the music, as well as the powerful lines we have come to expect of one of the finest poetic craftsmen of our time," one of America's "greatest living poets."[17]

Reviewers on the national scene, though qualified in their praise and sometimes puzzled, also called attention to outstanding qualities of the work. In the *Christian Science Monitor,* Janet Overmeyer contrasted Carl Sandburg's easy-to-understand poetry and his tendency to glorify America's past and its ordinary citizens with Gwendolyn's more complex approaches to language and her tendency to glorify nothing: "Miss Brooks' particular, outstanding genius is her unsentimental regard and respect for all human beings, even the gang kids, as indicated in three poems about them. ('Their country is a Nation on no map.') She neither foolishly pities nor condemns—she creates. From her poet's craft bursts a whole gallery of wholly alive persons, preening, squabbling, loving, weeping; many a novelist cannot do so well in ten times the space." The reviewer compared the form of the poem "In the Mecca" to that of a fugue, as any single section "makes indirect comment on others, until all combine in a rich tapestry of not-so-separate-after-all lives."[18]

M.L. Rosenthal, writing in the *New York Times Book Review,* called the title poem "overwrought with effects" and said the poet seemed to back away from "her overpowering subject." But he concluded that the poem "had the power of its materials and holds the imagination fixed on the horrid predicament of real Americans whose everyday world haunts the nation's conscience intolerably." Rosenthal mistakenly saw the title poem apart as "the real interest of the book," and looked for the registration of a single horror—the murder of Pepita. Thus he ignored ways in which other stories in the title poem and others in the book form a symphony of themes. William Stafford, in *Poetry,* credited the book with a special kind of complexity, although he found some references confusingly local. Marie Miller in the *Journal of Negro Education* commented only on the poem "In the Mecca," but recognized the poet's intent to create a larger picture. The brief *Virginia Quarterly Review* statement recognized that Gwendolyn was speaking with a new voice and in a new manner, "better than the earlier work in its honesty, poorer in its loss of music and control. Perhaps the exchange was necessary; it proves that Gwendolyn Brooks, the poet, is still alive in the fullest sense." Other reviews recognized the militancy or the political quality of the poems but also a loss of lyricism. While praising her discovery of new attitudes and treatment of new themes, Walter Waring, writing in *Library Journal*, spoke of her "abandonment of lyric meters of her earlier work for those of exhortation."[19] Generally, however, reviewers who responded in terms of wholes, whether the whole title poem or the whole book, were able to report a more powerful impact than those focusing closely on the framework story of the bereaved mother. In approaches to both art and writing style, *In the Mecca* is overwhelmingly a consolidation rather than a stylistic change for Gwendolyn.

Meanwhile, the poet expressed and committed her black sensibility through a number of activities. She was now making steady outlays of money—to help publish young black poets, to support writing contests, to provide needy writers with financial help, and to help underwrite black publishing. As one of her older friends put it, "Gwendolyn always loved nice things, but now that she is making money she simply gives it all away." Naturally, among so many instances of spontaneous giving she would occasionally find herself exploited through a plea that merely dressed itself in the name of the cause. Although money was lost, she usually brought misuse firmly to an end. As one of her young friends put it, the word was out that "when Miss Thang says hang it up, then hang it up, Brother." But in general she was pleased. During the summer of 1969, she sent two young writers to Africa at a cost of $4,000. She felt that the trip changed their lives and was therefore quite happy about it.

Gwendolyn kept busy giving readings at various colleges under the auspices of the Adult Education Council and dreaming about more ways to make money. The council, which was sounding out magazines regarding prebook publication of her autobiography, reported excitement and interest. She dreamed of a fee of $125,000, the amount she understood that *McCall's* had paid Liz Carpenter for a capsule of her book on Lady Bird Johnson and to Dr. Christiaan Barnard for his story. "I may sound 'presumptuous.' But I do expect the book to sell very well. And you GY

[Genevieve Young] and I—at *last*—will make a fortune."[20] Her hopes were kept high by the news that Ann Pinchot had received $162,000 for the paperback rights to a book. Publishers, however, wanted first to see Gwendolyn's book, or much of it, and she had little time for writing.

During 1967–68, Gwendolyn's renewed spirit of commitment had impact at home. In 1968, Nora, preparing to travel to France and England after graduating from Hirsch High School, found her high ambitions of getting a permanent opposed by Gwendolyn's allegiance to the movement for natural hair styles. When Nora put up a fight, Gwendolyn called Don L. Lee, who had become Nora's adopted big brother. Nora, though embarrassed and threatening to hide out in her room, continued to battle for the permanent, and got her first "natural" only when she was caught in the rain in Paris.[21]

Tensions occurred also between Gwendolyn and her husband, Henry. Nora was amused to see her mother, outraged by something her father had said, stamp her foot and exclaim, "You middle-aged people make me so mad!" Gwendolyn's response was, of course, a product of the strong commitment she was making to youth and of her feeling of new life from their energy. Apparently Henry at times felt that Gwendolyn was accepting certain ideas from the young that she had ignored when he had advocated them in the past. Perhaps partly because of his background in business, he had spoken for years of the need for black unity that Gwendolyn was now stressing.

Nora too was often at odds with Henry. She felt that he praised her cooking more than her numerous scholastic achievements. They would argue over whether an award to a black woman should not have gone to a black man and whether it was an emasculation of the black male. Nora would argue spiritedly that she was willing to respect any black man who got ahead of her but that she was not going to step back so he could have the illusion that he had earned the front position. She was strongly backed by Gwendolyn. Actually, the argument was newer in its application than in its existence. Henry had long felt that whites would often do for a black woman what they would not do for a black man, who was a greater challenge to their superiority. Rather early in Gwendolyn's career, when he had looked over a detailed itinerary for one of her engagements, with tickets for her purchased in advance, he stated that whites would not have made such arrangements for a black man.

Unresolved personal problems were apparently masked by other subjects of disagreement. On the one hand, Gwendolyn felt that she and Henry got along well on the level of companionship. "We could talk to each other about anything—writing, politics." He encouraged her writing and was pleased when she received rewards. Yet she knew that, "being a man," he had problems adjusting to her activities. She did her part to "uphold his faith in himself. I wouldn't talk about my own affairs unless he brought them up, and I tried to make sure that things I said would not be taken amiss." She felt that her kind of "walking on eggs" arose in part from the fact that both wrote and that it was "hard on the man's ego to be married to a woman who happens to get some attention before he does." She gave him credit for behaving better than any other man she could imagine in his position. For his part, Henry had a rather thick unpublished novel and sent out stories from time to time. The two discussed his literary ambitions, and she felt that he was an excellent writer who would get a good deal of attention when he put his literary ambitions fully to the test.[22]

Nora's viewpoint was that, though the family talked to each other a lot, the subjects were most frequently public issues. Talking did not get down to internal feelings, self-analysis, and interrelationships. However, when Nora was seventeen, she and her mother were able to break through this focus on the public and get down to "how we felt about each other, and the things that were going on inside ourselves." The process made them feel more like friends than is usual in the conventional relationship of mother and daughter.

No doubt the family situation also reflected changes within Gwendolyn's own personality, a matter of conflict between the traditional concepts of the roles of man and woman and her strong feelings of contemporary womanhood. It was observed within the family that Henry from time to time manifested the traditional man's self-assertion by not making repairs in the house when Gwendolyn thought they should be done. She would sometimes call in someone else to do the work, an act that in the pre-1967 days would upset both her and Henry. Gwendolyn felt that she was doing something wrong but something that nevertheless had to be done. Now she had begun to feel more secure, not just about blackness but about going out and doing things for herself or simply holding beliefs that could cause conflict.

It was one of Nora's adolescent escapades that brought into the open the tensions surging under the surface of the family's relations. She realized later that her mother at that time was already at the crack-up point. Returning from a date at 12:30 P.M., thirty minutes late, she found Gwendolyn even more disturbed than usual by her tardiness. Henry was also very upset and ordered Nora to her room. Amidst her mother's tears and her father's attempted discipline, Nora defiantly refused to go. She recalled later that the order caught her by surprise, since her father had rarely offered to discipline her, being mainly a person with whom she fussed over issues, played chess, and went to the movies. Discipline had come from her mother and, to a small extent, from her brother when he was a part of the household. Suddenly, Henry seized his daughter and pushed her toward her room. She tripped and fell against the piano, cutting her head seriously enough to require several stitches. The blood flowing, of course, did nothing to mitigate the mounting sense of hysteria. It was the first time Nora had seen her mother cry.

The sudden breakthrough of underlying tensions made clear that the frayed strings of family togetherness were broken. The marital separation did not take place immediately but something over a year later, in December 1969, when Henry moved out.

Gwendolyn felt the pain of separation from the person with whom her history and her memories had become inevitably intertwined. But the next stage was a feeling of release, of being able, at her age and with both children grown, to give attention to whatever came to mind without having to be preoccupied with preparing three family meals a day or humoring a man. She began to love being in the house by herself and felt that she appreciated aloneness more than a married woman should. She turned more to writing, reading, and the public commitments that were now expressing her individual life.

She had a strong interest in both Broadside Press and Third World Press, the latter founded and headed by Don L. Lee. She and Don usually paid the expenses incurred by Broadside in publishing their work and helped at times to defray publication costs for other writers. In preparation was her first book to be published by Broadside, a three-part poem entitled *Riot*, which dealt with the disturbances in Chicago after the assassination of Martin Luther King, Jr., in 1968.

Gwendolyn kept active in civic and cultural activities, but what became more and more noticeable was the growing awareness of her in the black community. On October 6, 1968, she was honored at a program sponsored by the Frank London Brown Society, entitled "Black History and Culture Comes Alive." *Negro Digest* had over the years published articles and poetry by her and articles about her; the *Chicago Defender* had taken frequent note of her activities; and *Ebony* had included references to her in various articles. But the *Ebony* of July 1968 went much further; in the article "Gwendolyn Brooks: Poet Laureate," by Phyl Garland, it told the story of her relationship to young blacks and celebrated her life and achievements. Such attention might have been expected, of course, for a poet laureate of the State of Illinois who had also won the Pulitzer Prize, but the article was distinctly black-oriented.

Black audiences varied in their attitudes toward her. For the very young she was "the sister who had come home"—that is, she had arrived at *their* point of "enlightenment." Gwendolyn encouraged such ideas by the extent of praise she lavished upon them and by her manner of quoting them— sometimes in almost textbook fashion. She had particular respect for Walter Bradford and Don L. Lee, who often encouraged her to read materials that would give her a more systematic view of the actual goings-on in America. She particularly responded to Ferdinand Lundberg's *The Rich and the Super-Rich* (1968); its exposure of the control of America and its resources by the few made hollow the pretensions of the American Dream. She was startled to discover that what she had thought was accidental and removable by time's improving hand was in fact highly systematic and doggedly inter-woven in American institutions. "Later, the kids in my writing class would talk about what was going on. And I'd listen and say, 'What? you don't mean it! Is that really true?' "[23]

To Ida Lewis she explained that through the 1940s and 1950s and to a degree up to 1967, she had had too much faith in integration, Christianity, and the world in general. "People were really good, I thought; there was some good even in people who seemed to be evil. It's true that I didn't know very much about wicked people or who they were. It was a good world, the best of all possible worlds. I believed everything. But then, I wasn't reading the books I should have read, when I was young. If I'd been reading W.E.B. DuBois, I would have known more, but I didn't even hear of *The Souls of Black Folk* until I was well grown."[24] Ironically, it would become a com-monplace realization that the North afforded such soundly educated persons as Gwendolyn a solid knowledge of European concepts, while it was the South that made inescapable some understanding of what DuBois was up to. Special community awareness groups changed the odds.

Deep reading for Gwendolyn had been Ralph Waldo Emerson's "Self-Reliance" and "Compensation" ("If you lost something here, you got it in some form over there. That thought made me happy."). There is perhaps something of a paradox here: The very unawareness that allowed Gwen-dolyn to accept "Self-Reliance" as a factual description of the power and imperatives to be derived from the self alone may have helped her to struggle over the years so unflaggingly for artistic achievement. And adopting the principles of "Compensation," allowed her to remain undaunted by dis-couragement in one part of her life while continuing to drive for a favorable outcome in other areas. But her recognition of her overall lack of knowledge of the social arena, despite living in a tough, raw, down-front city like Chicago, made her feel that she had been utterly ignorant. "I didn't know anything. I was naive, I was shy, and a very sweet girl. Sweet and ignorant. Some of it stuck—until 1967."[25] The systematic quality of American oppression became apparent only then.

The young were impressed by her humanity, craftsmanship, and honest portrayals of black life in America. They were simply surprised that, seeing their experiences as she clearly did, she could be startled by the conclusions they were making and fail to understand the wider forces of oppression. She found Walter Bradford dealing with her quite gently, yet holding her to strict account for her responses. He did not correct her directly when he felt she was in error, and sometimes he simply went on to another subject. But gradually she found herself understanding something she had not understood before. Never harsh, impetuous, or deflating, never rough or cold or acting as if he would consign her to the lower depths, Walter nevertheless managed to be firm. She had the impression that she would not get away with anything; that she would be steadily encouraged to form new views. Walter, it seems, had a like response; despite what he sometimes considered unusual behavior, he felt always from Gwendolyn a maternal encouragement.

On the other hand, she found her early relations with Don Lee more direct and of precise accounting. He displayed a careful admiration of her— so careful that she was always surprised when she encountered evidence of it. But his facial expression usually changed dramatically when she displayed some evidence of unawareness. He became instantly stern. She felt that it was his preference to smile tenderly upon little old ladies. "But, poof! There is an EMERGENCY. The childlike smile disappears." Gwendolyn felt that "While dispensing mercilessness," at programs, he looked "variously like the best paintings of Jesus . . . or like various serious students or like an elastic salon."[26] She seemed to enjoy the moment when a black woman, after praising her reading at the Pittsburgh International Poetry Forum, stated that Don frightened her. Gwendolyn reportedly replied, "He should."

The under-thirty group thus valued Gwendolyn from its appreciation of her true qualities. Perhaps with excessive solemnity, they were also often self-congratulating about being in the vanguard and saw her as the bridge by which they were crossing over into new territory. Older blacks or those who had come to set still deeper value upon craft evaluated her from that position, sometimes to the detriment of the under-thirty group. After meeting her in October 1970, the young radical critic-poet Larry Neal wrote her a reverent letter thanking her for her example of craft and devotion and urging her not to be easy on the younger poets. "Sister, Please, Please, Please, don't let some of us so-called 'young' writers intimidate you. You have done your work and you are giving us a legacy. Some of us may not know it, but we owe you so much. Not only you but Dudley [Randall], Robert [Hayden], [Ralph] Ellison, and all others who have fought the spiritual fight for us. I am not afraid to say it: you birthed many of us. Speaking for myself, I have tried to attain some of the *craft* that is indicated in your work. And I know that the word 'craft' is frowned upon by many of my generation. But craft, to me, is still important. Many times, poets younger than me have asked me about poetry. And so many times, I have recommended your work to them; told them to note the economy of language, the various twists and inflections that I hear in your poems. And most of all the love that simply swells over a sincere reader of your visions."

He felt within Gwendolyn a "fragility" that perhaps allowed her "to be bothered by those of us who have just begun to learn what a serious thing it is to shape words into felt-visions. But don't. Try to understand that we are searching ourselves. We don't really know all there is to know, and you will have to help us. Therefore, don't be easy on us. We need the strictness of a mature hand to guide us." He did feel, nonetheless, that the older artist gains from the energy of the younger ones.[27]

In an interview with me, Larry Neal was quite specific as to the qualities he admired in Gwendolyn and her work. Since he had read her as an undergraduate, his relationship to poetry and to Gwen's works came prior to the movement. He also read early the Harlem Renaissance writers, who made him understand that poetry was important beyond polemics. He had never felt that Gwendolyn should be militant; Gwendolyn's value, he felt, lay in a cosmology, a literary mind, and a holistic vision. Unlike many blacks who were returning to the community in the sixties, she had never been alienated from black life, as evidenced by how completely she saw her people. Neal pointed out that Gwendolyn had a clear understanding of the textures and rhythms of Afro-American life and their relationship to art. On the other hand, she could be polemical in good taste. Her devotion to form and craft revealed her knowledge of what it took to master an art. Her example of organization in poetry would have benefited the revolutionaries in their own field.

His only criticism was that she should have been harder on the younger writers, and that she could have taught them more of her "real secrets." Gwendolyn herself was aware of being careful, as evidenced by her comments to Phyl Garland. "Just now, there's such a gush of raw vigor that I'm careful about it when it comes into my hands. I don't want to do anything that would impede that vigor. There's something very special happening in poetry today and I see it happening chiefly among the young blacks. I think that later they will take out some of the unruly roughness, but right now, I'm just glad to see it coming out. I think after all of the activity there will be an intense interest in saying things more effectively, using language more effectively." In the Stavros interview she suggested that she hoped the artistic concerns in her 1950 *Phylon* statement would be applicable again in twenty years, after the 1960s crises had been dealt with. "By then the rawness will have come to some maturation. Hopefully something will have been decided, and the poets will then have time to play more with their art." Later, in an interview with Jill Oppenheimer, she conceded that "in the beginning there were poets writing poems that consisted chiefly of expletives, 'Kill the honky, kill the honky.' . . . When they found out the magical things words can do, they employed them in other ways." By 1975 she would also find younger poets "doing the kinds of things they used to tell me I should not do . . . concerning themselves with obscurities and irrelevancies."[28]

The somewhat-over-thirty portion of her black audience continued to feel that she had already registered more deep things concerning blacks than most other writers, and found her achievement in the great depths and beauties of her explorations. John O. Killens was impressed by "her tremendous humanity." Having been a part of the Harlem Writers Workshop, which resulted in sixteen novels, seven nonfiction works, five plays, and six movies, he had been close to the birth pangs of a number of writers. He was peeved with the condescending attitude with which Gwendolyn was introduced at the 1967 Fisk Conference and annoyed by the fact that a young group that arranged for her to visit Howard University paid her only one-third the fee it paid LeRoi Jones.[29]

The Chicago over-thirty group tended to have the same reverence for Gwendolyn's achievement prior to 1967. Hoyt Fuller felt that she had kept the younger group from going hog-wild. Lerone Bennett said that "Gwendolyn Brooks has always been committed and lyrical and relevant. Before it was fashionable, she was tone deep in blackness. In the fifties, she was writing poems about Emmett Till and Little Rock and the black boys and girls who came North looking for the Promised Land and found concrete deserts. In fact, she has always written about the sounds and sights and flavors of the black community."[30]

Such persons as journalist Francis Ward and his wife, Val Gray Ward, also felt that Gwendolyn had been at home in blackness all the time. Val was taken aback by the credit that Gwendolyn gave to the younger group for her awakening to a new consciousness. As a reader and dramatizer of poems, she felt that Gwendolyn had always been conscious and had been "doing fantastic" writing all the time. Participating in the explosions of the workshops with the younger group, she sometimes challenged their concept of a poem. Although she dramatized several, she objected to the amount of profanity, which sometimes precluded her using them in churches, where most blacks were still to be found. For her, some of the profanity could be labeled simply self-hate. She cited Margaret Walker's poem of revolutionary power "For My People," which had not a single word of profanity.

Despite such differences, the community in its ever-increasing awareness of Gwendolyn and her achievements was united in revering her, regardless of differences in their language. When Val Gray Ward suggested that the community should tell Gwendolyn how it felt about her while she was so alive in their hearts, the movement began to create what was to be called a "Living Anthology." Writers, musicians, painters, photographers, actors, and dancers came, as Hoyt W. Fuller put it, "from everywhere for the love-fest." They gathered in the heart of the black community at the Affro-Arts Theater on Drexel near Thirty-fifth Street. Walter Bradford, as moderator, steered the program in an easy-going fashion that kept alive a rising tide of excitement and, at the same time, allowed for adjustments in the program as late-comers arrived by automobile, bus, and plane from all over the country. For about three hours, both the over-thirty group and the younger group had their moments on the stage, and brief speeches, poetry, and music rolled forth in celebration. As Gwendolyn herself described it:

The most stirring tribute of my life, the most significant, was the extraordinary one created for me by Val Gray Ward, "our own" actress—her performing group, Kuumba, and many other young black artists of Chicago—on December 28 of 1969, at the Affro-Arts Theater. . . . On my night, as on other rich occasions, we had Phil Cohran and his Artistic Heritage Ensemble, making black music, sure and strong and passionate, in the big barny place . . . Darlene and her dancers, hot flesh-wire across the stage . . . the poets, giving freely of themselves to the huge crowd they knew *wanted* their product . . . the Kuumba players, Val's group, which is now presenting Root Theatre throughout the country . . . The Pharoahs . . . the Malcolm X Community College Chorus . . . black stars!—Lerone Bennett, Don L. Lee, Walter Bradford, Dudley Randall, Margaret Danner and Margaret Burroughs, Eugene Perkins, Sonia Sanchez, Sigmonde Wimberli, Carolyn Rodgers, Ronda Davis, Cynthia Conley (Zubena), Maxine Elliston, Johari; black painters with their portraits of myself, Jeff Donaldson, now chairman of Howard University's art department, Jon Lockard, Edward Christmas (who painted me into The Wall of Respect) . . . Norbert Wilkinson, who is Sika Dwimfo, one of our black jewelers. . . . And—the Blackstone Rangers came, in force!—with tokens of affection, earnest personal congratulations.[31]

At the end, speaking in a firm voice, she expressed simple thanks for the tribute.

Later, what the organizers of the program had called a "living anthology," with additions from some persons unable to attend, became formalized as *To Gwen With Love* (1971). Thus what had probably been the case for quite some time was now a matter of record: she was the prophet recognized in her own country.

10

Brave New World

Gwendolyn continued to look for ways in which she could express her commitment to ideology, and to develop a financial base. She remained enthusiastic about her autobiography and the money it would probably make, although Genevieve Young, her editor at Harper & Row, cautioned that "the world of art and the world of commerce seldom converge. All we have ever been able to do is to publish the best book the author is capable of writing in the best way we know how, and I promise we will do the best with yours."[1] The poet was obviously hoping for income to sustain her 1969 decision to give up teaching, despite lucrative offers from Northwestern University, the University of Washington, the University of California–Los Angeles, Loyola, Sarah Lawrence, Purdue, the University of Wisconsin, Lockhaven, Macalester, and Lake Forest. Refusal of local teaching options cost her nearly $38,000 in full-time and part-time opportunities. Nonetheless, she maintained a grueling road schedule for readings at colleges, feeling like a new person physically and emotionally. She had given concrete expression to her determination to be a writer, not a teacher, and the notes from which she would work out her autobiography were filling up a box, underlining the fact that she had made a formal start. She was ready now, she felt, "to starve in difficult ecstasy."[2]

In the late fall of 1970, Gwendolyn startled Harper & Row by securing an aggressive agent, Roslyn Targ. A Harper editor felt that a difficult author had found a difficult agent. Roslyn Targ soon confronted the editor with a series of imperative queries and requests: information at once on what efforts had been made to secure British publication and foreign publication in general.[3] In the next request, Mrs. Targ asked that rights on books currently out of print revert to the author: *The Bean Eaters, Annie Allen, A Street in Bronzeville,* and *Maud Martha.* To prevent such a reversion, Harper editors began thinking about republishing all the books in the fall of 1971 in a Gwendolyn Brooks omnibus. Feeling that Mrs. Targ's being away in Europe gave time for the necessary research on sales figures, they searched diligently also for clean copies of the books.[4]

Another action of Gwendolyn's had jolted the company and made its view of the omnibus more urgent as a means of protecting the company's interest. The poet had had lunch with Genevieve Young and another Harper official, without mentioning either that she had acquired an agent or that a black publisher would henceforth publish her works. Harper & Row gleaned the second bit of information from a report by Thomas A. Johnson in the *New York Times* regarding Yale University's "Conference on the Role of Black Women."[5] Besides reporting that Gwendolyn, Maya Angelou, John Henrik Clarke, and Shirley Graham DuBois had been brought to Yale as Chubb Fellows, Johnson reported that "Miss Brooks also announced that a black publishing firm, Broadside Press, would print her writings from now on."

Gwendolyn had in fact first turned to a black publisher with the publication of *Riot*, a three-part poem, in 1969. She had written to Harper about it, although the company did not publish individual poems.[6] Her latest move also startled her friend Dudley Randall of Broadside Press; when she asked Randall about publishing her autobiography, he at first refused, feeling that a small press could not do the full job she deserved. When Gwendolyn became annoyed and implied that she would find another black publisher, Randall consented. Don Lee felt that this was a bit much, "because I knew deep down inside that very few people in the movement would be making that type of commitment." He observed that his judgment was borne out by the fact that several black writers were now making it by leaving black publishers for white ones. He was impressed with Gwendolyn's political stance in switching publishers. Not that she had lacked a political or black focus earlier, but she was now concerned with such matters as expressing how she saw things and how she operated in the world. Thus, for him, her leaving Harper was the ultimate political move. She had won the Pulitzer Prize and become known through the work the company had published. Since blacks, in commercial appeal, were now beginning to have their day, she could have made the most money by remaining with a large publisher. Harper was now pushing her books and trying to get translations in other countries. "I think that move and some other things she did in that period really sealed my bonds with Gwen as a life bond because she did things that were essentially out of the ordinary."[7]

Meanwhile, work continued on the "omnibus." At one point in the negotiations, Roslyn Targ accused Harper of treating Gwendolyn shamefully in the past. Harper replied that, although Gwendolyn's success was due to her talent and reputation, her editors over the years had given her full devotion, and accused Mrs. Targ of negotiating in an adversary fashion. In an interview with me, Mrs. Targ explained that she had not been referring to lack of promotion because of race. Her feeling was that any author without an agent was automatically exploited, because publishers arbitrarily created their own star system and pushed the stars primarily. At any rate, Harper brought forth the omnibus in 1971. Apparently one compromise was the poet's acceptance of Harper's advice to call the new book *The World of Gwendolyn Brooks* instead of *The Gwendolyn Brooks Omnibus*. Gwendolyn won her battle for a "fat book," but at the cost of a lower advance, to keep expenses down and the price for the book within the range of her audience. Harper had wanted to include within the omnibus only *A Street in Bronzeville, Annie Allen, The Bean Eaters,* and *Maud Martha*. Perhaps Gwendolyn's greatest victory was the inclusion of *In the Mecca*. "MOST IMPORTANT," she wrote Mrs. Targ, "is the fact that, without 'In the Mecca' only inadequate impression of me is possible. Conceivably, the 'Omnibus' will be in print for many years—but my work is changing and is going to continue to change, and the first hints of the change are in the Mecca book. The 'Omnibus' as they [Harper] are planning it would NOT stamp me as part of this eruptive time, which I AM!"[8] Time, of course, has proved her right.

In an ironic reversal of the New York radio station's refusal to air "of De Witt Williams" because of the expression "plain black boy," the Bobbs-Merrill Company wrote that several cities had refused to buy its *Developmental Reader* because it included a section of *Maud Martha* entitled "We're the Only Colored People Here." Since the word "colored" had become quite unpopular, Bobbs-Merrill wanted to substitute "black" in the title. Gwendolyn felt that the change would have been out of line with the times and the tone of the book. The compromise: "Maud Martha at the Movies"; the original title was retained for *The World of Gwendolyn Brooks*.

The late sixties and the seventies were thus to be the stage on which Gwendolyn worked out increasingly more concrete rituals of commitment. By 1971 the poet made a trip to Africa, following her daughter's period of study at the University of Dar es Salaam. Gwendolyn enjoyed the feeling of blacks' land under her feet. With the racial division of the world a simple fact, she could feel, on a rather simple psychological level, that since she was black she was in her own land. But she was not indulging in sentimentality. History and language were difficulties not to be glossed over. She was in the presence of nuanced African gestures, mannerisms, and words from which several centuries separated her. Indeed, her time had obviously been spent in accumulating a deep sense of the nuances of the English language. Thus, in Africa veils sometimes seemed to rise and obscure meaning, although she had moments of full communication. She gained enough from this first trip to feel that she could continue to negotiate with her heritage in trips she would make to other parts of Africa—Ghana, for example, in 1974.

After having given up teaching in June 1969, she was lured back in 1971 by City College of New York, with a one-year appointment as Distinguished Professor of the Arts. She enjoyed working with the novelists Joseph Heller and John Hawkes, and the interchange with students was close and intense. However, a mild heart attack on Christmas Day caused her to give up her Monday–Tuesday commuting to and from Chicago, and since she did not intend to give up living in Chicago, she ended her teaching career. This career she had successfully pursued at Columbia, Elmhurst College, Northeastern Illinois State College, and the University of Wisconsin at Madison, where she was Rennebohm Professor of English. The experience had a central place in her confronting the spirit of the young.

One of Gwendolyn's most challenging commitments stemmed from her desire to create the kind of poetry that would appeal to the ordinary black, who was likely to feel that the art was unappealing. What was to give her both trouble and challenge over the years was that her standard of effectiveness included the degree to which her poetry could communicate to these non–poetry lovers. She had seen the Beat Poets widen the audience for poetry. The young black poets had done so too. The haunting scenes in which she saw blacks confronting each other with love at the dedication of the Wall and later in a tavern reading remained with her. She would speak of the experience in almost religious tones to Ida Lewis in 1971: The Wall "was something new, to see all those black people out on the street together, loving each other. Phil Cohran's group, the Artistic Heritage Ensemble, played the music; the poets read—I read. It was wonderful." As late as 1977, in an interview with Gloria Hull and Posey Gallagher, she struck a similar chord, after stating that I, her biographer, had little sympathy with her constantly announced concern for taverneers. "However, I feel that I was right when in the late sixties, I believed that Blacks should care for each other, nourish each other and communicate with each other. And if that was the right decision, I cannot forget the people who have grown up feeling that they hate poetry; that they would spell the word with a capital P and look upon it with great awe. I feel that there are poems which these people could enjoy. There are already some and I would like to contribute to this literature which, if they knew it was called literature, they would probably turn away from."[9]

Yet there were tensions between this goal and her definition of the effective poem. To D. H. Melhem, Gwendolyn spoke of a process she termed "clarifying rather than simple." The clarifying development is represented by a syntax that, when it does not remain close to the usual subject–verb–object (or complement) order, is modified as we do in actual speech. Also, the poem's reference system tends to be devoid of old teasing ambiguities. In *a capsule course in Black Poetry Writing* (1975), she advised the beginning poet: "Try telling the reader a little less. He'll, She'll love you more, if you allow him to do a little digging. Not *too* much, but *some.*" In *Young Poet's Primer* (1980), she advised, "Your poem does not need to tell your reader everything. A *little* mystery is fascinating. *Too much* is irritating." In an interview with Jill Oppenheimer at the University of Wisconsin, Gwendolyn defined poetry as "the very sifting of life. . . . Think of life as a rough powder that you pour through a sieve. Well, the finest part of it that comes through will be the poetry. Poetry is a concentration; you can get the essence of a novel into a short poem."[10]

Such definitions and reflexes would not make it easy for her to write the kind of poetry that a non–poetry reading public would turn to. In addition, she enjoyed not only working with language but also making beautiful sounds—perhaps beautiful, she felt, because the ear was brainwashed. At any rate, such an indulgence conflicted with her desire to speak relevantly and immediately to blacks not interested in poetry. In the far-ranging interview with Hull and Gallagher, she also confessed that she sometimes feared she would not be able to achieve her goal, and that the fact that her best possibility of achieving it lay in prolific writing and was in conflict "with my compulsion not to write at *all* unless I'm really hotly inspired," and that she was in a "groping stage."[11]

More positively, she thought it possible that she and the interviewers were underestimating what she had already achieved "along these lines." She pointed to such earlier poems as "Ballad of Pearl May Lee," "when you have forgotten Sunday" (*A Street*), "We Real Cool" (*The Bean Eaters*), and "Steam Song" (*Beckonings*) as "poems where people can say 'Yeah, I've had that feeling myself.' " She showed an awareness that getting the right subject, telling a story, producing music, and brevity were other important elements in appealing to non–poetry loving audiences. Since she saw herself as consumed with the passion of ideas that had come to her in the sixties and were now built into herself, she felt she did not have to address blacks consciously. "I am THAT—so anything I write is going to issue from a concern with and interest in blackness and its progress." She gave herself range and variety: "Now that can include a funny poem, an entertaining poem, a love poem, a joy of living poem."[12]

The stridency of the women's movement had not yet invaded the central currents of the black movement and was thus not part of the challenge Gwendolyn faced at that time. By 1977, in her interview with Hull and Gallagher, she would criticize her poem "Steam Song" for containing the line: "My man is my only necessary thing." "I do not believe that a man is a woman's necessary thing—for heaven's sake! That's one I let slip by me." But at the 1970 Yale Conference on the Role of the Black Woman, Gwendolyn, Maya Angelou, Shirley Graham DuBois, and John Henrik Clarke "saw women's liberation as an activity for white, not black women." Mrs. DuBois, writer and widow of the late W.E.B. DuBois, pointed out that wherever "people are struggling, there are no men asking women to walk three steps behind them." Maya Angelou, who had raised the issue of male expectations of women, stated that black women had shared the middle passage, the auction blocks, "the lash and the cotton fields—now we can't share the same sidewalk?" Gwendolyn reportedly said, "Our black men have enough to do without worrying about black women either getting behind or in front of them." Clarke, historian and professor at Hunter College, said that, if asked for equality by a black woman, he would give it for fear of being asked for more. But overall it was felt that racial oppression was the commanding issue that blacks faced.[13]

Gwendolyn, who has numerous poems devoted to woman's life, though not in the fashionable confessional style, could thus face blackness as a single issue. In her autobiography she gives a fuller statement: "Black Woman must remember, through all the prattle about walking or not walking three or twelve steps behind or ahead of her male, that her personhood precedes her femalehood; that, sweet as sex may be, she cannot endlessly brood on Black Man's blondes, blues, blunders. She is a person in the world—with wrongs to right, stupidities to outwit, with her man when possible, on her own when not. And she is also here to enjoy. She will be here, like any other, once only. Therefore she must, in the midst of tragedy and hatred and neglect, in the midst of her own efforts to purify, mightily enjoy the readily available: sunshine and pets and children and conversation and games and travel (tiny or large) and books and walks and chocolate cake."[14] She also spoke of *Riot* (1969), a poem in three parts that treats the implications of Chicago street disturbances after the 1968 assassination of Dr. Martin Luther King, Jr. She described it as an effort to communicate with large numbers of people which was only sporadically successful. She felt also that it was too meditative.[15] Nevertheless, her subject matter was one that would immediately get the attention of a mass audience.

Riot opens with the comic downfall of white John Cabot, symbolic of

European cultural pretensions, amidst the upsurge of angry Blacks. The second part, "The Third Sermon on the Warpland," deals with blacks' need for awareness and their confused awakening in the manner of the Phoenix. The already-aware people are such gang leaders as Richard, Bop, Rico, Sengali, Jeff, Geronimo, and Lover; they refuse foolish confrontations with the police, whose provocations they know from old experience.

The meditative portions are in the "Third Sermon on the Warpland": the comments of the Black and White Philosophers and individual lines eulogizing the dead Motherwoman and commenting on a "clean riot":

> A clean riot is not one in which little rioters
> long-stomped, long-straddled, BEANLESS
> but knowing no Why
> go steal in hell
> a radio, sit to hear James Brown
> and Mingus, Young-Holt, Coleman, John,
>   on V.O.N.
> and sun themselves in Sin.
>
> However, what
> is going on
> is going on.

The passage has the ordinary speech, loose rhythms, and communal reference points that could communicate with a mass audience. But the descriptive sections too quickly leave directness for the metaphorical. "The young men run. / The children in ritual chatter/scatter upon/their Own and old geography." One feels that in such passages she is in territory that some of the younger writers, with their freer use of street language, would handle more effectively. Thus Gwendolyn's old style invaded the new one she was attempting to create.

Ironically, the first and third sections of *Riot*, which derive from older resources, are the most effective in the poem. Val Gray Ward gave a very successful dramatic reading of the section on the downfall of John Cabot under the onslaught of pigfoot, chitterling, and cheap chili-eating blacks at the celebration for Gwendolyn at the Affro-Arts Theater on December 29, 1969. The poem draws strong contrasts between the poor and the wealthy and aristocratic John Cabot similar to that found in "The Lovers of the Poor."

> John Cabot, out of Wilma, once a Wycliffe,
> all whitebluerose below his golden hair,

> wrapped richly in right linen and right wool,
> almost forgot his Jaguar and Lake Bluff;
> almost forgot Grandtully (which is The
> Best Thing That Ever Happened to Scotch);
>   almost
> forgot the sculpture at the Richard Gray
> and Distelheim; the kidney pie at Maxim's,
> the Grenadine de Boeuf at Maison Henri.
>
> Because the Negroes were coming down the
>   street.

Cabot's pride and sense of exalted superiority make him an excellent satirical target. Actually, the poem moves into burlesque with the comments of Cabot, and creates a fine ironic line for its ending: " . . . and he cried "Lord! / Forgive these nigguhs that know not what they do."

The last section of *Riot*, "An Aspect of Love, Alive in the Ice and Fire," though different in thought, had something of the light touch and simplicity of "To Be In Love" (*Selected Poems*), which simply celebrates the exalted state resulting from the emotion: "To be in love / Is to touch things with a lighter hand. / In yourself you stretch, you are well." It follows the romantic idea of the individual seized by great passion. "An Aspect of Love," on the other hand, addresses the unity of the lovers and celebrates the new concepts of black manhood and womanhood involved in love in a new and revolutionary way. Thus the ice and fire, as in Robert Frost's "Fire and Ice," have to do with destruction but also with creation.

> It is the morning of our love.
>
> In a package of minutes there is this We.
> How beautiful.
> Merry foreigners in our morning,
> we laugh, we touch each other,
> are responsible props and posts.

After their mutual discoveries of each other, the lovers must respond to the world, and here the manhood theme predominates:

> You rise. Although
> genial, you are in yourself again.
> I observe
> your direct and respectable stride.
> You are direct and self-accepting as a lion

in African velvet. You are level, lean,
remote.

As William H. Hansel points out, the lovers' "communion endures, regardless of separation."[16] The situation of the lovers is as effectively evoked
as that of Cabot, whereas the riot section needs sharper evocation.

Family Pictures (1970) was a step forward into the new direction Gwendolyn
wanted to claim for the future. The theme is largely solidarity and the
consequences of blacks' strangerhood in America. The volume is marked by
an insistent simplicity, although some of the old devices appear in "To
Keorapetse Kgositsile (Willie)": unusual metaphors ("kitten Traveler") and
occasionally complex diction. The opening poem, "The Life of Lincoln
West," which first appeared as prose in Herbert Hill's anthology *Soon, One
Morning,* required only minor alterations to give it poetic form. Such a poem
reminds us that across the body of her works are several "simple" poems that
an audience not accepting of poetic conventions could understand, and that
her novel *Maud Martha,* rooted in the familiar subject of domesticity,
contains a readily understood prose of poetic intensity. One can illustrate
the technique of "The Life of Lincoln West" by drawing from any part of the
poem: "Even Christmases and Easters were spoiled. / He would be sitting at
the / family feasting table, really / delighting in the displays of mashed
potatoes / and the rich golden / fat-crust of the ham or the festive / fowl,
when he would look up and find / somebody feeling indignant about him."
Imagery and diction remain realistic and simple, and syntax has a friendly
familiarity. The narrator is an intimate chorus who stands on no ceremony
in addressing the reader and presenting a story—a special attraction for
people in general. Playing its part in the solidarity theme, the poem thus
portrays the birth in a small boy of what the sixties and seventies called
Black Consciousness. Presented as prose, the piece had evoked sustained
applause from the 1967 Fisk Black Writers Conference.

The title *Family Pictures* implies that the author will present some
striking likeness of the "kinsman" or "kinswoman" and perhaps a warm
memento. "To Keorapetse Kgositsile (Willie)" (an introduction to his book
My Name is Afrika), "To Don at Salaam," and "Walter Bradford"—poems
under the title "Young Heroes"—and possibly "Paul Robeson" best achieve
the objective. "To Don at Salaam" is marked by extreme simplicity throughout but is flawed by a line that moves too close to well-worn popular song:
"Your voice is the listened-for music." "Walter Bradford," however, is likely

to require a reader's reference to the printed page for understanding, since it moves simple metaphors into an allegorical drama:

> Just As You Think You're "Better Now"
> Something Comes To The Door.
> It's a Wilderness, Walter.
> It's a Whirlpool or Whipper.
>
> THEN you have to revise the messages;
> and, pushing through roars of the Last Trombones of seduction,
> the deft orchestration,
> settle the sick ears to hear and to heed and to hold;
> the sick ears a-plenty.

The rest of the poem encourages Walter to feel that his qualities are more than adequate for meeting the problems, and to retain commitment. The total poem addresses itself to Walter's leadership of people who are frequently confused by various seductions of society. The poem's allegorical method can be easily compared to certain earlier ones: "Do not be afraid of no" (*Annie Allen*), "The Explorer" (*The Bean Eaters*), and sections of "In the Mecca." "Young Africans," a celebration of the move for rebirth of a people by young revolutionaries, reveals both the old style found in "Walter Bradford" and a bit of the new simplicity. "Paul Robeson" contains a good deal of the new simplicity beginning with his "Warning," the second movement of the poem, which follows description of earlier despairing songs:

> forgoing tearful tale of bale and barge
> and other symptoms of an old despond.
> Warning, in music-words
> devout and large,
> that we are each other's
> harvest:
> we are each other's
> business:
> we are each other's
> magnitude and bond.

In pushing the theme of black solidarity, Gwendolyn thus worked under the pressures of the old reflexes and goals and those of a stripped-down simplicity, the dual drives later mentioned in the Hull and Gallagher interview. She was, on the whole, satisfied with the "Young Heroes" section but tended to feel later that the volume veered off into the pedestrian. Certainly the last two poems are slight ones. "Song: The Rev. Mubugwu

Dickinson Ruminates behind the Sermon" in the process of acknowledging his futile doctrine, by a kind of contrast reminds us of the earlier more effective "The preacher: ruminates behind the sermon" (A *Street in Bronzeville*). "Speech to theYoung. Speech to the Progress-Toward" remains broad and abstract.

Certain of the poems had roots of varying depths in Gwendolyn's life. Her admiration for Kgositsile derived from the deep impression made by his personality and his poems. A black South African by birth, Kgositsile revealed absolute commitment to freedom, mastery of poetic techniques, and mastery of African, black American, and European cultures. She felt that Walter Bradford had had a "high influence on my life." He and Don L. Lee (Haki Madhubuti) were family in a very real sense: "He and Haki are equal in my estimation. They are, in a way, sons of mine. I've even written about this but never did publish it although I will sometime. We still [in 1977] think of ourselves as mother and sons. And they have been more like sons to me than my own son because they have ideas that are like my own. And they have just been more the way a mother dreams of—affectionate, and we have a sharing of ideas."[17] Thus she extended herself through the role of mother into this new and challenging world.

Gwendolyn had always created with an awareness of history, as evidenced by her war sonnets and by "Negro Hero" in A *Street in Bronzeville* and by poems of social comment in other volumes. The sixties and seventies, however, revealed her as a woman directly and obviously at the center of historical struggle. Her poetry named specific people, scenes, and places, as in "In Montgomery," which was commissioned by *Ebony* magazine and appeared in its August 1971 issue with full illustrations of places and people. In it, the poet visits Montgomery, Alabama, scene of the famous bus boycott led by Martin Luther King, Jr., and finds the spiritual high tide of King's day not expired but at a low ebb against white supremacy. Many of the people are unaware of their history, especially certain of the young and the old.

"In Montgomery," a very long poem, Gwendolyn called "verse journalism," claiming the category as her original contribution to genres. It afforded her a tremendous range of experimentation with approaches to simplicity. Its realism ranges from direct, prosy statement to a heightening produced by a variety of devices: alliteration, gestural images, familiar but not trite metaphors, repetition, and biblical imagery, allusions, and rhythms, among others.

> I came expecting
> the strong young—
> up of head, severe,

> not drowsy, not in-bitten, not
> outwitted by the wiles of history.
> For the old tellings taught me
> that all of Before was rehearsal,
> that the true trends, the splendors, the splurges
> were to be lit by the young
> (who would give up life, limb and the length of a
> morrow for the Necessary Dream.)
>
> I came expecting
> the noble old
> whose names would be WAY!
> and DIRECTION! and STRIDE!
>
> I did not come expecting in History City
> the leaning and lostness,
> glazed paralysis, and the
> death-rattle of elderly vision

This passage reveals a structuring by parallelism, repetition, antithesis, and serial listings reminiscent of Walt Whitman.

Irony too finds use:

> My work: to cite in semi-song the
> meaning of Confederacy's Cradle.
> Well, it means to be rocking gently, rocking gently!
> In Montgomery is no Race Problem.
> There is the white decision, the white and pleasant
>   vow
> that the white foot shall not release the black neck.

She reaches into the biblical area for expressions and rhythms that have fused themselves into black experiences:

> Blackness is what stood up
> and clawed the oppressive ceiling
> till, behold, there was light,
> and clawed the oppressive walls
> till, behold, there was room to extend!
> Blackness remembered the Bible.
> It was blackness that re-said:
> How forcible are right words!
> and: Set thine house in order;
> and: They have sown the wind, and they shall reap
>   the whirlwind;

and: A new commandment I give unto you, That ye
         love one another;
and: Weeping may endure for a night, but joy
         cometh in the morning.
And blackness stretched forth the rough hand
to the white hand,
and cherished it into the clearing.
This blackness forgave what it would not forget.
And marched on remarkable feet.[18]

The poem contains scattered examples of words that gain dramatic impact by metaphorical use or simply by being adjacent to each other: "the leaning and lostness, / glazed paralysis"; "His voice is eventful but it does not scramble"; "weeps, out of stretchy eyes"; "will speak, spurt and spar for black children: / is spark plug or spasm."

After *Family Pictures* and "In Montgomery," Gwendolyn did not follow quickly with other poems, being busy with a variety of activities. Besides her usual heavy schedule of readings, she was at work on her autobiography. In 1970 the Internal Revenue Service asked for nearly $10,000 to be applied to her 1968 income tax. Interviews covered old grounds and some new ones. *You and Your World* praised the poetry and stated that, although Gwendolyn felt it was good for blacks to pull together, she wrote for everyone.[19] Whites continued to question her confining herself to black audiences, although Gwendolyn would point out that whites had access to most of the work she had created.

On May 1, 1970, she presented one of her poet laureate awards to Carolyn Rodgers for her book *Songs of a Black Bird* at the Society of Midland Authors' 55th Annual Dinner and Presentation of Awards. She joined Galway Kinnell, Stanley Kunitz, and Denise Levertov at the 15th Annual Poetry Day of the Modern Poetry Association, held in honor of the late Henry Rago, editor of *Poetry* from 1955 through 1969.

On a tour of the South, she read poetry at Alabama A&M University and endowed a three-year annual Gwendolyn Brooks Poetry Prize with $300. The university's Department of English and Foreign Languages later assumed the financial responsibility for continuing it.[20] Alabama A&M, Clark College, Atlanta University, and others were later included in her gifts for student scholarships, after she had heard from students how difficult it was for them to finance their education. A single gift was for $2,000, although her mother was uneasy regarding Gwendolyn's giving away large sums of money without thinking more about how to secure her own future welfare. Some of the student recipients eventually became outstanding in their communities.[21]

Amid such matters, Gwendolyn grieved on the passing of the family dog, Fluffy, whom Nora had chosen at the animal shelter in 1961. Like most pets, he had established his own place within the family pattern and contributed to its warmth.

Her writing time was invested largely in her autobiography. Like most of Gwendolyn's works, it would carry a strong individual stamp, and like Maud Martha it would insist to some extent upon its own definition of the genre. Combining memoir and the confessional, Gwendolyn threw light upon crucial areas in her life and the circumstances influencing them. She included also key interviews; an appendix containing "marginalia" (mainly literary commentary); a "Collage" of comments upon persons, places, and her own experiences; and the obituary for Fluffy. Report from Part One covers the essentials without giving sensational details or focusing closely upon emotionally charged experiences. Her intraracial bouts with prejudice are given largely in summary form; the process of self-search and the passages of introspective musings characterizing many contemporary autobiographies are conspicuous by their absence. The topic of marriage is an excellent example of Gwendolyn's refusal to agonize in public. Her marriage is discussed in a few paragraphs and the breakup is described as follows: " 'Everyone' felt the marriage was not only successful but a model for other marriages. We were separated in December of 1969. We understood that our separation was best for the involved. (That won't be enough for the reader but it is enough for me.)"[22]

Report from Part One has its own kind of strengths. In the first place, it is a storehouse of information about the poet's life and works. Though presented with composure, the events described frequently have the benefit of Gwendolyn's comic eye, fresh phrasing, understatement, and appropriate seriousness. The book places order on the chaos of life and suggests that it can be richly engaged and enjoyed. Thus the book withstands repeated readings, an assessment that cannot always be granted to more sensational types of autobiographies. It must be said, however, that Gwendolyn's method reveals the persistence of the traditional woman of decorum within the new modern woman. Beneath the attractive surface is also the principle, though not the rigidity, of her mother's reticence.

While questioning Gwendolyn during the 1977 CLA Journal interview, Gloria Hull asked for some preview of what would be included in her updating of Report from Part One. Gwendolyn spoke of American blacks and the possibility that they might acquiesce in being sent to kill their black brothers in Africa. Gloria pointed out that this would be commentary on world conditions and that Gwendolyn was "a very reticent person" and had "the nicest way I know of finessing personal questions into something else." It seemed to Gwendolyn, however, that she was "always spilling out."

In a sense, both were right. The poem "when you have forgotten Sunday" would be received by any reader as a segment of her married life without its being so labeled. Such works as *Annie Allen* (particularly "The Anniad") and *Maud Martha* also cut deeply into Gwendolyn's personal life, but since they also take advantage of the artist's privilege to deliberately distort and of Gwendolyn's capacity for confronting agony with her comic sensibility, the reader lacking her comments in *Report* would be able to make only crude guesses regarding specific events. Perhaps her most daring personal poem is "A Lovely Love," but who would be able to pierce Lillian's passionate encounter and find that the experience was really that of Gwendolyn and the black painter Ernest Alexander? How Gwendolyn ultimately regarded such matters is apparent in her comments on *Maud Martha* in her autobiography and her final comments to Gloria Hull on updating *Report*.

In *Report*, she opens her comments on *Maud Martha* with the statement: "An autobiographical novel, I believe, is a better testament, a better thermometer, than a memoir can be. Who, in presenting a 'factual' account, is going to tell the absolute, the inclusive, the horrifying or exquisite, the 'incredible Truth?' One wishes to spare—to spare others and one's self. May not one add, multiply, subtract?—without wanting to. But an 'autobiographical novel' is nuanceful, allowing. There's fact-meat in the soup, among the chunks of fancy: but, generally, definite identification will be difficult."[23] In the interview, when Ms. Hull pressed for personal details that would appear in an updated edition, "So you do not foresee having in there . . . . " Gwendolyn completed the statement: " . . . HOT! Ain't gone be *nothing hot!*"[24]

Yet, earlier in the interview, she had more freely discussed the updating of her autobiographical novel. Gwendolyn would bring Maud Martha up to her own age and supply her with two more children; then Maud's husband would die in a bus fire like one that actually happened in Chicago in the 1950s. "Wasn't that nice of me? I had taken him as far as I could. He certainly wasn't going to change. I could see that." The husband was a narrow, small-minded sort, a fact creating a considerable gulf between him and Maud. Did Gwendolyn kill him in the novel because he would not change? Ms. Hull queried. Gwendolyn did not answer directly but pointed out that she wanted Maud Martha to have additional adventures and probably get involved with another man when she was almost Gwendolyn's

age, "certainly fifty." The chapter would end with Maud feeling an "unbid-
den relief." Maud indicates the feelings that she will have of "intense regret"
when she finds in a drawer some little "memento of the past," but for the
time being she "is thinking passionately about the cake that's going to be at
the wake and how good it's going to be." She will later travel to Africa.
Gwendolyn agreed with Ms. Hull that she was putting a lot of herself into
the sequel of *Maud Martha*: "Yes, I will, as I did with *Maud Martha*. That has
much autobiography though I've twisted things." But she also expected to
use her imagination more.

There seems to be in the passage much of the intense frustration that
Gwendolyn at one time felt in her own marriage. In *Annie Allen*, she caused
the inconvenient and irascible husband to die of an incurable "overseas disease" after his return from World War II. Maud's elation is also Gwendolyn's
after her own separation, as is apparent in certain sections of her 1971
interview with Ida Lewis. To the comment that Gwendolyn really seemed as
though she were starting a new life spiritually, she responded, "It's true that
my life is developing new dimensions. A concrete example, that serves
pretty well metaphorically, is that I got on an airplane for the first time last
spring. That really opened up geography to me. Now I just run up the
'gangplank.' This is what the last three years have been like for me: a challenge, bringing more freedom of movement. It's just fine to be airborne."[25]

She felt the same freedom and elation in regard to writing works other
than poetry. She spoke with some astonishment of the prospect of writing
verse plays and short novels of 15,000 to 25,000 words each. She was
inspired to reach an audience of "people who generally don't have a long
attention span," the audience that would not be interested in a work of
600,000 words. She found it an exciting prospect. And whereas she had
once opposed rawness in poetry, she now presented it as a sort of challenge:
"Dare to be raw sometimes, Poet! Dare to extend, with something more of
clangor. Dare—sometimes—to concern yourself with seeable, feelable,
hearable people. Again: sometimes. Not all the time, but sometimes."[26]

Gwendolyn had been surging beyond traditional bounds since 1967,
and in the early 1970s she was releasing herself fully. She seemed again the
girl who rebels at confinement to the front yard, who wants "a peek at the
back / Where it's rough and untended and hungry weed grows" ("a song in
the front yard" from *A Street in Bronzeville*). Like Big Bessie of "The Second
Sermon on the Warpland," she would stand "bigly—under the unruly
scrutiny, . . . in the wild weed." She herself was blooming "in the noise and
whip of the whirlwind."[27]

In this spirit she was ready to assist others in tackling ground that was undomesticated among blacks. After getting a commitment from Broadside Press to bring out the autobiography, she encouraged Dudley Randall to pioneer as a literary agent in selling the paperback rights. In this spirit of self-determination, she felt that where blacks did not have experience they must get it. (Randall, for a period, was able to interest Bantam, but when they saw the manuscript they said it was not their type of book. Randall tried several other companies and got the impression that they were looking for something with more jolts for the reader.)

On the domestic scene, Gwendolyn's compulsion toward a radical freedom ebbed and was drawn back into a sense of freedom within traditional family order. Knowing how much her mother had favored her marriage, Gwendolyn decided in 1973 that one way to make Keziah's eighty-fifth birthday memorable would be to have Henry join them for dinner. When she phoned Henry, he accepted the invitation and spoke of poems he had been writing. He recited some of them over the telephone, and Gwendolyn felt they were very good. "I said, 'Those poems have got to be published.'" Henry began taking her out to dinner, where they continued to discuss their poetry. Their reconciliation seems to have come about as a natural result of this contact.

It is not clear whether they were able to work out old grievances and misunderstandings or whether they simply considered them part of a past to be forgotten. Gwendolyn's stress upon the role of poetry would seem to imply that their common interest in literature was sufficient, but of course the reader will realize that their having been drawn together into courtship and marriage by their interest in poetry had not been able to prevent the agonizing separation. Could poetry and other binding experiences now do what they could not do earlier? Apparently, like Maud Martha of the sequel, Gwendolyn had opened up a drawer of her history and seen some memento of the past. The reunited couple took a trip to London as their second honeymoon, had a good time, and through 1977 were still finding that being together was the right thing. Out of the experience came her poem "Shorthand Possible."

> A long marriage makes shorthand possible,
> The everything need not be said.
> Much may stay within the head.
> Because of old-time double seeing,
> Because of old-time double being.
> The early answer answers late.
> So comfortably out of date!
> The faded photographs come clear

To dazzle down the now and here.
I said: "Someday we'll get Franciscan China."
You said, "Some day the Defender will photograph your house."
You said, "I want to have at least two children."[28]

Poetry remained a continuous struggle. In the late 1970s, she would agree with Gloria Hull that there was present in her new work a dichotomy between her distinctive style of the past and her new style, and she would add that *Beckonings* (1975) "is the great failure among all of my books."[29] One has to keep in mind here that *Beckonings* contains only twelve poems, and that she is comparing it with some rather formidable predecessors. But certainly there are distracting elements in the volume—what she and Gloria Hull called "dual impulses." "Boys. Black." had appeared in *Ebony* in August 1972 and is thus one of the earliest poems in *Beckonings*. It has a prophetic tone and urgency and reflects anxiety regarding blacks' failure to retain the high level of consciousness they had achieved, a matter that would be more fully expressed by other poems of *Beckonings*. Subtitled "a preachment," the poem begins with the urgency of a mother calling her sons abruptly into action:

> Boys. Black. Black Boys.
> Be brave to battle for your breath and bread.
> Your heads hold clocks that strike the new time of day.
> Your hearts are
> legislating Summer Weather now.
>   Cancel Winter.

In rapid succession appear the simple symbols—clocks, Summer Weather, and Winter. One is reminded by "Summer" of the expression "long, hot summer," which during the riot years implied destruction of aspects of an ignoring economic system. Gwendolyn's approach would seem to include the broader sense of creative spirit.

> Up, boys. Boys black. Black boys.
> Invade now where you can or can't prevail.
> Take this:
>   there's fertile ground beneath the pseudo-ice.
> Take this:
>   sharpen your hatchets. Force into the green.
> Boys, in all your Turnings and your Churnings,
> remember Afrika.

"Afrika" does not carry real force, since it remains rather abstract where it should be vitalizing. It is difficult to feel how Afrika will thus make a difference in the boys' strivings. They are said to know little of "that long leaplanguid land." The speaker explains that the union of American Blacks "is the dwarf magnificent"—that is, a magnificent replica of Africa on a small scale. By this time the poem has incorporated the more complex diction found in the earlier style.

> In the precincts of a nightmare all contrary
> be with your sisters hope for our enhancement.
> Hurry.
> Force through the sludge.
> Wild thick scenery subdue.
>
> Because
> the eyeless Leaders flutter, tilt, and fail.
> the followers falter, peculiar, eyeless too.
> Force through the sludge. Force, whether
> God is a Thorough and a There,
> or a mad child,
> playing
> with a floorful of toys,
> mashing
> whatwhen he wills. Force,
> whether God is spent pulse, capricious, or a yet-to-come.

The preceding stanza, the most complex in the poem, reminds us of the poet's skepticism in *A Street in Bronzeville* about God's action in the lives of mankind, or the general human bewilderment to be opposed, reflected in *The Bean Eaters*. In the last two stanzas, the development is akin to the simpler style of "In Montgomery," with its biblical tones, familiar diction, and elemental parallelism.

> Beware
> the easy griefs.
> It is too easy to cry "ATTICA"
> and shock thy street,
> and purse thy mouth,
> and go home to thy "Gunsmoke." Boys,
> black boys,
> beware the easy griefs
> that fool and fuel nothing.
>
> I tell you
> I love You

and I trust You.
Take my Faith.
Make of my Faith an engine.
Make of my Faith
a Black Star. I am Beckoning.

The poem must be judged to have the power of its passion. The firm mother is speaker, with the rhythms of such an imagined mother's urgencies. Gone is the contemplative mother of "the children of the poor" and her bemusement at the task of helping black children to stand upright in a racist and otherwise confusing world. "Boys. Black." fit in well in the August 1972 issue of *Ebony*, which was devoted to the black male. Nevertheless, it is only partially a poem that would appeal in the tavern or call to blacks across the board.

"Boys. Black." pleads directly for solidarity and reveals the unease Gwendolyn was experiencing. "The Boy Died in My Alley," a much later poem not published until 1975, also reveals the persistence of the old artistic reflexes with the newer responses. A poem that dramatizes the speaker's feeling of complicity in the deaths of boys who are destroyed, "The Boy Died in My Alley" seemed to Gwendolyn to represent her struggling toward the newer simplicity. But she felt that it was amiss in "leading toward the traditional, almost irresistibly, in several parts." And neither the rhyming nor "the very close rhythm" was part of the structure toward which she now aspired. The poem begins with the pattern of the ballad stanza of European tradition and does not escape from its mold, since the rhythm, incremental repetition, and structure keep us mindful of the form. The diction is occasionally both overly literary and melodramatic ("careening tinnily down the nights / across my years and arteries"). In the end one has a picture of guilt and an awareness of a missing responsiveness to which all might give attention. But the studied character of the poem reduces its emotional impact, and its self-conscious devices leave us too aware of being carried through a literary exercise.

"Boys. Black." and "The Boy Died in My Alley" are two of the dozen poems in *Beckonings*. Others are celebrations of group solidarity or strengthening: "Five Men Against the Theme"; "To John Oliver Killens in 1975," "Steam Song" (man-woman love); and "Elegy In a Rainbow" (on the evolution of an appropriate Christmas for blacks); "A Black Wedding Song" (exhortations for couples to be strong in their love, which must face the world); "Horses Graze" (analogous to qualities blacks might treasure); " 'When Handed a Lemon, Make Lemonade' " (transforming bitterness into the palatable); "Sammy Chester Leaves 'Godspell'" (a celebration of African vitality); and "Friend" (a celebration of "evening" love).

Gwendolyn held stubbornly to the theme of black solidarity and was greatly concerned about the rapid diminishment of solidarity and its supporting symbols during the 1970s. She was amazed to see black women begin once more to straighten their hair; they looked unnatural to her. The reversion suggested such low pride that blacks felt other people's hair was more beautiful than theirs. "That nice togetherness that was developing, a lot of us are losing. Once again we're emphasizing the individual loving self above the group."[30] She looked to the vogue of Alex Haley's *Roots* to restore pride, but Haley was soon under a variety of attacks.

Although she did not feel that blacks would go all the way back to "the utter slavery" mentality,[31] it was out of concern for pride and solidarity that she wrote three more "preachments"—two poems and a brief statement that she would eventually publish as *Primer For Blacks* (1980). The title poem begins:

> Blackness
> is a title,
> is a preoccupation,
> is a commitment Blacks
> are to comprehend—
> and in which you are
> to perceive your Glory.

With humor and irony, the poem comments on the power and triumph of black blood. The fourth and most philosophical stanza calls on blacks "to Comprehend, / to salute and to Love the fact that we are Black, / which *is* our 'ultimate Reality.'"

"A Primer For Blacks" ends with a call to defecting blacks:

> ALL of you—
>   you proper Blacks,
> you half-Blacks,
> you wish-I-weren't Blacks,
> Niggeroes and Niggerenes.
>
> You.

One of the other poems, "To Those of My Sisters Who Kept Their Naturals" is subtitled: "Never to look a hot comb in the teeth." The first stanza celebrates the attractive qualities of black womanhood that manifest

themselves "below the richrough righttime of your hair." The next praises
the women for not worshiping whiteness, and the last celebrates hair as
"The natural Respect of Self and Seal! / Sisters! / Your hair is Celebration in
the world!" The last piece, "Requiem Before Revival," again criticizes
imitative blacks but looks forward to their awakening, since even the
blighted ones possess a "yearning toward Black validation." The essay and
the poems use devices of Don L. Lee and Sonia Sanchez, poets Gwendolyn
felt were able to reach all kinds of blacks: name-calling, insinuation, comic
reduction of the offending black, and so forth. Although Gwendolyn
doesn't venture far into street language, she reproduces the situation:
"Swarms of Blacks have not understood the mechanics of the proceeding,
and they trod along to the rear of Pied Piper whites, their strange gazes fixed
on, and worshiping, each switch of the white rear, their mesmerized men-
talities fervently and firmly convinced that there is nothing better than
quaking in that tail's wake."[32] They fail, however, to imitate one white
habit—the secret of so-called supremacy, which is simply to impose yourself
upon the world repeatedly whether it wants you or not.

   Primer For Blacks concludes on an optimistic note: "In spite of all the
disappointment and disillusionment and befuddlement out there, I go on
believing that the Weak among us will, finally, perceive the impressiveness
of our numbers, perceive the quality and legitimacy of our essence, and take
sufficient, indicated steps toward definition, clarification."

   Gwendolyn was satisfied that in writing *Primer For Blacks* she had been
able to hold at bay most of the impulses demanding beautiful sounds and
complexity, and that her subjects were those that would interest all blacks.
She was not at the end of the struggle, however, as would be shown by *To
Disembark* (1981), a collection of poems written since 1969 which included a
new group not heretofore published, under the title "To the Diaspora." The
omitted poems were often the very simple ones of earlier volumes, apparently considered too simple: from *Family Pictures*, "Estimable Mable," a
couplet expressing uncertainty about the probability of Mable's response to
the speaker; and "Love You Right Back," a poem of two stanzas pointing out
that love of whatever quantity the speaker offers to Mable will not be
enough; from *Beckonings*, "Steam Song," "Elegy in a Rainbow," "Horses
Graze," and "Friend." Certainly, they were slight poems and could detract
from the urgency she was giving the black solidarity theme, for the message
of the volume is that which she describes in her poem entitled "Paul
Robeson": "we are each other's / harvest: / we are each other's / business: / we
are each other's magnitude and bond."

   In addition to omitting certain poems, Gwendolyn revised others. "Five

Men Against the Theme 'My Name Is Red Hot. Yo Name ain Doodley Squat,'" originally celebrating Hoyt Fuller, Lerone Bennett, Dudley Randall, Haki Madhubuti, and Lu Palmer, she combined with "To John Oliver Killens in 1975." By concentrating on a single man and his qualities, the consolidation gave more force to the theme of constructive doings while reducing the length of the first poem by four lines. The result also is that the abstract and allegorical character of the opening lines benefits by the contrasting specificity of the Killens poem. Killens, the novelist, is well known in radical and literary circles in Chicago and elsewhere, although his name and role recognition among a cross-section of blacks or taverneers would not be so easy to predict. The next stanza of the poem, along with introductory comment by the poet, eases matters to some extent by concentrating on his qualities. The final stanza calls for his aid. Individual images are at times startling: "with you, the word kindness was not / a *jingling thing* but an / *eye-tenderizer,* a / *heart-honeyer*" (emphasis added). One feels once more the intent craftsman twisting words into new applications of meaning.

"Boys. Black." is revised and becomes, in *to disembark,* "Another Preachment to Blacks," as the poet felt that the first version was too preachy. Certainly the new version seems to gain more impact by having been broadened to include all blacks rather than males only, and it is more realistic in not asking blacks to draw inspiration from Africa, a land they are told they know little of. But, as an individual poem, the first version, with its image of the firm mother, seems to utilize persona and tone more rousingly.

The section "To the Diaspora" dramatically emphasizes the poet's role as nurturer and prophet. With confident authority, the speaker of the poem "To the Diaspora" instructs a friend regarding the achievement of Africa within the self. "Music For Martyrs" is a sardonic comment on the murder of Stephen Biko, and "A Welcome Song for Laini Nzinga" celebrates the birth of Haki's daughter and draws her warmly into the kinship group.

Other than "To the Diaspora," the most ambitious new poems are "To Black Women" and "To Prisoners." Neither poem should be very difficult in terms of the accessibility of its overall message, but both are highly concentrated. By creating allegorical journeys and obstacles, they go frankly for essence. Perhaps women will argue that all parts of "To Black Women" are immediately accessible to them whether or not they are poetry initiates. The poem urges them to maintain their goals and rich values despite the bitter struggles they have had to wage. Its management of tone is highly effective, and its flavor is suggested by the opening stanza.

> Sisters,
> where there is cold silence—
> no hallelujahs, no hurrahs at all, no handshakes,
> no neon red or blue, no smiling faces—
> prevail.
> Prevail across the editors of the world!
> who are obsessed, self-honeying and self-crowned
> in the seduced arena.

The rest of the poem enlarges upon the obstacles faced but also emphasizes the qualities of beauty and excellence that black women retain:

> But there remain large countries in your eyes.
> Shrewd sun.
> The civil balance.
> The listening secrets.
>
> And you create and train your flowers still.

"To Prisoners," like "To Black Women," is firmly structured, goes for essence, and should have an intense appeal for its audience, who would certainly grasp the overall message. The poem urges prisoners to cultivate strength and spirit and self-mastery in order to conquer the onslaught they are bound to receive. Its drift and flavor may be quickly gained from its first stanza.

> I call for you cultivation of strength in the dark.
> Dark gardening
> in the vertigo cold.
> in the hot paralysis.
> Under the wolves and coyotes of particular silences.
> Where it is dry.
> Where it is dry.
> I call for you
> cultivation of victory Over
> long blows that you want to give and blows you are going to get.

The remainder of the poem varies its call for endurance and spirit. It begins on a more immediately realistic level, with such expressions as "what wants to crumble you down, to sicken / you." The last lines, however, are more symbolic, as Gwendolyn calls for healing and enhancement, among other things, "in the chalk and choke"—in the context, a quite subtle use of diction. But the poem, simply as a poem, is closely woven.

In *To Disembark*, Gwendolyn showed that she was continuing to write strong poems, that she was devoted to black solidarity, that she could find subjects to which an audience would respond intensely, and that she could create simple poems. But whether she could address a cross section of blacks with the consistency of a Langston Hughes is a question that has not yet received a decisive answer. The works reflect her knowledge of the devices making for simplicity and other qualities that would appeal to a broad audience. But, as she acknowledged, she was also impelled by the need to create beautiful sounds and to respond fully as a devoted craftsman.

Would a goodly body of simple poems emerge from the sheer quantity of her more recent work? She did not feel as prolific as of old, and she has an aversion to writing without the force of inspiration. The questions appeared likely to stay with her.

In the midst of readings, recognitions, and civic activities, Gwendolyn in 1978 suddenly faced the decline of her mother, although the evidence of that decline was clear in hindsight. The changes made Gwendolyn more aware of the necessity to crystallize the meaning of her mother's strong presence within her, and gradually carried her back through family discussions and her own memories of decisive encounters. For Keziah, the experience combined the impact of age and the erosion of the order in which she had lived with a simple but firm sense of certainty.

Keziah had not long before achieved, at the age of 88, publication of *The Voice and Other Short Stories*, a series of autobiographical pieces and reflections on which she had worked for several years. The event had been celebrated at a book party among old friends and new. Gwendolyn was completing the organization of fifteen young writers on her block, two of whom would be sent during the summer to Nigeria and two to Ghana. On Sunday, when Gwendolyn went by Keziah's to take her to church, she found that her mother had completely forgotten what was normally the high point of each week, although her mind had been quite clear up to that date. The two looked at each other in astonishment. Keziah got ready for church but could not seem to get over her forgetfulness.

In fact, other symbols of the order in which Keziah had invested herself were crumbling. Her street, South Champlain, had deteriorated. No longer was it the attractive block of family homes, well-kept lawns, and comfortable wide porches to which she had moved in 1921. Urban blight had invaded, and predators made their appearance. Keziah had been startled to find herself jostled and her pocketbook snatched by two youths one day as she returned from shopping. Fortunately, two other youths who knew her chased the thieves, who dropped the pocketbook. But the damage had been done. A world in which mythical boys helped old ladies cross the street had clearly been replaced by one in which one might be brutalized for small change. Order was at best shaky. Revealing in every article her passionate commitment to order, grace, and decorum, her book mildly comments on the needs of age and the brashness of youth in the essay "Can Senior Citizens Avoid Boredom?": "Picture one in his seventies taking his morning neighborhood walks, ever fearful that some careless lad, with no respect for age, makes it mandatory to leave the walk to escape a catastrophe. This happens regularly."[33] Although she could say that "special housing for senior citizens is one of the greatest assurances of a long, contented life," she actually found her own home, where she had lived for over sixty years, well-nigh indispensable to her sense of order and tranquility. When Gwendolyn took her mother to her home while Henry worked on Keziah's exploded furnace boiler, she found her mother extremely uncomfortable at the idea of being away from her own place. Thus Gwendolyn and the other family members had to adjust to Keziah's insistence on living alone and to derive security from keeping her and the house under close scrutiny and frequent visitation. But they were unable to prevent the house from being burglarized while she was out or to keep her from feeling deeply the violation of privacy.

Eventually, Keziah's health declined. She seemed to lose interest in eating and in taking the medicine that had been prescribed for hypertension. Against her will, she had to be hospitalized. When Gwendolyn was able to bring her back home under the supervision of a nurse and doctor, Keziah was gratified. Gwendolyn speaks of how happy she herself had been to get her mother out of the hospital and back into her own home. "I am peaceful," Keziah responded. "Thank you." But as Gwendolyn gave her a bath the next morning, she sensed that the resistance to handling, which had represented her mother's independence, was gone. Keziah did not care how she was turned, made little response to queries regarding her condition, and would not eat, although she seemed to be getting along all right. She did better with a nurse, but while Gwendolyn was fulfilling an engagement at the University of Vermont on March 14, Keziah died quietly and peacefully.

In 1975 Gwendolyn had characterized Keziah as she saw her at that time.

> My mother sits in yesterday,
> and teeters toward today,
> and topples toward tomorrow's edge,
> and panics back away.

Yesterday taught her to contrive,
to dredge-up and to thoroughlize
—fitting her for some reckonings
with the not-old and with surprise.[34]

Keziah had remained close to the model of the woman of neighborhood, club, old friends, and church, although she often surprised Gwendolyn with her feeling for things beyond this area. After considerable discussion and argumentation, she understood something of the goals of the order-challenging rebels of the 1960s. At the tenth anniversary celebration of the Institute for Positive Education, a group of young people dedicated to creating an unbrainwashed education for blacks, she enjoyed the ceremony and the beauty. Haki Madhubuti, leader of the group, asked her to stand and celebrated her as a worthy elder. She appreciated the respect shown by representatives of a generation who were often suspicious of those over thirty. Her own existence, though full of struggle, had been peaceful, and she was shocked at the treatment of blacks portrayed in the televised version of Alex Haley's *Roots*. To the journalist Hoke Norris of the *Chicago Tribune*, she stated that "I was so disgusted with the way our people were treated, that I started several times not to listen or look anymore because I didn't think that anybody would treat our people that badly. I was just so angry. . . . I would think one night that I wouldn't listen the next night, but before the next night appeared I'd decide that maybe it wouldn't be so bad. Maybe I could stand it a little better. So I just went on and heard every one of the installments. Don't think that I think that all the Whites are the same, because I have some very good Whites as friends. But there are a lot of them that are still that bad, or would be if they could."[35]

Keziah also found it difficult to accept the new freedom Gwendolyn exercised after the breakup of her marriage in 1969. On her reconciliation with Henry, Gwendolyn discovered that Keziah had objected to her having a young man take care of the house when she was commuting to New York to teach, although the man entered as she left and left when she returned. Her mother had asked Henry to get the man out of his house and to remove any possible appearance of indecorum. But such conflicts did not break into the persisting comradeship in which each woman recognized the strength of the other. Just as Gwendolyn had asserted her independence as an adolescent by a stony silence when punished by her mother and father, so Keziah refused while in the hospital to cede her independence for invalidism. She met excessive attention with a frown or an abrupt admonishment.

Gwendolyn concerned herself with the essential values that Keziah had deeply embodied and that she had sometimes fought within herself. At church, at the celebration of the Feast of the Pentecost and Mother's Day, she was aware of the congregation singing all the songs that had meant so much to her mother and that now seemed to come laden with her presence: "Near the Cross," "Come Holy Spirit, Heavenly Dove," "Our Father Who Art in Heaven." That last was the last song she had heard her mother sing during her illness. As the two quietly watched television, someone on the screen began to sing it. Suddenly Keziah picked up the song and sang it through.

Afterword

George Kent's biography of Gwendolyn Brooks ends in 1978 with the death of Keziah Brooks and a remembered image of her, singing. The poignancy of the image emphasizes Kent's appreciation that the familial context, with which his study begins, is a continuity. Brooks's "duty-loving" mother, who had so faithfully served her daughter's talent, persisted in expressing her own aspirations until the end of her life.

Keziah Brooks died on March 14, 1978, after a long illness through which her daughter had nursed her. The poet's career and its social context would become her path of adjustment to deep grief and awareness of loss, for the world still claimed and acclaimed her. In January 1978, she had helped celebrate Carl Sandburg's one-hundredth birthday memorial. In June, she received an honorary doctorate of letters from the City College of the City University of New York. Later that summer, she journeyed to England and France with her cousin, Gail Willis. Upon her return home, she resumed an intensive schedule of cross-country readings and workshops. The road that Merdice, "the bolted nomad" of "To a Squirrel" had longed for, was again the poet's own. And new honors lay ahead.

On January 3, 1980, at the invitation of President Jimmy Carter and Mrs. Carter, Brooks read at the White House. Along with twenty other distinguished poets, including Sterling Brown, Lucille Clifton, Josephine Jacobsen, Robert Hayden, and Stanley Kunitz, she joined in "A Salute to Poetry and American Poets." Brooks, who read with Richard Eberhart, recalls the occasion with pleasure. One of the selections that she read was "the mother," her still-controversial poem on abortion. Brooks was later appointed to Carter's Presidential Commission on the National Agenda for the Eighties.

Brooks made an important publishing decision in 1980. Just as she had moved in the 1960s and 1970s to support the Black press, she now resolved to produce her own works. She had enjoyed editing *The Black Position*, an annual that she founded in 1971, when it was published by Broadside Press, and later, when she herself published it. She liked having total responsibility for creative control. She put forth both *Primer For Blacks* (Black Position Press) and *Young Poet's Primer* (Brooks Press) in 1980. They are now issued by The David Company of Chicago.

Brooks as teacher and her abiding concern with young people show clearly in *Young Poet's Primer*. Directly addressing new poets in a friendly manner, the author gives thirty-three basic suggestions on the writing of poems and concludes with a short bibliography of useful reference works. Not only a writer but a doer, Brooks organized a local teenagers' forum for her block, 74th and Evans Avenue, and kept it active for four years. In the summer of 1981, she sent two members of the club, high school students Georgette Smith and Wendy Boswell, with her own daughter Nora as chaperone, to Africa. They visited Ghana and, en route, England and France. The poet's interest in the young received public recognition when the Gwendolyn Brooks Junior High School was dedicated at Harvey, Illinois, on November 24, 1981.

Seven months later, Brooks herself would again travel abroad. In July 1982 she visited the Soviet Union as guest of a conference of prominent Soviet and American writers, including Harrison Salisbury, who organized the trip, Erica Jong, Arthur Schlesinger, Jr., Robert Bly, Susan Sontag, Irving Stone, and Studs Terkel.

Third World Press had wanted to publish a Brooks anthology from the 1960s through the 1980s. In 1981 it brought out *To Disembark*. The following year, another call for an anthology came from Marc Crawford, writer, editor, and teacher, who had featured Brooks in his magazine supplement *Tone* and had "assigned" the writing of "Boy Breaking Glass." He asked for permission to reprint material for a tribute issue of *Time Capsule*. Brooks, with my assistance, selected "Twenty-Four Poems from Four Decades," published in the Summer/Fall 1983 issue. The handsome, oversized format included critical pieces on the poet by both Dudley Randall and myself.

In 1983 Brooks returned to Brooks Press with *Very Young Poets*, "Dedicated to all the children in the world." Clear, simple, and practical, the twenty "Little Lessons" prepare the young poet—or the aspiring poet of any age—to consider the world and books with affection and wonder. The author's maternal approach nurtures the beginner.

Along with its literary significance for Brooks, 1983 was a momentous political year for Chicago. She joined Artists for Washington in the mayoral contest, and Harold Washington became the first Black mayor of the city, succeeding Jane M. Byrne. Brooks read at Washington's first inauguration. Addressing him (in "Mayor Harold Washington") as "Mayor, Worldman, Historyman," she wrote, "Beyond steps that occur and close, / your steps are echo-makers." She later published three Chicago-oriented poems in *Mayor Harold Washington and Chicago, the I Will City*. She also read at his second inauguration four years later. Following his untimely death in 1987, her poem in memoriam, "Last Inauguration of Mayor Harold Washington," highlighted a special December 8 tribute edition of the *Chicago Tribune*.

Brooks was named Consultant in Poetry to the Library of Congress for 1985-86. Besides her formal task of inviting and introducing outstanding poets for monthly readings, she regularly invited students and local poets to read informally in her office, after which she took them to lunch. Her appointment book was a mass of scheduled visits to schools and community groups. She seemed to turn down no request for her time and energy. Her procession of honorary doctorates has grown to exceed fifty.

Even though she was immersed in local and national happenings, events abroad deeply stirred Brooks's consciousness. The ongoing turmoil and tragedy in South Africa moved her to write and publish *The Near-Johannesburg Boy and Other Poems* (1986), dedicated to the students of Gwendolyn Brooks Junior High School. She called her new imprint The David Company, after her late father, David Brooks. In the title poem, she speaks as the defiant young boy whose father has been murdered and whose brave mother, outwardly, "is still this loud laugher!" The boy walks with "a hundred of playmates to where / the hurt Black of our skin is forbidden." The poem conveys the resolution of the youths and the uncertainty of the outcome. "We shall flail in the Hot Time" says the boy. Brooks's verb expresses precisely her disquieting vision. "Early Death," comprising two poems—"Of the Young Dead" and "To the Young Who Want to Die"— recognizes the problem of despair among teenagers, as she puts it, "of any race or 'persuasion.' " Divinely compassionate "Infirm" states, "Everybody here / is infirm," and goes on to assert the beauty of all human beings.

As the rights to Brooks's publications with Harper & Row gradually reverted to her, Brooks arranged to publish her own anthology, *Blacks*, under the imprint of The David Company. The omnibus comprises five books of poetry, her one novel, *Maud Martha*, and other works. Among the many celebrations of its appearance was the notable reception organized by Sonia Sanchez at Temple University. Even though printing and distribution have presented problems, Brooks remains determined to produce her books through totally independent enterprise.

On June 7, 1987, the poet celebrated her seventieth birthday. Pleased by the excitement surrounding the event, she was somewhat amused by the surprise accorded her youthful energy, especially by the young. "They seem to be impressed that I'm seventy," she wryly observed. The day's festivities in the city centered on her annual Poet Laureate Awards on June 7, 1987, at the University of Chicago. Although the awards were customarily given to elementary and high school pupils, Brooks, assisted in the presentations by her daughter Nora, marked the special occasion by giving additional prizes to thirty-two outstanding adult poets of Illinois. Many were familiar on the Chicago literary scene: Michael Anania, Henry Blakely, Walter Bradford, Maxine Chernoff, Reginald Gibbons, David Hernandez, Paul Hoover, Angela Jackson, Haki Madhubuti, Lisel Mueller, John Frederick Nims, Sterling Plumpp, Eugene Redmond, and Carolyn Rodgers. The rest of the awards—which totaled over $7,000—were conferred upon elementary and high school students whose parents and teachers were asked to comment briefly on their accomplishments. The celebration was marked by affection and warmth, the kind of atmosphere Brooks creates with ease.

The Poet Laureate Awards, initiated and funded by Brooks herself, have encouraged the writing of poetry throughout Illinois. Since 1969, the ceremony has become a popular public function. In 1987 it was duly covered in the Chicago press, with photographs of Brooks surrounded by several very young prize recipients, as she blew out the candles on her birthday cake. The historic assembly of prominent adult winners, however, went largely unnoticed. The poet and editor of TriQuarterly, Reginald Gibbons, did take note of the gathering in his appreciation in the Chicago Tribune on July 12.

Haki Madhubuti (Don L. Lee), whom Brooks regards as her spiritual son, planned his own surprise to honor her birthday. Secretly, he edited a tribute anthology, Say That the River Turns: The Impact of Gwendolyn Brooks (Third World Press, 1987), featuring poetry, prose, and reminiscences by a wide variety of writers, among them her husband and her daughter, who directs Chocolate Chips Theatre Company, an adult troupe for young people's theatre. Nora's lively appraisal astutely describes "Mama as Midwife" assisting in the birth and development of new writers, and "Mama as Mapper" who "delineates and defines the scenery of now." In his introduction to the book, Madhubuti refers to Brooks as "a Living National Treasure":

It is her vision—her ability to see truths rather than trends, to seek meaning and not fads, to question ideas rather than gossip—that endears her to us. Her uniqueness with language is common knowledge and few would argue with the fact that she has helped to set new standards for poetry in the twentieth century. She is a slow and careful writer. In the totality of her work there is little that will not stand the test of close, critical examination. . . . She has the stature of a Queen Mother, but is always accessible and giving. Ms. Brooks is a woman who cannot live without her art, but who has never put her art above or before the people she writes about.

This general acknowledgment was evident when she became, in effect, the representative Black dignitary participating in "A Tribute to the Bicentennial of the Constitution," held on September 17, 1987, at the Supreme Court of Illinois.

Three months later, on December 11 and 12, Madhubuti organized the Third World Press's "20th Anniversary Conference on Literature and Society" at Chicago State University, with Brooks and, as she observes, "many other 'family.' " Although the conference was celebratory, its tone was one of vital urgency, as witnessed by its dedication to the memory of Mayor Harold Washington, John Oliver Killens, and James Baldwin, all of whom had died in 1987. Panel members ranged from academics like Eugenia Collier, poet and critic Eugene B. Redmond, and producer and editor Woodie King, Jr., to radical thinker Frances Cress Welsing, who attracted a large, enthusiastic audience for her lecture "The Problem of White World Supremacy."

Third World Press gave awards to Brooks, the other workshop leaders, including Chancellor Williams (who was too ill to attend), Ruby Dee (accepting for herself and husband Ossie Davis), and other prominent guests, such as Margaret and Charles Burroughs and keynote speaker Susan Taylor of *Essence* television and magazine. Brooks established her own Third World Press annual award of two $500 prizes, the George Kent Award. She personally presented the initial grants to Mari Evans and Sonia Sanchez.

In Brooks's workshop at the conference, moderated by Sterling Plumpp, she, Evans, and Sanchez discussed "The Writer and His/Her Social Responsibility." Evans enjoined writers to channel their work politically, as in the 1960s, and quipped, "You can't sit in your ebony tower. . . . One of our responsibilities is to deal with the issues of our times." Sanchez called for teachers to "expel the myths," showing students, for example, that Rudyard Kipling's "The Charge of the Light Brigade" is "a poem about imperialism" and that Joseph Conrad's *Heart of Darkness* dehumanizes the image of Blacks. Brooks made the point that more writers should portray "The BLACK FAMILY," the words capitalized for emphasis, and described a childhood evening, with her mother playing the piano and the rest of the family singing. "Think of it," she wryly exclaimed, "a Black family singing!"

Another significant event in Brooks's career took place in December 1987, this time in absentia. Early in the year she had become the first Black woman to be elected an honorary fellow of the Modern Language Association (Ralph Ellison and James Baldwin had preceded her). On December 29, the first MLA special session on her work, "Cultural Approaches to Gwendolyn Brooks's Afro-American Aesthetics," was held at the MLA convention in San Francisco.

What lies ahead for the poet? Current projects include a sequel to her autbiography, *Report from Part One,* and a short book of poems, "Winnie," inspired by Winnie Mandela. She travels (by train) as much as ever, giving readings, lectures, and workshops, visiting schools and prisons, going where she is needed. Her advice to the young, and to all Blacks, still firmly holds:

Conduct your blooming in the noise and whip of the whirlwind.

D. H. MELHEM
September 1988

Notes

Publisher's Note: Dr. Kent's source notes were in an unfinished state at the time of his death. For invaluable assistance in providing full information, we are grateful to D. H. Melhem. Thanks go also to Jean F. Preston, curator of manuscripts, Princeton University Library; and to Donna Slawsky, corporate librarian, Harper & Row, Publishers.

1. Beginnings

1. In presenting the early life of Gwendolyn Brooks, I am indebted to the following sources: extensive conversations with Miss Brooks, her mother, Keziah Brooks, and other family members; poetry notebooks from the juvenile writing period; Miss Brooks's autobiography, *Report from Part One* (hereafter cited as *RPO*); and Keziah C. Brooks, *"The Voice" and Other Short Stories* (Detroit: Harlo Press, 1975; hereafter cited as *The Voice*). On the "Paul Laurence Dunbar" quotation, see *RPO*, 56; cf. *The Voice*, 56.

2. Richard Wright, *American Hunger* (New York: Harper & Brothers, 1944), 1, 3.

3. *RPO*, 57.

4. Ibid., 55.

5. Ibid., 57.

6. Ibid., 50.

7. *Negro Story*, March–April 1945.

8. Jill Oppenheimer, interview, *subject to change*, Oct. 1975, 10.

9. Ida Lewis, "Conversation: Gwendolyn Brooks and Ida Lewis: 'My People Are Black People,' " *Essence*, April 1971, reprinted in and hereafter quoted from *RPO*, 167–82, quotation from 173.

10. Ibid., 174.

11. Arvarh E. Strickland, *History of the Chicago Urban League* (Urbana: Univ. of Illinois Press, 1966), 104, 109.

12. *The Voice*, 134.

13. Ibid.

2. Into the Morrow

1. Charles H. Lynch, "Robert Hayden and Gwendolyn Brooks: A Critical Study," Ph.D. diss., New York University, 1977, 133.

2. GB's scribbled comment in Glenda Estelle Clyde, "An Oral Interpreter's Approach to the Poetry of Gwendolyn Brooks," Ph.D. diss., Southern Illinois Univ., 1966, 20.

3. *RPO*, 190.

4. Margaret Taylor Burroughs in Lynch, "Robert Hayden and Gwendolyn Brooks," 136.

5. Author's telephone interview with Mrs. Frances Matlock.

6. *RPO*, 57–58.

3. Struggles, Triumphs

1. *RPO*, 58.

2. Michel Fabre, *The Unfinished Quest of Richard Wright* (New York: William Morrow, 1973), 128.

3. St. Clair Drake and Horace R. Cayton, *Black Metropolis: A Study of Negro Life in a Northern City* (New York: Harcourt, Brace, 1945), 261.

4. Quoted from Abraham Chapman, ed., *Black Voices* (New York: St. Martin's Press, 1968).

5. Fabre, *Unfinished Quest*, 129.

6. Author's interview with Burroughs.

7. *RPO*, p. 12 of photo insert.

8. *New Challenge* (Fall 1937); complete version in *Amistad II*, 1971.

9. George Stavros, "An Interview with Gwendolyn Brooks," *Contemporary Literature* 2 (Winter 1970):1-20; reprinted in and hereafter cited from *RPO*, 147–66, quotation from 161.

10. *Chicago Tribune Magazine*, Jan. 22, 1978.

11. Ibid.

12. *The Voice*, 123.

13. *RPO*, 66.

14. Richard Wright to Edward C. Aswell, Sept. 18, 1944, Harper & Row Author files, Princeton University Library. All quotations from Harper & Row correspondence for 1944–1958 are quoted by permission of Harper & Row and Princeton University Library.

15. GB to Elizabeth Lawrence (hereafter cited as EL), Sept. 28, 1944.

16. GB to EL, March 25, 1945.

17. Margaret Walker, "New Poets," *Phylon*, Special Issue, "The Negro in Literature: The Current Scene," ed. Mosell C. Hill and M. Carl Holman, vol. 11 (4th Quarter 1950): 349, 351–52.

18. *CLA Journal* 7 (Dec. 7, 1963): 114–25.

19. Lewis interview, *RPO*, 175.

20. GB to EL, March 12, 1945.

21. *RPO*, 72.

4. Bright Waters

1. Genevieve Taggard to EL, undated (*ca* early July 1948), quoted in GB to EL, July 17, 1948.

2. GB to EL, July 17, 1948.

3. EL to GB, March 3, 1949; GB to EL, March 12, 1949.

4. Langston Hughes to EL, June 19, 1949.

5. Alfred Kreymborg to EL, Nov. 26, 1949.

6. J. Saunders Redding, "Cellini-like Lyrics," *Saturday Review of Literature*, Sept. 17, 1949, 23, 27.

7. Stavros interview, *RPO*, 158, 159.

8. GB to EL, Sept. 5, 1949.

9. GB to EL (telegram), May 2, 1950; letter, May 14, 1950.

10. Author's interview with Henry Blakely, Jr.

11. Strickland, *History of the Chicago Urban League*, 156–63.

12. *Negro Digest*, Feb. 1950.

13. *RPO*, 203–4.

14. *Phylon*, Special Issue, "The Negro in Literature" (4th Quarter 1950): 296.

15. Ibid., 312.

16. Stavros interview, *RPO*, 149.

17. GB to EL, July 17, 1948.

18. Ibid.

5. A Complicated Universe

1. GB to EL, April 16, 1951.

2. Keziah Brooks, *The Voice*, 133.

3. GB to EL, Feb. 24, 1953.

4. GB to EL, Oct. 20, 1952.

5. GB to EL, Dec. 31, 1952.

6. EL to GB, Jan. 23, 1953.

7. GB to EL, Feb. 14, 1953.

8. EL to GB, Feb. 24, 1953.

9. GB to EL, Feb. 24, 1953.

10. EL to GB, March 2, 1953.

11. GB to EL, March 13, 1953.

12. EL to GB, April 1, 1953.

13. GB to EL, April 6, 1953.

14. Dorothy B. Fiske, Harper & Row, to GB, May 28, 1953.

15. GB to Dorothy B. Fiske, June 17, 1953.

16. Robert Hillyer to EL, Sept. 7, 1953.

17. Worth Tuttle Hedden to EL, Sept. 8, 1953.

18. Ann Petry to EL, June 11, 1953.

19. GB to EL, June 17, 1953.

20. GB to EL, Oct. 9, 1953.

21. Inez Stark Boulton to EL, Nov. 3, 1953.

22. EL to Inez Stark Boulton, Nov. 5, 1953.

23. *RPO*, 191–93.

6. Reachings

1. EL to GB, March 10, 1954.

2. Strickland, *History of the Chicago Urban League*, 225.

3. EL to GB, March 10, 1954.

4. GB to EL, March 19, 1955.

5. GB to EL, May 5, 1955.

6. GB to EL, March 19, 1955.

7. GB to EL, May 15, 1956.

8. Quoted in ibid.

9. Ursula Nordstrom to GB, Feb. 7, 1957.

10. Ursula Nordstrom to GB, June 1957.

11. EL to GB, date unknown.

12. GB to EL, April 7, 1958.

13. Sonia Sanchez, *We Be Word Sorcerers: 25 Stories by Black Americans* (New York: Bantam, 1973).

14. EL to GB.

15. EL to GB, Feb. 9, 1959, Harper & Row files, New York, N.Y. All Harper & Row correspondence for 1959–1971 is quoted by permission of Harper & Row.

16. GB to EL, Feb. 16, 1959.

17. D. H. Melhem, "Gwendolyn Brooks: Prophecy and Poetic Process" Ph.D. diss., CUNY, 1976, 223.

18. GB to EL, April 2, 1959.

19. Reader's reports and EL comments on *The Bean Eaters,* undated.

20. EL to GB, Dec. 10, 1959.

21. GB to EL, Jan. 8, 1960.

22. Peter Viereck to EL, Dec. 25, 1959.

23. Lynch, "Robert Hayden and Gwendolyn Brooks," 162.

24. *RPO,* 78.

25. EL to GB, Aug. 31, 1960; Academy of American Poets to EL, Oct. 13, 1960; and author's telephone interview with GB, Sept. 30, 1980.

26. GB to Ann Flagg, *Harper's,* Dec. 6, 1960.

27. John McGiffert, WCBS TV, to GB.

28. GB to EL, Feb. 15, 1961.

7. Foreshadowings

1. GB to Herbert Marks, Feb. 1, 1962, enclosing GB to John V.B. Sullivan.

2. GB to EL, Jan. 11, 1961; EL to GB, Jan. 26, 1961.

3. GB to EL, Aug. 22, 1962.

4. EL to GB, Aug. 29, 1962.

5. Harvey Curtis Webster, "Pity the Giants," *Nation,* Sept. 1, 1962, 96.

6. In Robert Cromie, "Frank London Brown: An Appreciation," *Chicago Scene,* April 12, 1962, 25.

7. GB to EL, Feb. 28, 1963.

8. EL to GB, March 18, 1963.

9. Ibid.

10. GB to EL, March 20, 1963.

11. EL to GB, March 25, 1963.

12. GB to EL, April 19, 1963.

13. Ibid.

14. Telegram, GB to EL, Aug. 12, 1963.

15. EL to Gordon Gould, *Chicago Tribune*, July 14, 1963.

16. *RPO*, 78.

17. Ibid., 81.

18. Gwendolyn Brooks, "I Don't Like to Think of Myself as a Poet," *Panorama Magazine*, *Chicago Daily News*, Sept. 28, 1963.

19. Author's interview with Lerone Bennett, Jr., Oct. 21, 1981.

20. *RPO*, 208–9.

21. Ibid., 74.

22. EL to James F. Mathias, secretary, John Simon Guggenheim Memorial Foundation, Feb. 25, 1964.

23. *RPO*, 198.

24. *Chicago American*, sect. 2, 13.

25. *RPO*, 198.

26. Ibid., 198–99.

27. John Hope Franklin, *From Slavery to Freedom* (New York: Alfred A. Knopf, 1979), 636.

28. Lerone Bennett, *Before the Mayflower* (Chicago: Johnson Publishing Co., 1962), 354.

29. William Targ to GB, May 30, 1964.

30. EL to GB, June 30, 1964.

31. GB to EL, July 1964.

32. Discussion of the Asilomar Conference is based on a report in *Newsweek*, Aug. 24, 1964; Kenneth Rexroth, "Panelizing Dissent," *Nation*, Sept. 7, 1964; and Hoyt W. Fuller's reports in *Negro Digest*, Sept. 1964, and *Ebony*, Nov. 1964.

33. Author's interview with GB.

34. "The Nationalization of Gwendolyn Brooks," *Chicagoland*, Sept. 1969, 19.

8. Changes

1. *RPO*, 146.

2. Conrad Kent Rivers, "The Day King Marched in Chicago," *Negro Digest* (March 1966), 54–58.

3. *Tuesday Magazine*, Sept. 1965, 37; *Bulletin*, May 20, 1965.

4. The two preceding paragraphs are based on Robert Glauber's interview with GB, "Gwendolyn Brooks Speaks of Poetry," *Illinois Bell News*, Feb.–March 1965, 3–9.

5. Ibid.

6. *Negro Digest*, June 1965, 57.

7. Ibid.

8. Ibid., 81.

9. *Negro Digest*, June 1966, 62–63.

10. Ibid., 58.

11. *Negro Digest*, July 1966, 49–50.

12. Ibid.

13. *Aurora Borealis*, April 4, 1966, 18; *Illinois Bell News*, Aug. 15, 1966, 1.

14. *Negro Digest*, Oct. 1966, 51–52.

15. Ibid.

16. *Phylon*, Special Issue, "The Negro in Literature," vol. 11 (4th quarter 1950): 312.

17. *Negro Digest*, July 1967, 91–92.

18. RPO, 84. Discussion of the Fisk Conference is based on a tape of the proceedings.

19. RPO, 85.

20. Ibid.

21. Milner's statement is based on his essay in *The Black Aesthetic*, ed. Addison Gayle, Jr. (Garden City, N.Y.: Doubleday/Anchor, 1971), 291.

22. Lynch, "Robert Hayden and Gwendolyn Brooks," 152.

9. Recognized in Her Country

1. Author's interview with Walter Bradford.

2. RPO, 200.

3. *Ebony*, Dec. 23, 1967, 48–50.

4. RPO, 152.

5. Author's interview with Walter Bradford.

6. Stavros interview, *RPO*, 152–53.

7. Lewis interview, *RPO*, 181.

8. RPO, 183.

9. EL to GB, Oct. 4, 1967.

10. GB to Genevieve Young (hereafter cited as GY), Oct. 4, 1967.

11. *Harper's*, Dec. 1950.

12. *Ramparts*, Dec. 14, 1968, 53–58.

13. Stavros interview, *RPO*, 152.

14. "Gwendolyn Brooks: The Heroic Voice of Prophecy," *Studies in Black Literature*, Autumn 1976, 1–3.

15. GB to GY, Nov. 26, 1969.

16. GY to GB, Sept. 13, 1968.

17. *Chicago Sun-Times*, Aug. 25, 1968, sect. 3, 1 and 4; *Chicago Daily News*, Aug. 31, 1968.

18. Sept. 19, 1968, 13.

19. *New York Times Book Review*, March 2, 1969; *Poetry*, March 1969; *Journal of Negro Education*, Winter 1970; *Virginia Quarterly Review*, Winter 1969; *Library Journal*, August 1968.

20. GB to GY, Nov. 26, 1969.

21. Author's interview with Nora Blakely.

22. Ida Lewis interview, *RPO*, 178–80.

23. Ibid., 175.

24. Ibid.

25. Ibid.

26. Author's interview with GB; David Llorens, "Poet Is Acclaimed Creator of Black Art," *Ebony*, March 1969, 72.

27. Larry Neal to GB, Oct. 1970.

28. Phyl Garland, "Gwendolyn Brooks: Poet Laureate," *Ebony*, July 1968, 56; Stavros interview, *RPO*, 150; Oppenheimer interview; Gloria T. Hull and Posey Gallagher, "Update on Part One: An Interview," *CLA Journal*, Sept. 1977, 20, 34.

29. Author's interview with John O. Killens.

30. Author's interview with Hoyt Fuller; Lerone Bennett, Introduction to *To Gwen With Love*, ed. Patricia Brown et al. (Chicago: Johnson Publishing Co., 1971).

31. *RPO*, 197.

10. Brave New World

1. GY to GB, June 24, 1970.

2. GB to GY, Aug. 9, 1969.

3. Harper memorandum, Gunilla Dronvall and Ann Harris, Dec. 3, 1970.

4. Letter to Elizabeth [Lawrence] Kalashnikoff, Dec. 15, 1970, no signature on copy.

5. *New York Times*, Dec. 14, 1970.

6. GB to GY, Aug. 9, 1969.

7. Author's interview with Don L. Lee.

8. Roslyn Targ to Ann Harris, quoting GB, Feb. 1, 1971.

9. Lewis interview, *RPO*, 175; Hull and Gallagher interview, 22.

10. Gwendolyn Brooks et al., *a capsule course in Black Poetry Writing*, 10; Brooks, *Young Poet's Primer*, 5; Oppenheimer interview, 10.

11. Hull and Gallagher interview, 23–24, 33.

12. Ibid. 22, 25.

13. *New York Times*, Dec. 14, 1970.

14. *RPO*, 204.

15. Hull and Gallagher interview.

16. "The Role of Violence in Recent Poems of Gwendolyn Brooks," *Studies in Black Literature*, Summer 1974, 26.

17. Hull and Gallagher interview.

18. *Ebony*, Aug. 1971, 42–48.

19. April 15, 1970, 4.

20. Mattie D. Thomas to GB, May 23, 1974; *Huntsville* (Alabama) *Times*, May 12, 1974.

21. Author's interview with GB.

22. *RPO*, 58.

23. Ibid., 190–91.

24. Hull and Gallagher interview, 30.

25. Lewis interview, *RPO*, 182.

26. *RPO*, 199.

27. *The World of Gwendolyn Brooks*, 426.

28. Since published in *The Near-Johannesburg Boy and Other Poems* (Chicago: The David Co., 1986), 28.

29. Hull and Gallagher interview, 21.

30. Ibid., 24.

31. Oppenheimer interview, 10.

32. *Primer For Blacks*, 15.

33. *The Voice*, 27.

34. Since published in *TriQuarterly*, July 1989.

35. *Chicago Tribune*, Jan. 22, 1978.

Selected Bibliography

Principal Works by Gwendolyn Brooks

A Street in Bronzeville. New York: Harper & Brothers, 1945.
Annie Allen. New York: Harper & Brothers, 1949.
Maud Martha. New York: Harper & Brothers, 1953.
Bronzeville Boys and Girls. New York: Harper & Brothers, 1956.
The Bean Eaters. New York: Harper & Brothers, 1960.
Selected Poems. New York: Harper & Row, 1963.
We Real Cool. Detroit: Broadside Press, 1966. [Reprinted from *The Bean Eaters*]
The Wall. Detroit: Broadside Press, 1967.
In the Mecca. New York: Harper & Row, 1968.
Riot. Detroit: Broadside Press, 1969.
Family Pictures. Detroit: Broadside Press, 1970.
The World of Gwendolyn Brooks. New York: Harper & Row, 1971. [Includes *A Street in Bronzeville, Annie Allen, Maud Martha, The Bean Eaters,* and *In the Mecca*]
Aloneness. Detroit: Broadside Press, 1971.
Black Steel: Joe Frazier and Muhammad Ali. Special Broadside. Detroit: Broadside Press, 1971.
[Editor]. *A Broadside Treasury.* Detroit: Broadside Press, 1971.
[Editor]. *Jump Bad: A New Chicago Anthology.* Detroit: Broadside Press, 1971.
[Editor]. *The Black Position.* 1971–. [Annual]
"In Montgomery." *Ebony,* Aug. 1971, 42–48.
Report from Part One. Detroit: Broadside Press, 1972.
The Tiger Who Wore White Gloves, or *What you are you are.* Chicago: Third World Press, 1974.
Beckonings. Detroit: Broadside Press, 1975.
[With Keorapetse Kgositsile, Haki R. Madhubuti, and Dudley Randall]. *A Capsule Course in Black Poetry Writing.* Detroit: Broadside Press, 1975.
Primer For Blacks. Chicago: Black Position Press, 1980.
Young Poet's Primer. Chicago: Brooks Press, 1980.
To Disembark. Chicago: Third World Press, 1981.
"Twenty-Four Poems from Four Decades." *Time Capsule,* Summer/Fall 1983.
Very Young Poets. Chicago: Brooks Press, 1983.

Mayor Harold Washington and Chicago, the I Will City. Chicago: Brooks Press, 1983.
The Near-Johannesburg Boy and Other Poems. Chicago: The David Company, 1986.
Blacks. Chicago: The David Company, 1987. [Includes *A Street in Bronzeville, Annie Allen, Maud Martha, The Bean Eaters,* "New Poems," *In the Mecca,* selections from *To Disembark,* and *The Near-Johannesburg Boy and Other Poems.*]
Gottschalk and the Grande Tarantelle. Chicago: The David Company, 1988. [Includes "Winnie."]
Winnie. Chicago: The David Company, 1988.

Index